Discovering God's Blueprint for Your Career

Discovering God's Blueprint for Your Career

A Christian's Job Search Guide

John S. Lybarger, MBA, PhD & William L. Donelson, MDiv

iUniverse, Inc.

New York Lincoln Shanghai

Discovering God's Blueprint for Your Career
A Christian's Job Search Guide

iUniverse, Inc.

For information address:
iUniverse, Inc.
2021 Pine Lake Road, Suite 100
Lincoln, NE 68512
www.iuniverse.com

ISBN: 0-595-30848-1

Contents

Preface ix

   Why Discovering God's Blueprint for Your Career? ix

   Why Us? x

   Clients' Testimonials x

   What Will I Learn? xi

Chapter One: Finding Yourself Unemployed 1

   Unexpected Job Loss—Paul Williams' Story 1

   Strategies for Understanding Job Loss 3

Chapter Two: Discovering Your Job Matches 21

   Actions for Identifying Your Spiritual Gifts 23

   Paul Williams' Profiles Career Coach Results 24

Chapter Three: Your Career and Education History 35

   Paul Williams' Personal Career & Education Inventory *36*

   Paul Williams' Functional Skills Checklist *44*

   Paul Williams' CAR Story Examples *57*

   Industry Checklist *60*

Chapter Four: SALT—Factors Affecting Your Career Search Length 68

   SALT—Scope, Activity, Liabilities and Timing 68

Chapter Five: Creating Your Career Search Activity & Scope Action Plan (ASAP) 91

   ASAP Goals & Tracking Worksheet 101

Chapter Six: Milestone One—Getting Job Interviews 106

   Milestone One Tools 106

   Résumé Formatting 108

   Résumé Styles 109

   Introductory Résumé *109*

   Internet Résumé *117*

   Letter Résumé *121*

   Value—Proposition Letter *124*

   Constructing the Value—Proposition Letter *124*

Chapter Seven: Writing Compelling Job Search Letters 127

    Twelve Letter Writing Essentials 127

    Cover Letter—Direct Mail 128

    Cover Letter—Classified Advertisement 129

    Cover Letter—Recruiting Firm 130

    Networking Letter—Industry Influential 131

    Networking Letter—Colleagues, Friends, Acquaintances 134

    Reference Contact Letter 135

    Alumni Executive Letter 137

    Follow-up Letters 138

    Thank You Letters 142

Chapter Eight: Milestone Two—Winning Job Offers 149

    Milestone Two Tools 149

    Common Interview Questions and Suggested Replies 150

Chapter Nine: Milestone Three—Negotiating & Accepting a Position 163

    Milestone Three Tools 163

Fifty Strategies—Discovering God's Blueprint for Your Career 175

Becoming a Christian 177

    God's Plan for Our Lives 177

    We Are All Sinners 178

    Death is the Penalty for Our Sins 178

    Jesus Christ Died in Our Place for Our Sins 178

    Forgiveness Requires Confessing Jesus Christ as Savior and Lord 178

    Your Personal Decision 178

Appendix—Career Search Forms 181

    Job Search Checklist 182

    Personal Career and Education Inventory 183

    Functional Skills Checklist 197

    Functional Skills Summary 207

    CAR Stories 208

    Career History & Goals Worksheet 215

    Industry Checklist 217

    Career Obstacles Checklist 223

    ASAP Goals & Tracking Worksheet 226

    Interview Preparation Checklist 229

    Negotiations Worksheet 230

    Negotiations Preparation Checklist 231

    Negotiations Questions 233

Biography—John S. Lybarger, MBA, PhD 235

Biography—William L. Donelson, MDiv 237

Acknowledgements

John would like to thank Margie, his loving wife of twenty-two years, for her unselfish support and encouragement while he completed this project. He also wants to thank his children, Ashley and Ryan, for their patience and understanding while he stayed locked up in his office for hours on end during late evenings, and over many weekends.

Bill is grateful to his family and friends who have offered encouragement, support and patience throughout this writing project. He also wants to thank his colleagues in the career development field for their insights, suggestions and feedback on the manuscript as it developed.

Profiles International Inc. of Waco, Texas generously granted us permission to reprint the *Career Coach Report* and *Brief Career Coach Profile Summary*. The report and profile in this guide illustrate Paul Williams' *Career Coach* results. Paul Williams is a fictional character, created specifically for this project. Any resemblance to actual persons living or dead is purely coincidental and unintended by the authors.

Many friends, colleagues and clients contributed to the success of this project. We are honored to have been a part of hundreds of clients' lives during their job searches. Paul Williams' story is a composite of so many real-life job seekers' journeys.

Specifically, we want to thank Gerry Harrington and Jeanna Finch for careful and thoughtful editing and suggestions for improving the manuscript. This book would not be the same without the input and thoughtful recommendations they both provided. All mistakes and errors are our own.

We also want to acknowledge Dr. Christofer French for his thoughtful review and comments. He directed the career development department at the Denver Paralegal Institute for several years, and wrote *The Professional Paralegal Job Search* in 1995. Robert Gerberg, Sr. was one of our mentors in career planning and career marketing. He wrote *The Professional Job Changing System—An Easier Way to Find the Right New Job,* in 1997. We are both indebted to his mentoring and expertise over the years.

John S. Lybarger, MBA, PhD   William L. Doneslon, MDiv
2004   2004

Preface

This guide is written for Christians who are currently unemployed or facing pending unemployment. A biblical approach is taken throughout the book that offers a Christ-centered strategy for understanding your spiritual gifts, your natural skills, talents and abilities, and your vocational calling.

If you don't yet know Jesus Christ as your personal savior and Lord, you may find this material confusing. If you aren't sure about your salvation, please consider studying the section at the end of the guide on "Becoming a Christian" before attempting to use these strategies.

Daily, a believer loses a job, faces pending unemployment, or finds themselves currently under-employed. When one of these events occurs, two steps usually follow. First, you find yourself asking God for direction and guidance. Secondly, you start searching for a new position. If you have found yourself in one of these circumstances, then you know that it isn't nearly as easy as you thought it would be to find your next job. This guide is for you. It will assist you in keeping Christ at the center while paving the way to a successful job search!

Why Discovering God's Blueprint for Your Career?

Discovering God's Blueprint for Your Career—A Christian's Job Search Guide is a guidebook for your job search journey. By reading and using this guide, prayerfully considering the Holy Spirit's leading, and seeking wise counsel from your pastor, spiritual director or a Christian career coach, you will learn how to find a job that fulfills your calling and spiritual vocation.

Additionally, you will learn how to avoid the "activity pitfall." Many job seekers spend valuable time engaging in activities that fail to produce desirable interviews and job offers! By using these strategies, you can learn how to use the Internet and the Web's vast resources to your advantage. Without a clear plan and specific goals, you can easily get lost in the eUniverse! You can discover and avoid the time-stealing behaviors that will detract from a successful job search today.

Grab a highlighter and pen and find a comfortable work space. Carefully study this guide. Highlight important ideas that will help you in your search. Underline the sections you find most helpful. By marking up your guidebook, you can easily find information later. With proper use, it will become your personal journal and map for your job search journey.

These strategies will help you identify where God wants you to be in your next job. You will have everything you need to you reach your destination successfully. Now, you can discover and begin a new job in a company and industry you choose, based on your spiritual gifts, natural skills, talents and abilities.

By studying and using this guide, you will learn 50 strategies that will:

- Direct you toward discovering God's blueprint for your career

- Guide you in discovering your spiritual gifts

- Enhance your effectiveness in getting job interviews, winning job offers, and negotiating and accepting a desirable position

- Help you find job matches that are the right fit for you in a wide variety of positions, occupations and industries

Why Us?

Dr. Lybarger and Mr. Donelson each share a passion for ministry—guiding believers along successful career paths that God leads them to follow. They both live in suburbs of Denver. Together, they bring over thirty years experience, coaching managers and executives in career development. Their clients have come from Global/Fortune 1000 companies, family-owned businesses, and public agencies in the city, state and federal sectors.

Dr. Lybarger earned both the Master of Business Administration and the Doctor of Philosophy (psychology) degrees from California Coast University, the Master of Science degree in counseling from California State University at Fullerton, and the Bachelor of Science degree in Christian education at Biola University.

He has conducted more than 600 executive coaching sessions, utilizing assessments, improving individual performance, increasing job match, reducing workplace conflict, and strengthening team relationships in the public and private sectors. As a master trainer and facilitator, he has led more than 500 training programs with more than 7,000 participants, from front-line employees to senior level executives in churches, Christian organizations and in some of North America's leading firms.

Mr. Donelson earned the Master of Divinity degree in counseling from Denver Seminary and the Bachelor of Science degree in accounting from the University of Wyoming, where he was an outstanding graduate of the College of Commerce and Industry. His diverse career experiences in counseling, the pastorate, human resources management, organizational development, and public speaking give him a unique perspective, as he consults with clients from a broad spectrum of industries and experiences.

He has coached over 500 executives from Global and Fortune 1000 companies, blue chip firms, and government organizations, as well as smaller businesses, both public and private. His skilful ability to focus clients on their strengths and match them to career opportunities has led to numerous coaching successes.

Clients' Testimonials

"In my estimation, a master résumé writer—certainly one of the nation's top writers—is John Lybarger, MBA, PhD, President of Lybarger & Associates Inc. in Denver." Gerry Harrington, former executive producer, CNN.

"John was a significant resource in my job search. He is extremely creative, resourceful, persistent, and a great source of positive feedback and ideas. I would not have found the opportunities I did without John's help." Dick Mosher, former associate general counsel & assistant secretary, Maytag Corporation, and chairman, International Affairs Committee of American Corporate Counsel Association

"…you might want to consider hiring a résumé doctor…But be careful. Résumé revamping is a largely unregulated field rife with sham grammarians, sloppy formatters, and pricey 'career-repurposing' poseurs who promise access to 'hidden job markets' that don't exist…Among those we felt helped craft the clearest, most data-filled résumés…John Lybarger in Denver." Michelle Conlin, editor, *Business Week*, The Résumé Doctor is In, July 14, 2003

"I have worked with Dr. Lybarger for over seven years on a variety of projects. We have worked as trainers on the same training team, as designers in a variety of curriculum development projects and on several coaching-consulting projects. What I like the best about my relationship with him is that when I think about integrity, character and hard work I think of John. I'm the lead in a national coaching contract program, and I give the hardest clients to John because I know he has the expertise to handle difficult clients. I have given him a variety of international participants and he has consistently delivered across organizational, cultural and language barriers. I know I can always count on John's consistent delivery." Maria Valdes, PhD, senior associate program director, Western Management Development Center, Office of Personnel Management, United States Government

What Will I Learn?

In *Chapter One: Finding Yourself Unemployed*, you will meet Paul Williams. He receives news that his position is being eliminated as soon as a pending acquisition is completed.

After hearing this shocking news, Paul begins experiencing the thoughts and emotions associated with losing his job. If your circumstances are similar to Paul Williams', you aren't alone! Discover the strategies for understanding and managing your feelings about your job loss as you follow Paul's journey from being terminated, to landing a desirable, new position that fulfills his spiritual and vocational calling.

Paul meets with his pastor for spiritual direction and prayer support. During their meeting, Pastor Chuck suggests that Paul might benefit from talking with a Christian career coach. He tells Paul that a career coach can provide valuable assistance with discovering spiritual gifts, identifying natural skills, talents and abilities; and helping with planning a strategic job search.

Everyone who loses a job experiences overwhelming feelings and grief, loss and sadness. Understanding the stages of job loss prepares you for managing your thoughts, feelings and behaviors as you move through each stage.

Coping with your job loss can be challenging and rewarding. This major life change impacts almost every aspect of your daily life. Learn how to manage this change and trust the Lord to comfort and direct you through it. The pain, suffering, and damage that often results from unemployment and unclear direction about where to go next can be minimized.

First, you can create and maintain a healthy, personal lifestyle. Plan your diet with nutritious, balanced meals. Make sure you get plenty of exercise—God's natural stress-reliever. Set aside a regular time daily for prayer, scripture reading and meditation. Make enjoyable leisure activities a routine, high priority in your weekly schedule. Don't neglect fellowship activities with family, friends and colleagues. Open yourself to advice, opinions and feedback from other believers.

Secondly, consider planning a spiritual retreat. Taking time to retreat from your busyness and frenetic activities allows you to slow down, rest, and center your heart, mind and soul on spiritual things. Doing appears to be so much easier than being for most people in American culture. Setting aside some time to be present—in the moment—and to center your thoughts on Christ helps you to listen to the Holy Spirit and hear his voice speaking to your soul.

Third, you can help yourself avoid the "activity pitfall" by writing down your action plan. Remember, those who fail to plan, plan to fail! By carefully studying this guide, you will learn specific strategies for targeting your job search, focusing your activities on fruitful endeavors and reaching your goals.

Finally, maintaining a positive outlook throughout your job search will enhance your ability to cope with job loss. Your thoughts affect your feelings, and your feelings influence your behaviors. By focusing your thoughts on what God wants you to do and where he is leading, you will create positive feelings about your job search. When you feel optimistic and confident that the Lord is in control, you will have more energy to take action and increase your search activity.

During Mr. Williams' meetings with his career coach, he is introduced to the importance of identifying his natural talents, strengths, and abilities; and discovering job matches that capitalize on his abilities and interests. He takes the *Career Coach* assessment, which is designed to measure these factors.

In *Chapter Two: Discovering Your Job Matches*, you will see Paul's *Career Coach Report*. You can read his coach's interpretation and suggested applications of these results. Discover how the *Career Coach* can help you identify job matches for your career planning too.

Chapter Three: Your Career and Education History shows you how Paul created a summary of his career and education experiences using the Career & Education Inventory. A worksheet for your use is provided in the Appendix. Carefully document all your accomplishments in each section.

This inventory covers:

- Education History
- Work History
- Military Service
- Continuing Education & Professional Development
- Honors, Awards and Professional Recognition
- Community Service
- Charitable Activities
- Professional Associations
- Leisure Activities

By carefully completing this comprehensive inventory, you will gain several advantages. First, capturing your history in a snapshot summary gives you the opportunity to review it from beginning to end. Secondly, by reflecting on your past accomplishments, you can see the depth, breadth and scope of your talents, strengths and skills. Third, many job seekers have said that this exercise helped them tremendously. By completing it, they came to realize that God has been faithfully leading, guiding and preparing them for their vocational calling for many years. They also realized more clearly that they had significant worth and value for a variety of prospective employers!

Fourth, you will organize your achievements in preparation for writing your résumés and completing employment applications. This saves you valuable time and effort throughout your job search because you will have all the information you need in one place.

Finally, through this exercise you will create a concise summary of your professional development. This summary will assist you in planning your next steps which may include seeking additional training, completing more education or obtaining work experience in other functional areas.

Storytelling is a powerful, age-old method of communication. Prior to recorded history, key events were passed on from one generation to another orally. Historians were the storytellers. They spoke of the community's traditions, accomplishments and achievements. Both the Old and New Testament scriptures are filled with stories and parables that illustrate God's guidance, plan, direction, hope, and love for each one of us.

The CAR story concept is the application of storytelling to your career search. The acronym stands for *C*hallenges, *A*ctivity and *R*esults. By developing CAR stories—stories that clearly and concisely illustrate the *C*hallenges you faced; the *A*ctivity you engaged in, and the measurable *R*esults you achieved—you will be prepared to write your résumés, draft compelling letters, and excel in interviews and negotiations.

How long will my career search last? This question haunts every job seeker. ***Chapter Four: SALT—Factors Affecting Your Career Search Length*** *answers* this question by assisting you in evaluating the:

*S*cope of your search, setting your

*A*ctivity goals, managing your

*L*iabilities/Career obstacles, and assessing the

*T*iming factors involved.

Paul Williams' Career Obstacles Checklist is provided for your review, along with his notes about each area of concern. In-depth explanations of each career obstacle follow, and they are accompanied by practical examples. These scenarios illustrate how each career obstacle can be managed effectively.

You can use the Career Obstacles Checklist to record your individualized, career obstacle assessment. Then, you can prayerfully plan your personal strategies for managing each one. Study the in-depth descriptions and scenarios for your specific areas of concern.

Developing your search action plan is essential. ***Chapter Five: Creating Your Career Search Activity & Scope Action Plan (ASAP)*** leads you through the identification of activity and scope targets, and goal setting. Eight target and activity areas are described. They include:

- Industries
- Geographic locations
- Employers
- Positions and functions
- Recruiters
- Key industry leaders
- Investment firms
- People in your network

Each of your goals should be SMART focused: Specific, Measurable, Action-oriented, Results-driven and Time-limited. You can review Paul Williams' ASAP Goals & Tracking Worksheet to see how he focused his activities for maximum results. An ASAP Goals & Tracking Worksheet is provided for your personal use in the Appendix.

Chapter Six: Milestone One—Getting Job Interviews. The skills and tools you need to reach this first milestone include: writing effective résumés and collecting the equipment necessary to maximize your effectiveness in written communications and interviews.

Take some time to review Paul Williams' original résumé and the evaluation of its weaknesses. Then study his new set of résumés. These have been designed for a variety of uses in his job search. Each application is explained in detail. You will also find specific guidelines for developing each résumé style for your own search. These résumé styles include:

- Introductory Résumé Style

- Internet Résumé Style

- Letter Résumé Style

- Value—Proposition Letter

When you carefully study this section and apply the instructions given, you will be prepared to create your own persuasive résumés. You'll have everything you need to get job interviews for the positions you want in the companies you choose.

In *Chapter Seven: Writing Compelling Job Search Letters,* you will learn the Twelve Letter Writing Essentials for crafting clear, concise and compelling job search letters. Examples are provided from Paul Williams' career search illustrating:

- Cover letters (direct mail, classified ads and recruiting firm mailings)

- Networking letters (industry influentials, colleagues, friends and acquaintances)

- Reference contact letter

- Alumni executive letter

- Follow-up letters

- Thank you letters

In *Chapter Eight: Milestone Two—Winning Job Offers,* discover how to use the Interview Preparation Checklist and the CAR story concept for successful interviewing. Common interview questions and suggested replies are provided to assist you as you prepare for each interview. You will also be introduced to behavioral-based, structured interview questions and how to prepare for answering these types of questions persuasively.

Chapter Nine: Milestone Three—Negotiating & Accepting a Position teaches you the tools for negotiating competitive offers and accepting desirable positions. You will be able to review Paul Williams' Negotiations Preparation Worksheet and Checklist. Study the guidelines for preparing your own negotiations questions. Your own Negotiations Preparation Worksheet and Checklist are in the Appendix.

The *Appendix: Career Search Forms* provides you with all the worksheets and checklists you will need for your job search. Each one has been presented in this guidebook as an example from Paul Williams' job search. You may duplicate each form for your personal use.

Chapter One:
Finding Yourself Unemployed

Unexpected Job Loss—Paul Williams' Story

"Please meet me in my office at 4pm to discuss the merger, Bill." Paul deleted the text message from his cellphone and added the appointment to his Palm Pilot for later that day. The recent takeover of KCMA Radio by the nation's largest radio broadcasting company was creating numerous changes for everyone. He couldn't help but wonder what was next.

It was almost noon and he had a lunch appointment scheduled with Sarah Culver, vice president of marketing at Gart Sports in downtown Denver. The last quarter's advertising campaign had been a huge success and it was time to plan the fourth quarter campaign. Winter sports equipment and apparel accounted for a large portion of the seasonal sales in the Rocky Mountain region stores.

At 37, Paul had reached a comfortable level of success. He seemed to have found a niche in the broadcasting industry—selling advertising, designing marketing strategies and partnering with clients to increase their revenue and market share.

For over three years now, he had been working at KCMA Radio as the sales manager. Bill Thompson, the vice president of sales and marketing was his immediate supervisor. Leading a team of six, he grew their advertising revenue by 20% annually for three consecutive years. Paul loved sales and working with people. Others admired him and enjoyed working with him too.

In June 2004, KCMA Radio had been acquired by the nation's largest radio broadcasting company in a hostile takeover move. Reflecting back on his career at KCMA, Paul realized that his sales successes had contributed to making the company a desirable acquisition target. He couldn't help but wonder if this would backfire now, negatively impacting his position with the new owner.

Driving south on I25, Paul was headed back to KCMA's corporate offices in Colorado Springs. His appointment with Sarah in Denver had gone extremely well. She had increased her quarterly advertising budget by 15%. Paul was feeling ambivalent. On the one hand, he was elated over his continuing sales successes. On the other hand, he was worried about his future.

A similar takeover event happened back in November 2000, when Paul was at Channel 5 News as a regional sales associate. The television station had been acquired by a global network and he was laid off. It took him six months to find a new position. That was one of the most difficult periods he had ever gone through in his life. His faith and trust in the Lord were tried and tested in so many ways.

KCMA Radio occupied the top floor of a new building in a corporate parkway located just north of Colorado Springs and southeast of the Air Force Academy. The building was burnt sienna-colored with smoked-glass and chrome trim. The view of Pike's Peak to the west was spectacular. With a summit at 14,110 feet, it is Colorado's 31st highest mountain.

At 4pm, Paul went up to meet Bill in his office. Bill said, "Paul, please sit down. I have some disturbing and unexpected news. I've just learned today that our entire sales and marketing division is being eliminated. We will all be let go on October 31st 2004. I didn't see this one coming, but I guess it makes sense to them. The new parent company claims their corporate sales and marketing division can absorb our work so we are no longer needed."

Paul replied, "Don't they have any idea how this change could impact our customers? I know if I leave, many of my accounts would want to follow me to another station. Don't they see any value in us as the employees of KCMA? Did they just buy us like a commodity, without any consideration for us as people? It just doesn't make any sense to me, Bill."

"I know, Paul, it seems like so many takeovers end this way for the employees of the smaller company. There just doesn't seem to be any loyalty anymore by corporations to their workers. Everyone is looking out for "Number One.""

Later that evening, Paul called his pastor, Chuck Truman, for spiritual counsel and support. They agreed to meet for coffee at 7am the next morning at Starbucks.

After getting their lattes and baguettes, Paul and Chuck found a table for two outside the store. It was a crisp, cool morning at 40 degrees Fahrenheit and 22% humidity. Several other tables were also occupied by patrons. Some were catching up on the news with the Denver Post or the Wall Street Journal; others were busily reviewing Palm Pilots and catching up on e-mails before starting their busy days.

Together, Paul and Chuck prayed diligently for guidance and direction. Then, they searched God's word for encouragement. Paul took comfort in several passages including:

> *"For I know the plans I have for you," says the* LORD. *"They are plans for good and not for disaster, to give you a future and a hope."* Jeremiah 29:11 (NLT)

> *"He renews my strength. He guides me along right paths, bringing honor to his name."* Psalm 23:3 (NLT)

> *"The* LORD *says, 'I will guide you along the best pathway for your life. I will advise you and watch over you.'"* Psalm 32:8 (NLT)

Pastor Chuck told Paul, "I believe that you should think and pray about talking with a career coach. The economy is really tight right now and jobs are hard to find. This may also be an important time in your life to reflect on God's blueprint for your career. A Christian career coach can help you explore and identify your gifts and calling, along with your natural talents, skills and abilities."

"Then, the two of you can work together to match your calling with various careers. I know several men and women in our church who have taken this route. They have found the right jobs with the right companies—where they can use their God-given abilities to glorify Him, and feel satisfied and fulfilled in their work. Here is his name and phone number, why don't you give him a call this afternoon?"

"I'm not sure I need any help, Chuck. Except for my unemployment following Channel 5 News, I've always found a job on my own. But, then again, those six months were really a difficult struggle for me and for my family. I don't want to have to go through that again unnecessarily. Maybe I will give him a call. Thanks for suggesting him to me."

Paul had finally landed at KCMA Radio after a long and difficult period of unemployment, back in 2001. Now, he was facing being out of work once more. He couldn't help asking himself, "Why is God allowing me to go through this again? What lesson is there in this for me? Did I miss something last time?" During his evening devotions, he read Psalm 37:34, which gently reminded him, *"Don't be impatient for the LORD to act! Travel steadily along his path."* (NLT)

The next day, Paul realized that almost every job he had previously held had just seemed to open up. Suddenly, it dawned on him that he hadn't really given much thought to what his gifts and calling might be for a career. That seemed like something only people in full-time ministry had to struggle with and he had always worked in secular jobs. Acting upon this realization, Paul called the career coach and made an appointment. In his heart, he felt that this was the Lord's direction at this point in his career.

Strategies for Understanding Job Loss

If your circumstances are similar to Paul's, you are not alone! There's nothing wrong with the way you are feeling right now. Often, being unemployed is not your fault. Even if you were terminated for cause, your future is not hopeless. Throughout this guide, you will find hope and encouragement along with strategies for managing obstacles to your career search.

Strategy #1 Understand the Job-Loss Cycle

> *"Have mercy on me, LORD, for I am in distress. My sight is blurred because of my tears. My body and soul are withering away. I am dying from grief; my years are shortened by sadness. Misery has drained my strength; I am wasting away from within."* Psalm 31:9-10 (NLT)

Regardless of how it happens, job loss is usually painful. It is, after all, a form of death—death of dreams, predictability, routines, and security. Understanding that these feelings are normal and that almost everyone who loses a job goes through predictable stages may be helpful.

Elizabeth Kübler-Ross, MD first wrote about these stages in her seminal work, *On Death and Dying*. After studying many terminally ill patients, she identified five stages of the death and dying process: Denial, Anger, Depression, Bargaining and Acceptance.

You will move in and out of these same stages as you progress through the job-loss cycle. You may spend more time in some stages and less time in others. Sometimes you will have one foot in one stage and the other foot in a different stage. The cycle is a process and everyone goes through it a little differently. In fact, you may obtain your next position before you've progressed to the acceptance stage.

> *Losing your job triggers a grief and loss process.*

Each stage has several elements. You may not experience all the elements within each stage. You may have additional experiences not listed.

Jeremiah speaks eloquently about his grieving and loss in Lamentations 3:20-25. *"I will never forget this awful time, as I grieve over my loss. Yet I still dare to hope when I remember this: The unfailing love of the LORD never ends! By his mercies we have been kept from complete destruction. Great is his faithfulness; his mercies begin afresh each day. I say to myself, 'The LORD is my inheritance; therefore, I will hope in him.' The LORD is wonderfully good to those who wait for him and seek him."* (NLT)

Denial

Denial is a process of deluding yourself into thinking or believing something that is not true or real. Often, you don't even realize you are doing it! This is because you actually believe the lies you are telling yourself. It isn't until after you pass through denial that you can see you were actually in it—hindsight is always twenty-twenty!

Your feelings are normal. Given your present circumstances, it's logical that you would be having these emotions. At first you may experience shock or numbness, especially if you were caught by surprise when you lost your job.

You may find yourself thinking:

God, I can't believe this is happening to me!

Lord, I know I'm going to wake up soon from this terrible nightmare!

I feel like I'm a robot—on autopilot, I can't control anything.

I feel numb, like my whole body was injected with Lidocaine.

God, has someone made a mistake? This can't be true!

Make a list of the feelings and questions you have asked yourself in the Denial stage below.

Why was it me?
How was I worse than others? How were others better than me?

_____

_____

_____

Set aside some devotional time to pray about your feelings and questions. Remember God's promise to us in Romans 8:28. *"And we know that God causes everything to work together for the good of those who love God and are called according to his purpose for them."* (NLT) When you are struggling with denial, it's easy to avoid accepting God's planning and purpose.

Make a conscious effort, in faith, to ask him and he will gladly tell you. James reminds us:

"If you need wisdom—if you want to know what God wants you to do—ask him, and he will gladly tell you. He will not resent your asking. But when you ask him, be sure that you really expect him to answer, for a doubtful mind is as unsettled as a wave of the sea that is driven and tossed by the wind. People like that should not expect to receive anything from the Lord. They can't make up their minds. They waver back and forth in everything they do." James 1:5-8 (NLT)

Paul speaking:

"My first step was to contact a few colleagues and close friends in other companies. I sent out some e-mails and made several phone calls. It seemed like everyone I talked to was either in the same boat I was—looking for their next move—or they were still employed but didn't know of any companies that were hiring now. It seemed like the sales job market had simply vanished.

Over the next several weeks, I kept asking myself questions, like, 'How could my company do this to me after all my loyalty and service? Why didn't I see this coming? Should I ask about transferring to another department, or offer to take a pay cut?' I found myself drawing irrational conclusions: 'I don't know if I can ever trust another employer again!' Or, 'I doubt if there are any companies out there today that are loyal to their employees.'

My career coach explained the stages of job loss to me and gave me some strategies for coping with my pending unemployment. He helped me understand that my thoughts and feelings were normal for anyone in my circumstances. I guess misery loves company—I did feel better after our appointment. I was looking forward to doing some of the exercises he assigned me. I knew the Lord had been faithful in the past and I was confident he would see me through this trial too. I remembered Hebrews 11:1, '*It* [faith] *is the confident assurance that what we hope for is going to happen. It is the evidence of things we cannot see.*" (NLT)

God has a plan for your future too. Seek his guidance and direction now. He will not fail or abandon you in your time of need. Trust him with what you cannot yet see, take initial steps now in the confidence that he will direct your path.

Strategy #2 Accept Help from Others through Each Job-Loss Stage

"The heartfelt counsel of a friend is as sweet as perfume and incense." Proverbs 27:9 (NLT)

Family members, friends and coaches can help you break through your denial by confronting you with its reality. If you are willing to listen and hear their logic, you may be able to break free from denial's grip.

Once you are released from denial, you will pass directly into anger. Your anger may be targeted toward your previous employer, boss, industry, co-workers, God, and even yourself.

Anger

Anger is a secondary defensive reaction. It is an emotional response to primary emotions like hurt, fear and shame. Anger covers or masks these primary emotions and temporarily makes you feel better about your circumstances. This is why you may occasionally shout at someone or make an aggressive comment, and then burst into tears. The hurt, fear or shame you are feeling beneath the anger breaks through the defensive anger barrier and expresses itself spontaneously.

You may experience feelings of anger, bitterness or resentment toward your former employer and/or supervisor. Or you may direct these feelings toward yourself.

David expressed his anger and rage toward God on numerous occasions.

"O LORD, God of my salvation,
I have cried out to you day and night.
Now hear my prayer;
listen to my cry.
For my life is full of troubles,
and death draws near.
I have been dismissed as one who is dead,
like a strong man with no strength left.
They have abandoned me to death,
and I am as good as dead.
I am forgotten,
cut off from your care.
You have thrust me down to the lowest pit,
into the darkest depths." Psalm 88:1-6 (NLT)

"O God, take up my cause!
Defend me against these ungodly people.
Rescue me from these unjust liars.
For you are God, my only safe haven.
Why have you tossed me aside?
Why must I wander around in darkness,
oppressed by my enemies?" Psalm 43:1-2 (NLT)

Making statements or asking questions like these is not uncommon:

I knew s/he had it in for me as soon as s/he became my new boss!

How could my company do this to me after all my years of loyalty and service?

Lord, what did I do to deserve this?

Why didn't I see this coming?

God, I'll only trust you—I can never trust an employer again!

I can understand why some people go postal!

In the space below, list your feelings and questions that you have experienced in the Anger stage:

How did I let this happen?

They're missing out by letting me go.

How come they don't see what I put into my job?

During your quiet time, bring your questions to the Lord. Pour out your heart-felt feelings. He knows what you are thinking and feeling anyway.

> *"O LORD, you have examined my heart*
> *and know everything about me.*
> *You know when I sit down or stand up.*
> *You know my every thought when far away.*
> *You chart the path ahead of me*
> *and tell me where to stop and rest.*
> *Every moment you know where I am.*
> *You know what I am going to say*
> *even before I say it, LORD.*
> *You both precede and follow me.*
> *You place your hand of blessing on my head.*
> *Such knowledge is too wonderful for me,*
> *too great for me to know!"* Psalm 139: 1-6 (NLT)

> *"O LORD Almighty! You know those who are righteous, and you examine the deepest thoughts of hearts and minds."* Jeremiah 20:12a (NLT)

> *"Search me, O God, and know my heart; test me and know my thoughts."* Psalm 139:23 (NLT)

As you work through your anger and get in touch with your primary feelings of hurt, fear, and/or shame, you will experience feelings of relief. The pressure and stress will be lifted. In its place, you will begin to feel vulnerable, wounded, hurt and afraid. But you need not run from those feelings—God will meet you in the midst of them. Remember what Paul said to the believers in Corinth.

> *"Three different times I begged the Lord to take it away. Each time he said, "My gracious favor is all you need. My power works best in your weakness." So now I am glad to boast about my weaknesses, so that the power of Christ may work through me. Since I know it is all for Christ's good, I am quite content with my weaknesses and with insults, hardships, persecutions, and calamities. For when I am weak, then I am strong."* II Corinthians 12:8-10 (NLT)

When we come to terms with our personal powerlessness and weakness over our life circumstances, we can open ourselves to the power and strength of Christ within us. *"For I can do everything with the help of Christ who gives me the strength I need."* Philippians 4:13 (NLT)

Again, family members, friends and coaches can help you move through the anger stage. They can listen to your feelings, ask you clarifying questions, and encourage you to get in touch with why you are feeling so angry right now. Don't resist seeking accountability and wise counsel from other believers.

> *"Fools think they need no advice, but the wise listen to others."* Proverbs 12:15 (NLT)

> *"Get all the advice and instruction you can, and be wise the rest of your life. You can make many plans, but the LORD's purpose will prevail."* Proverbs 19:21 (NLT)

Following your breakthrough of the anger stage, you may begin to bargain. You may seek to find ways of making it all better, trying to make the present circumstances go away. Or, you may attempt to get your employer to reverse his or her decision.

Bargaining

Bargaining is about trying to negotiate or compromise. It is a strategy for seeking a way to make everything all right again. You may attempt to fill another position within your company, or try to negotiate with your manager for another chance to prove yourself. You may offer to take a cut in pay or hours, or you may offer to transfer to a less desirable position, or volunteer for relocation.

You may make statements or ask questions like:

I could take a pay cut.

I could transfer to another department.

I could take a demotion.

Please give me another chance. I know I can prove myself this time.

Record your thoughts, feelings, and behaviors from the Bargaining stage here:

Lord, I won't make same mistakes. I will put more time and effort. Please let me keep the job.
I will prove I can do better.

Take a few minutes to prayerfully consider your heart's motives. Are you willing to compromise your beliefs or your faith to get through this season of unemployment quickly? Remember, the Lord is faithful. He will make his plans clear to you in his timing. Trust him to reveal his path and wait patiently for his guidance. Oftentimes his ways are different than our ways. The path he illuminates is often beyond our wildest dreams and expectations.

"My thoughts are completely different from yours," says the LORD. "And my ways are far beyond anything you could imagine. For just as the heavens are higher than the earth, so are my ways higher than your ways and my thoughts higher than your thoughts." Isaiah 55:8-9 (NLT)

Similar to the previous stages, you can move through the Bargaining stage with support from family, friends and coaches. When you are willing to share your thoughts and intentions with others, you can usually get valuable feedback. People in your support system will tell you if your plans are logical or if you are attempting to undo the past.

"Plans go wrong for lack of advice; many counselors bring success." Proverbs 15:22 (NLT)

"Share each other's troubles and problems, and in this way obey the law of Christ." Galatians 6:2 (NLT)

When you pass through the Bargaining stage, you may find yourself feeling depressed. Depression is about feeling hopeless and helpless.

Depression

Depression is a combination of feelings like hopelessness, helplessness and despair. You may feel like you barely have enough energy or stamina to get through the day. Tomorrow may be something you hope never arrives.

When you are depressed, you may find yourself making statements or asking questions like:

> *Lord, I don't know if I can ever trust another boss again.*
>
> *I don't know if I can ever give my all to another company or job.*
>
> *I don't think there are any companies anymore that are loyal to their employees.*
>
> *I don't think any other company will want to hire someone like me.*
>
> *I'm too old to get a new job.*
>
> *My skills are too specialized to qualify me for anything else.*
>
> *Lord, I feel like I don't know who I am anymore without my job or career.*
>
> *I feel like I've lost my network and social support.*

Reflect on your thoughts, feelings and behaviors during your Depression stage. Record your responses in the space below.

I'm useless. No one wants me.

They will see me as a failure.

My life is meaningless.

They won't be impressed with me at all.

Depression will easily drive you into isolation, loneliness and withdrawal. You may be tempted to turn away from fellow believers and to question the Lord's presence. Find solace and comfort in the Word. Claim God's promises once again.

> *"I waited patiently for the LORD to help me,*
> *and he turned to me and heard my cry.*
> *He lifted me out of the pit of despair,*
> *out of the mud and the mire.*
> *He set my feet on solid ground*
> *and steadied me as I walked along."* Psalm 40:1-2 (NLT)

> *"But I called on your name, LORD, from deep within the well, and you heard me! You listened to my pleading; you heard my weeping! Yes, you came at my despairing cry and told me, "Do not fear."* Lamentations 3:55-57 (NLT)

When you are caught in the throes of depression, support from others is critical. Although you may want to isolate and withdraw, it's important for you to make every effort to seek out and accept support whenever it is offered to you. Press through these initial urges. Seeking comfort and encouragement from God, family, friends and coaches will help you restore your faith, hope and trust in the future. Others who know you and believe in you can be crucial sources of caring, support and encouragement at this time.

Learning to let go of the past and embrace the future is a painful and productive beginning. Holding on to what you once had does not bring it back. Let go, fear less and live for today.

Letting Go

"To let go doesn't mean to stop caring,
    It means I can't do it for someone else
To let go is not to cut myself off,
    It's the realization I can't control another
To let go is not to enable,
    But to allow learning from natural consequences
To let go is to admit powerlessness,
    Which means the outcome is not in my hands
To let go is not to try and change or blame someone else,
    It is accepting that I can only change myself
To let go is not to care for another,
    It's to be supportive
To let go is not to judge,
    But to allow others to effect their own outcomes
To let go is not to be protective,
    It's to permit another to face reality
To let go is not to deny,
    But to accept
To let go is not to nag, scold, or argue,
    But to search out my own shortcomings and correct them
To let go is not to adjust everything to my desires,
    But to take each day as it comes and cherish the moment
To let go is not to criticize and regulate anyone,
    But to try to become what I dream I can be
To let go is not to regret the past,
    But to grow and live for today
To let go is to fear less and love more."

Author Unknown

Strategy #3 Commit to Daily Prayer and Meditation

"Be glad for all God is planning for you. Be patient in trouble, and always be prayerful." Romans 12:2 (NLT)

Spending time daily in God's Word, and in conversations with him are both essential—if you want to stay in an intimate relationship with Christ. He speaks to you primarily through the scriptures and through other believers. Make a commitment now to set aside time each day for prayer and thoughtful meditation. Focus your heart, mind and soul on seeking his will for you and the strength and guidance to carry it out in your life work and career.

Acceptance

In the final stage, you begin to accept that your job is gone. Often, acceptance of your job loss can be illusive. Sometimes, it only comes after getting settled into your next position. During the Acceptance stage, you will experience a feeling of serenity, inner peace and contentment. You will be at peace with yourself, your previous employer and your past supervisor—ready to move forward. You may make statements or ask questions like:

> *Losing that job was the best thing that ever happened to me!*
>
> *I never would have discovered my talents and calling if I had remained in that position.*
>
> *I know that losing my job wasn't personal; it was based on economic and business circumstances beyond my control.*
>
> *I have to come to believe now that God's hand was in my job loss, now I know he had something better in store for me all along!*

Paul speaking:

"Jumping into this process gave me hope. I couldn't see clearly where I would end up; but I had faith and hope that I could get to a better place—the place God wanted me to be next—with focused effort and an open heart on my part, strategies from my career coach and support from other family members and believers."

Keep in mind that God's peace far surpasses our human understandings. If we seek him first, he will guard our hearts and minds.

"Don't worry about anything; instead, pray about everything. Tell God what you need, and thank him for all he has done. If you do this, you will experience God's peace, which is far more wonderful than the human mind can understand. His peace will guard your hearts and minds as you live in Christ Jesus." Philippians 4:6-7 (NLT)

Strategy #4 Develop a Plan to Cope with Your Job Loss

"I told you my plans, and you answered. Now teach me your principles. Help me understand the meaning of your commandments, and I will meditate on your wonderful miracles. I weep with grief; encourage me by your word."
Psalm 119:26-28 (NLT)

Coping with your job loss can be challenging and rewarding. It is a major life change that impacts almost every aspect of your daily life. Learning to adapt and cope during this stressful time will reduce the damages you could potentially experience.

Paul created an action plan for coping with his job loss. Here are his goals and strategies:

1. I will contact one friend, colleague or customer daily by phone or by e-mail.

2. I will reach out to my family members and friends at least three times weekly for support, encouragement, prayer and accountability.

3. I will keep a daily prayer journal, tracking my thoughts, feelings and behaviors; and God's leading and direction, throughout my job search.

4. I will choose two or three Bible verses and use them daily to keep my heart focused on God's comfort, leading and guidance during my job search.

5. I will seek advice from my pastor, my coach and trusted family members and friends before making any significant decisions.

Create a personal action plan now for coping with your job loss. Reflect on your responses to the stages of job loss. Identify strategies you can implement to move forward. Record your personal goals below:

1. I won't stay discouraged and in despair, I will fight it by meditating on the Scripture and praying daily.

2. I will ask my family and friends to pray for me

3. I will talk to others to help me find direction.

4. I will stay productive and remain faithful in the search process.

Strategy #5 Create and Maintain a Healthy Physical Lifestyle

"Or don't you know that your body is the temple of the Holy Spirit, who lives in you and was given to you by God? You do not belong to yourself, for God bought you with a high price. So you must honor God with your body." II Corinthians 6:19-20 (NLT)

Creating and maintaining a healthy physical lifestyle should be your immediate focus when seeking to cope with your job loss. You may be tempted to change your current routines and replace them with destructive and debilitating activities. Frequently, when people experience depression they eat more, eat less, or begin eating unhealthy foods.

When you choose to eat more than usual, or to eat unhealthy foods, it functions as a self-nurturing activity that temporarily provides feelings of comfort, satisfaction and contentment. Although it's a quick fix, in the long run, it can result in numerous health problems. Weight gain, elevated cholesterol, high blood pressure, circulatory problems, increased body fat, and other metabolic conditions such as diabetes are not uncommon.

Your body is the temple of the Holy Spirit. God expects you to honor and care for your body as his holy dwelling place. We are to honor him with our bodies that are no longer ours, but his—purchased for a great price.

Before beginning any exercise routine, or making dramatic changes in your diet, always consult your primary care physician for advice and direction. Here are some suggestions for maintaining a healthy, physical lifestyle:

> 1. *Eat healthy foods*
> 2. *Monitor your weight and caloric intake*
> 3. *Exercise routinely*
> 4. *Enjoy leisure activities*

Family members, friends and coaches can be invaluable sources of support, encouragement, and assistance during this difficult time. Most will let you know how they can be of help to you. Don't hesitate to take advantage of their offers.

You will quickly discover that most people love to give their advice and opinions about anything and everything. Take it all in. Sift through it. Pray about it. Accept what you feel is of the Lord. Politely disregard the rest.

> 1. *Engage in social activities*
> 2. *Network with others who are unemployed*
> 3. *Talk to family, friends, and colleagues*
> 4. *Prayerfully consider advice, opinions and feedback from others*

Paul speaking:

"When we discussed the importance of creating and maintaining a healthy physical lifestyle during this transition phase, I realized that I had stopped doing a lot of healthy activities. I began a new exercise routine at the health club and stopped eating fast food regularly."

Strategy #6 Plan a Spiritual Retreat

"And now about prayer. When you pray, don't be like the hypocrites who love to pray publicly on street corners and in the synagogues where everyone can see them. I assure you, that is all the reward they will ever get. But when you pray, go away by yourself, shut the door behind you, and pray to your Father secretly. Then your Father, who knows all secrets, will reward you." Matthew 6:5, 6 (NLT)

Taking time to retreat from your busyness and frenetic activities allows you to slow down, rest, and center your heart, mind and soul on spiritual things. Doing appears to be so much easier than being for most people in American culture. Setting aside some time to be present—in the moment—and to center your thoughts on Christ helps you to listen to the Holy Spirit and hear his voice speaking to your soul.

On many occasions, Jesus sought solitude and engaged in prayerful communion with his Father. Mark reports one of these accounts in his gospel: *"The next morning Jesus awoke long before daybreak and went out alone into the wilderness to pray."* Mark 1:35 (NLT)

If you are not aware of a retreat center in your community, check with your pastor for local resources. Many communities have spiritual renewal and retreat centers available for anyone wishing to use them. There are several advantages to using these centers. Usually provisions are made for meals, sleeping, and bathing so you aren't distracted by planning or preparing for these needs during your retreat. Some centers also have spiritual directors on site that will meet and pray with you or give counsel.

Alternatively, you may want to plan your own retreat using a friend's cabin or condominium in the mountains, at a lake or in the desert. Check on the Internet for weekend rentals or try a Web site like priceline.com to bid for an inexpensive accommodation. You would probably want to locate something with a kitchenette so that meals can be taken in quiet solitude without the distraction of a busy restaurant and side conversations.

Paul speaking:

"Pastor Chuck told me about a retreat center located in Idaho Springs, about 30 miles West of Denver off of Interstate 70. I called and made a reservation for Friday night and Saturday. I was really looking forward to some solitude and quiet time.

I arrived at the retreat center at about 9am Friday morning. I was greeted by Mrs. Walker at the reception desk. She welcomed me to the retreat center, told me about the facilities and gave me directions to find my room.

The center was nestled in a grove of Aspens, spread out over about 3 acres of land. A stream ran through the property, from northwest to the southeast. The buildings were constructed of rough-hewn logs and stone. Inside the main lodge, there was a great room with a stone fireplace, several chairs, sofas and reading lamps. To the right of the great room was a dining area. Mr. & Mrs. Walker prepared the meals and served them family-style to guests. Meals were to be taken in silence so as not to distract guests from their contemplation.

Adjacent to the main lodge were two dormitory buildings. One was for women and the other was for men. Each dormitory contained six rooms and a community bath area. The rooms had a single bed, desk, chair and closet.

A walking path led to a footbridge over the stream and to a small prayer chapel. Inside the chapel were four wooden pews that could comfortably seat about five people each. At the front, there was an altar with a large Bible and some candles. Above and behind the altar there was a stained glass window with a dove ascending to heaven above an empty cross. Pictures adorned the walls on both sides representing scenes from Jesus' life.

Both Mr. and Mrs. Walker were available for spiritual direction and prayer. I scheduled a meeting with Mr. Walker for Saturday morning at 8:30am following breakfast.

I spent some time in my room before lunch—journaling my thoughts about my career, God's calling in my life, and my feelings about what to do next. Following lunch, I went down to the prayer chapel and spent about an hour in prayerful meditation, asking the Holy Spirit to give me wisdom, discernment, guidance and direction as I sought God's will for me in my job search.

Later that afternoon, I spent time reading the Scriptures and choosing some verses for memory work that I believed would help me stay focused on seeking the Lord's guidance and direction during this job seeking journey. I added these verses to my journal along with my initial thoughts about how God was speaking to me through his word.

After my evening meal, I went back to the chapel for more prayer time and meditation. Then, before retiring for the evening, I went up to the main lodge with my Bible and journal. I spent some quiet-time reading and continuing to journal in the great room near the fireplace. The crackling fire's warmth and the soft glow of the burning embers reminded me of the story in the book of Acts when the Holy Spirit was first poured out on believers. I felt his presence deep within my soul.

Following breakfast the next morning, I met with Mr. Walker. He asked me about my needs and what I was seeking from the Lord during my spiritual retreat. He shared some scripture with me, asked me several thought-provoking questions and then we spent some time together in prayer.

Saturday afternoon arrived and I packed up to return home. It seemed like the time had passed by so quickly. I felt a deep sense of personal renewal. Having the opportunity to focus completely on God and his will for me for the thirty-six hours was a tremendous blessing and I was very grateful. I realized that I needed to plan regular retreats in the future to help me keep my heart and mind centered on Christ and becoming all that he means for me to be as one of his followers.

Strategy #7 Ask Others to Pray for You and Your Job Search

"Confess your sins to each other and pray for each other so that you may be healed. The earnest prayer of a righteous person has great power and wonderful results." James 5:16 (NLT)

Scripture is quite clear when it comes to the power and effectiveness of prayer. Make up a specific prayer list and share it with your prayer partners. Commit to keeping them updated on answers to their prayers and your own throughout your job search. By keeping a prayer journal, you can track the results of your efforts.

"And the Holy Spirit helps us in our distress. For we don't even know what we should pray for, nor how we should pray. But the Holy Spirit prays for us with groanings that cannot be expressed in words. And the Father who knows all hearts knows what the Spirit is saying, for the Spirit pleads for us believers in harmony with God's own will." Romans 8:26-27 (NLT)

"Pray at all times and on every occasion in the power of the Holy Spirit. Stay alert and be persistent in your prayers for all Christians everywhere." Ephesians 6:18 (NLT)

Strategy #8 Write Down Your Detailed Job-Search Action Plan

"Show me the path where I should walk, O LORD; point out the right road for me to follow." Psalm 25:4 (NLT)

Avoid the "activity for activity's sake" pitfall! If you fail to create an action plan, you may remain unfocused, and your activity will likely result in disappointment.

Chapter Five: Creating Your Career Search Activity & Scope Action Plan (ASAP) leads you through the identification of activity and scope targets. Set aside time to think and pray about each strategy. Write out your goals. Share your plan with others and seek wise counsel. Modify it as you move forward and discover what God is calling you to do, where He wants you to be, and how you can successfully achieve it. Budget your time by devoting larger amounts to activities with a higher probability of success. Don't fall victim to your comfort zone!

"The steps of the godly are directed by the LORD. He delights in every detail of their lives." Psalm 37:23 (NLT)

"Seek his will in all you do, and he will direct your paths." Proverbs 3:6 (NLT)

Keep these simple guidelines in mind. Each one is outlined in detail in this guide. Take time to review each one periodically. Update them when changes occur or you modify your goals, objectives or search strategies.

---

1. *Compose your Personal Career and Education Inventory*

2. *Complete your Functional Skills Summary*

3. *Write your CAR stories*

4. *Finish your Career History and Goals Worksheet*

5. *List your industry preferences*

6. *Identify your SALT (Scope, Activity, Liabilities and Timing)*

7. *Create your ASAP (Activity & Scope Action Plan)*

8. *Track your progress*

Strategy #9 Maintain a Positive Outlook during Your Search

"Fix your thoughts on what is true and honorable and right. Think about things that are pure and lovely and admirable. Think about things that are excellent and worthy of praise." Philippians 4:8b (NLT)

You can change your attitude! Thoughts affect feelings, and feelings influence your behavior. By focusing your thoughts on positive beliefs and outcomes, you can influence your feelings about your present circumstances. When you begin to feel positive about yourself and your circumstances, you will have more motivation to engage in productive activities.

"So think clearly and exercise self-control." I Peter 1:13 (NLT)

Keeping a positive attitude will help you stay on track. Look for occasions to be grateful and thankful. Give praise to the Lord for his blessings. Share your victories and celebrate them with others. Be gentle and kind to yourself. Set realistic but aggressive expectations. Don't be afraid to pursue your dreams. Expect the unexpected. Seek spiritual insight and understanding and God will grant you wisdom.

"Cry out for insight and understanding. Search for them as you would for lost money or hidden treasure. Then you will understand what it means to fear the LORD, and you will gain knowledge of God. For the LORD grants wisdom! From his mouth come knowledge and understanding. He grants a treasure of good sense to the godly. He is their shield, protecting those who walk with integrity." Proverbs 2:3-7 (NLT)

---

1. *Engage in continuous learning and growing activities*

2. *Look for a lesson learned in rejections you receive during your search*

3. *Talk about your job search activities and results*

4. *Treat yourself with gentleness and kindness*

5. *Meditate on scripture*

6. *Empower yourself with words like "I can," "I choose," "I know," "I believe"*

7. *Seek out opportunities for temporary or volunteer work*

Paul set goals for creating and maintaining a healthy, physical lifestyle and a positive outlook during his job search. Here is what he wrote down:

1. I will eat healthy foods and monitor my weight daily.

2. I will exercise for thirty minutes, four times weekly with an exercise partner.

3. I will maintain my personal devotions, mediating regularly on encouraging scriptures.

4. I will spend at least thirty minutes daily and at least two hours weekly in leisure activities like reading for pleasure, gardening, hiking, rock-climbing, attending concerts and participating in fellowship activities with other believers.

5.   I will look for a lesson learned in any rejections I receive during my job search.

6.   I will seek out opportunities for temporary or volunteer work on a limited-activity basis.

In the space below, write down your personal goals for creating and maintaining a healthy, physical lifestyle and a positive outlook.

1. *I will eat well and stay active, helping out house chores. and to running errands*

2. *I will be deligent to fellowship with others at church.*

3. *I will make trips to my friends and spend time with them.*

4. *I will improve my resume and interview skills*

Paul speaking:

"Fearful of becoming a burden to my friends and colleagues, I had been withdrawing from them; effectively severing my support systems. I didn't think they would know how to help me. Moreover, I didn't want to make them feel uncomfortable over my situation, so I just pulled away and kept to myself.

My coach helped me to see my double standard. He asked me if I would feel uncomfortable, "put out," or taken advantage of by a friend or family member if they asked me for help in similar circumstances. I realized then that I would want to assist in any way I could—and I would probably feel hurt if they didn't look to me for support.

Not wanting to unintentionally hurt family or friends, I had withdrawn to protect them. I thought by isolating and not asking for help, I would avoid creating conflict in our relationships by making them feel obligated to assist me!

Together, my coach and I discussed the importance of social contact and fellowship with others in my circumstances. I decided to join both a job seekers' support group and a networking group. At first, I thought that being around other unemployed people would be depressing. To my surprise, I found that they were willing and eager to help me in my search. They welcomed my ideas and suggestions too. As people got interviews and found new positions, we celebrated their successes—finding more hope for ourselves along the way.

Networking was never one of my strong suits. Now I realized that I hadn't kept track of many contacts over the years. I guess I didn't think I would ever need them. When I first started putting my list together, I found myself limiting it to people I thought would be able to help me get a job. My coach quickly pointed out that everyone I knew should be on my list. "Who do you know who I need to be talking to?" was a question I needed to be asking everyone I could contact.

Through discussions with my coach, I realized that this journey was going to be much different than I had anticipated. Gradually the cloud over me lifted, and I began to get excited about what I was going to discover about God's will for me and where I was headed. Uncovering my talents, finding my spiritual gifts and discovering ideal job matches would give me the opportunity to find work that I love, express my passion and faith through my career, and enjoy fulfillment and satisfaction each day—knowing that I am becoming all that God wants me to be as his child."

Chapter Review

Finding Yourself Unemployed

Strategy #1 Understand the Job-Loss Cycle
- Denial
- Anger
- Bargaining
- Depression
- Acceptance

Strategy #2 Accept Help from Others through Each Job-Loss Stage

Strategy #3 Commit to Daily Prayer and Meditation

Strategy #4 Develop a Plan to Cope with Your Job Loss

Strategy #5 Create and Maintain a Healthy, Physical Lifestyle

Strategy #6 Plan a Spiritual Retreat

Strategy #7 Ask Others to Pray for You and Your Job Search

Strategy #8 Write Down Your Detailed Job-Search Action Plan

Strategy #9 Maintain a Positive Outlook During Your Search

Chapter Two:
Discovering Your Job Matches

Paul speaking:

"After helping me understand what I was experiencing and giving me some helpful strategies for moving forward, my career coach told me about the importance of uncovering my talents, discovering my spiritual gifts and identifying my ideal job matches."

Strategy #10 Uncover Your Natural Gifts and Talents

"God has given each of us the ability to do certain things well. So if God has given you the ability to prophesy, speak out when you have faith that God is speaking through you. If your gift is that of serving others, serve them well. If you are a teacher, do a good job of teaching. If your gift is to encourage others, do it! If you have money, share it generously. If God has given you leadership ability, take the responsibility seriously. And if you have a gift for showing kindness to others, do it gladly." Romans 12:6-8 (NLT)

Understanding your natural gifts and talents is the first step of the journey toward finding and enjoying your ideal career. You were born with natural talents. When you combine knowledge and skill to develop your natural talents, you create your strengths.

> *"Talent-naturally recurring patterns of thought, feeling or behavior."*

In *Now, Discover Your Strengths*, Marcus Buckingham & Donald O. Clifton define talent as "your naturally recurring patterns of thought, feeling or behavior." They go on to say: "Knowledge consists of the facts and lessons learned" and "skills are the steps of an activity."

Naturally recurring patterns of thought

Naturally recurring patterns of thought which result in talent can be identified as cognitive processes—how you mentally process information or think about it. The Profiles *Career Coach* is a very effective assessment published by Profiles International Inc. It identifies thinking style and a measurement of your learning index.

Naturally recurring patterns of feeling

Naturally recurring patterns of feeling that result in talent can be identified as affective or feeling responses. The process of using feelings can be identified by your temperament type. A common assessment of temperament type is the

Keirsey Temperament Sorter. It is based on Carl Jung's typology of two opposing ways of perceiving and two opposing ways of judging.

The Temperament Sorter identifies your preferences for mentally processing collected data (perceiving) and your mental processes for reaching conclusions from the information collected (judging). Additionally, it identifies your attitude toward using energy and relating to your environment.

Most of your psychological energy is consumed by your dominant psychological function and you enjoy engaging it. By doing so, you gain most of your skills and experience. The activities you engage in and the pleasure you experience as a result significantly influences your career choices and your interpersonal relationships.

You can take the Keirsey Temperament Sorter on-line. It can be found at http://www.advisorteam.com/temperament_sorter/register.asp. Or you can find it in the book, *Please Understand Me II: Temperament, Character, Intelligence*, by David Keirsey.

Naturally recurring patterns of behavior

Naturally recurring patterns of behavior that result in talent can be identified by assessing your behavioral style. The Profiles *Career Coach* assesses your style. It also measures behavioral traits and identifies personal strength areas.

Buckingham and Clifton include a one-time use access code to take the on-line strengths assessment (StrengthsFinder Profile) discussed in their book, *Now Discover Your Strengths*. This assessment identifies and describes your top five Signature Themes. The book provides a comprehensive overview of the themes and how they interact with one another.

The Gallup Organization asked 198,000 employees in 7,939 business units within thirty-six companies: "At work do you have the opportunity to do what you do best every day?" When responses were compared to business unit performance the following characteristics were discovered:

When employees answered "strongly agree" to this question, they were 50 percent more likely to work in business units with lower employee turnover, 38 percent more likely to work in more productive business units, and 44 percent more likely to work in business units with higher customer satisfaction scores (*Now, Discover Your Strengths*, p. 5).

Strategy #11 Discover Your Gifts

"God has given gifts to each of you from his great variety of spiritual gifts. Manage them well so that God's generosity can flow through you." I Peter 4:10 (NLT)

You have spiritual gifts that God has given to you. When you use them well, he is glorified. Others see Christ in you through your actions, words and deeds. If you are unsure of your gifts, ask the Lord to reveal them to you. Seek counsel from other Christians who know you well and ask them to tell you what gifts they believe God has given to you.

Actions for Identifying Your Spiritual Gifts

1. Search the scriptures for passages on giftedness, how God gives them and their individual purposes in your life and ministry.

    Psalm 139:13-16; Acts 2; 8:14-19; 10; 19:1-6; Romans 6:19-20; 12:4-8; I Corinthians 4:7; 12:4-6; 13:1; II Corinthians 5:17; 8:12; 9:6-7; Galatians 5:22; Ephesians 3:20-21; 4:7-8; 4:22-25; 5:8-17; Philippians 2:12-13; Colossians 1:28-29; I Timothy 1:18; 4:14; II Timothy 1:6; I Peter 4:9-10

2. Ask the Lord to give you wisdom and direction in discovering your gifts.

3. Reflect on the variety of ministries and work experiences you have had in the past.

4. Give careful attentiveness to your yearnings and sense of calling.

    *   What stirs you deep within your soul?

    *   Which activities fill you with a sense of fulfillment, completion and contentment?

    *   Describe your dream roles and responsibilities in detail

    *   Identify your creative drives and aspirations

5. Consider your natural talents and abilities—what seems to come natural to you? These may be indicators of your spiritual giftedness in undeveloped form. Typically, you will achieve success or demonstrate competency with certain skills, these may be other indications of your giftedness.

6. Approach other Christians who know you well and ask them for their input. Pay attention to feedback from others. Often comments like, "You are so talented at resolving conflict." "Your ability to lead others is exemplary." Or,"When you speak to groups, they always seem to come away motivated and inspired to take action."

Strategy #12 Discover Your Job Matches

"I have filled him with the Spirit of God, giving him great wisdom, intelligence, and skill in all kinds of crafts."
Exodus 31:3 (NLT)

Paul speaking:

"My career coach explained that there was an assessment available that I could take that would give me a clearer understanding of my strengths, personality and interests and then match me to a wide variety of occupations that would be strong fit for me.

By taking the Profiles *Career Coach* assessment, I gained insights into my thinking style, occupational interests and behavioral traits. I also learned how I match up with other successful people in a variety of careers who share similar talents and abilities with me. This gave me insights into a whole range of career possibilities!

My coach gave me my *Career Coach Report* and reviewed the results with me. I was excited to learn about so many different future possibilities. Having so many strong fits for such a variety of occupations was surprising. You can see my report below."

Paul Williams' Profiles Career Coach Results

SECTION ONE
Job Match

The *Career Coach* compares the results of your evaluation with the requirements for a variety of career fields described by O*NET (Occupational Information Network). The percentages below indicate the degree to which your results match each of the listed occupations. They are shown in descending order by percentage match within each group. You should consider those occupations where you show the highest match because they suggest a good job fit. Remember, these results reflect suitability only in terms of Thinking Style, Occupational Interests and Behavioral Traits as reported here. Other important components, such as educational level, specific skills and experience, should also be taken into account in examining career options.

Your results have been grouped into two categories. **Group One** indicates those occupations typically requiring education beyond high school; and **Group Two** indicates those occupations not typically requiring education beyond the high school level. Also provided is the O*NET SOC Code that may be used to research each occupation. To do this go to <u>on-line.onetcenter.org</u>, select Find Occupations and enter the appropriate SOC Code from the list below.

Group One: Advanced Training Required

O*NET SOC Code	Occupational Title	Job Match Percentage
29-1122.00	Occupational Therapist	89%
21-1014.00	Mental Health Counselor	88%
11-9061.00	Director, Funeral	88%
27-3043.02	Creative Writer	88%
41-3031.01	Trader/Stockbroker	88%
11-9031.00	Elementary School Principal	88%
29-1127.00	Speech Pathologist	87%
11-3021.00	IT Manager	86%
27-1025.00	Interior Designer	86%
29-1111.00	Registered Nurse	86%
29-1041.00	Optometrist	86%
27-3011.00	Announcer, Radio & TV	86%
11-1011.01	City Manager	86%
27-3011.00	Radio & Television Announcers	85%
53-2012.00	Executive Pilot	85%
25-2021.00	Elementary School Teacher	85%
11-3021.00	Software Manager	85%
15-1081.00	Network Specialist	85%
29-1123.00	Physical Therapist	84%
11-9081.00	Hotel Manager	84%
11-3042.00	Training & Development Manager	84%
21-1021.00	Social Worker	84%
15-1031.00	Software Engineer	84%

Group One: Advanced Training Required (Continued)

O*NET SOC Code	Occupational Title	Job Match Percentage
29-1011.00	Chiropractor	84%
27-3043.00	Writer/Author	84%
29-1051.00	Pharmacist	84%
11-3031.02	Bank Manager	84%
11-3031.02	Bank President	83%
29-1031.00	Nutritionist	83%
19-3031.03	Counseling Psychologist	83%
27-3022.00	Reporter/Correspondent	83%
15-1051.00	Systems Analyst	83%
11-9141.00	Property Manager	83%
21-1012.00	Vocational Counselor	83%
11-9031.00	Secondary School Principal	83%
33-1012.00	Police Chief	83%
11-9111.00	Administrator, Health Care	83%
19-3032.00	Industrial/Organizational Psychologist	83%
29-1031.00	Dietician, Chief	82%
17-1012.00	Landscape Architect	82%
13-2052.00	Financial Planner	82%
15-1031.00	Senior Software Engineer	82%
11-2021.00	Marketing Manager	82%
33-1021.01	Fire Chief	82%
27-3031.00	Public Relations Specialist	82%
23-1011.00	Lawyer, Corporate/Business	82%
23-1011.00	Lawyer, Trial	82%
17-1011.00	Architect	82%
11-3040.00	Human Resource Manager	82%
13-2072.00	Senior Bank Loan Officer	82%

Group Two: Basic Training Required

O*NET SOC Code	Occupational Title	Job Match Percentage
11-2022.00	Sales Manager	88%
43-1011.01	Help Desk Manager	87%
41-4012.00	Sales, Commissioned	87%
43-4051.00	Client/Customer Service Representative	87%
13-1121.00	Conference Coordinator	84%
27-4021.00	Photographer	84%
35-1012.00	Restaurant Manager	84%
13-1031.01	Claims Adjuster	83%
41-2031.00	Inside Sales	82%
11-3011.00	Office Manager	82%
47-2031.01	Carpenter, Finish	82%
41-2031.00	Sales Associate	81%

Group Two: Basic Training Required (Continued)

O*NET SOC Code	Occupational Title	Job Match Percentage
41-3041.00	Travel Agent	81%
13-1071.00	Employment, Recruitment & Placement Specialist	81%
43-6011.00	Administrative Assistant	81%
41-9022.00	Leasing Consultant	79%
43-6011.00	Executive Secretary	79%
15-1021.00	Computer Programmer	79%
13-1022.00	Wholesale & Retail Buyers	78%
11-9021.00	Construction Manager	78%
15-1041.00	PC Specialist	77%
39-6032.00	Transport Attendant	77%
43-6012.00	Legal Secretary	77%
35-1011.00	Chef	77%
43-5061.00	Inventory Control Manager	76%
43-9011.00	Computer Operator	76%
43-6014.00	Secretary	75%
47-2021.00	Brick Mason	75%
49-3023.02	Automotive Technician	75%
39-6031.00	Airplane Flight Attendant	75%
47-2031.02	Carpenter, Rough	75%
33-2011.00	Fire Fighter	75%
43-1011.01	Head Teller, Bank	75%
43-3061.00	Procurement Officer	74%
43-3071.00	Bank Teller	74%
43-4171.00	Receptionist	74%
43-4151.00	Order Expeditor	74%
43-4081.00	Hotel Desk Clerk	74%
43-3031.00	Accounts Payable Clerk	74%
43-3031.00	Accounts Receivable Clerk	74%
51-9071.01	Jewelers	73%
49-2094.00	Electronics Technician	72%
43-6014.00	Financial Secretary	72%
43-3031.00	Bookkeeper	71%
47-2111.00	Electrician	71%
51-1011.00	Quality Assurance Supervisor	70%
53-4013.00	Railroad Engineer	70%
43-4021.00	Courtesy Clerk	70%
37-1011.02	Maintenance Superintendent	70%
43-6013.00	Medical Secretary	70%

SECTION TWO
Understanding and Using the O*NET

O*NET OnLine is an application that was produced for the US Department of Labor by the National O*NET Consortium. It has been created for public use to provide broad access to the O*NET catalog of occupational information. By logging onto the site you will gain access to a wealth of information about the jobs listed in Section One. The web address listed below will take you directly to the site where instructions for using O*NET can be found. It is a helpful tool that you may use more successfully with the results of your *Career Coach Report*.

The occupational profiles on O*NET will help you understand various aspects of a particular job. These descriptions help build your understanding of the job just as the *Career Coach* helps build your self-understanding.

Each O*NET Occupational Profile provides extensive data. These are organized in several groupings:
Worker Characteristics—Abilities, Interests, Work Values and Work Styles
Worker Requirements—Skills and Knowledge
Experience Requirements—Training, Experience and Licensing
Occupation Requirements—Generalized Work Activities and Work/Organizational Content
Occupation Specific Information—Important Occupation-Specific Tasks
Occupation Characteristics—Outlook and Earnings
Related Occupations—A database of jobs similar in scope to your matched jobs list

O*NET is a user-friendly resource, providing an easy to understand frame of reference for its users. As a supplement to career counseling, the database provides complex data in a manner that offers utility and convenience to the user. By using it in conjunction with your *Career Coach Report*, the O*NET database can be extremely helpful in selecting your next career.

The O*NET Internet site is at this web address: online.onetcenter.org

SECTION THREE
Your Results

Understanding Your Report
Your *Career Coach Report* has a list of matching jobs with a percentage figure indicating how closely your results match the thinking style, occupational interests, and behavioral traits that have been determined as important for success in that job. The *Career Coach Report* helps you narrow your search and identify careers that may suit you best. Your *report* is divided into three major areas that are briefly described below.

Thinking Style
The *Career Coach Report* gives your results for Numerical Ability, Numerical Reasoning, Verbal Skill, Verbal Reasoning and an overall Learning Index. This is not a test of intelligence, but it does suggest how efficiently you assimilate and utilize various forms of information.

Occupational Interests

The Occupational Interests section reflects how you answered questions related to working in various occupations. From this information, you can see any clear preference or pattern of interests.

Behavioral Traits

Everyone can be defined partially by their behavioral traits, which are measured by your responses to the *Career Coach* questionnaire. This profile reflects your behavioral traits and can help you to find the jobs for which you may be best suited.

THINKING

Learning Index (An index of expected learning, reasoning and problem solving potential.)

- Your understanding and utilization of new information will be better than most individuals in the general population.

- You are an effective learner in most situations.

- You generally learn by paying attention to detail and determining how the information applies to various relevant areas of your work.

- You handle fairly complex tasks with relative efficiency, demonstrating strong problem-solving abilities.

Verbal Skill (A measure of verbal skill through vocabulary.)

- You are capable of precise communication even under the pressure of strict time constraints.

- You excel in a job that requires the accurate application of communication in order to make correct decisions.

- You are quick in communicating correct conceptual solutions to problems, using a diverse vocabulary.

- Your analysis of communication related concepts should be sharp and on target.

Verbal Reasoning (Using words as a basis in reasoning and problem solving.)

- You do not typically have any difficulty in effectively communicating thoughts and ideas to others.

- You are proficient in the use of words and language.

- You demonstrate adequate and, in some areas, good verbal skill.

- You probably assimilate verbal information as easily as the general population.

- Numerical Ability (A measure of numeric calculation ability.)

- You should be able to grasp common mathematical principals that apply to the job.

- You should be comfortable analyzing basic numerical material and performing some mathematical functions without relying on a calculator.

- You may need assistance with complex mathematics or technical calculations.

- You should be capable of learning to apply everyday mathematical principles to new, more complex problems as necessary.

Numeric Reasoning (Using numbers as a basis in reasoning and problem solving.)

- You demonstrate a relatively strong ability to solve problems of a numerical nature.

- You work well with numbers and numerical concepts.

- You grasp numerical concepts readily.

- You complete numerical problems with comparable success to the general population.

OCCUPATIONAL INTERESTS

- You scored highest in the Creative and the People Service themes on the interest inventory:

- You are attracted to positions where you can apply creative problem solving skills to people issues.

- The composite results here strongly suggest a person who is going to take a lot of pride in developing and training people.

- You will enjoy opportunities to create systems and anything that has to do with creative expression and aesthetics.

- You should be a motivated counselor, coach and general supervisor based on these interests.

BEHAVIORAL TRAITS

Energy Level (Tendency to display endurance and capacity for a fast pace.)

- You are a self-starter, an energetic personal producer; you show a high sense of urgency.

- You enjoy a quick pace and a fast track. You demonstrate a strong focus on critical deadlines and timely results.

- You would very likely enjoy positions which call for a high energy level, fast work pace and critical deadlines.

- You have an unusually high energy level and probably do not enjoy sedentary work.

- Assertiveness (Tendency to take charge of people and situations. Leads more than follows.)

- You tend to prefer solutions that are not risky and that have been proven to be effective in the past.

- You sometimes need to be in charge, to be the leader. However, not in all situations.

- You are careful in asserting yourself, tending to be more of a follower than a leader.

- You tend to be a good listener, to be more comfortable as a participant in a group rather than as the leader.

Sociability (Tendency to be outgoing, people-oriented and participate with others.)

- You are highly inclined to promote the benefits of teamwork; you tend to confer with others and to involve the team in the discussion of how things will be done.

- You spend a great amount of time interacting with people, engaging them in conversation and being concerned with interpersonal relationships. You would find it extremely challenging to work in isolation from other people.

- You are quick to initiate relationships, to interact easily; you fit in with all types of people.
- Your sociability is highly compatible with establishing a network of contacts. You are open to others, approachable and quick to share feelings and ideas.

Manageability (Tendency to follow policies, accept external controls and supervision and work within the rules.)

- You have a generally accommodating interpersonal style. You can usually work cooperatively with others.
- Your attitude is typical of most people regarding authority and rules, with a generally cooperative interpersonal style.
- You relate to most directives in a generally cooperative and accommodating manner, but may resent high pressure leadership.
- You relate to authority in a cooperative manner in most routine situations; however, occasionally you may express a need for more personal freedom.
- Attitude (Tendency to have a positive attitude regarding people and outcomes.)
- You have a highly positive attitude concerning risk, change and unexpected challenges.
- You express a positive attitude regarding supervision and external controls.
- Your attitude is highly compatible with confronting interpersonal problems and frustrations.
- You demonstrate a highly positive attitude regarding changes in policies and procedures.
- Decisiveness (Uses available information to make decisions quickly.)
- You are capable of responding to an emergency and of solving problems in a timely manner.
- You are not inclined to delay important decisions.
- You are typically decisive and inclined to act, effective in positions which require timely results.
- You stand firm on some decisions and may not be inclined to back down once a decision is made, unless under pressure.

Accommodating (Tendency to be friendly, cooperative, agreeable. To be a team person.)

- You are generally pleasant, friendly and patient. You are not inclined to show temper or frustration.
- You tend to be modest, not inclined to take or to maintain an extreme opinion or position.
- You express a desire to promote the benefits of teamwork and cooperation and are usually willing to share resources and information.
- You tend to have a cooperative outlook and are generally prepared to help others.
- Independence (Tendency to be self-reliant, self-directed, to take independent action and make own decisions.)
- You take on new developments independently, bringing in co-workers only when absolutely necessary.
- You likely prefer to run your own show and may quietly resist being restricted. You can become impatient with the traditionalist view that "we've been doing this for the last ten years, so why should we change?"

- You are highly independent, functioning well on your own, but could benefit by making room for the advice of others.
- You are an independent worker who prefers minimal guidance and coaching.

Objective Judgment (The ability to think clearly and be objective in decision-making.)

- Your judgment is best utilized in concrete situations and with tangible data.
- Your decisions might not consistently indicate objective judgment and logical deduction.
- Your judgment is compatible with routine problems and decisions.
- Your conclusions have a tendency to be inconsistent under pressure.

Paul Williams' Career Coach Profile Summary

Thinking Style

	1	2	3	4	5	6	7	8	9	10
Learning Index	1	2	3	4	5	6	**7**	8	9	10
Verbal Skill	1	2	3	4	5	6	7	8	**9**	10
Verbal Reasoning	1	2	3	4	5	**6**	7	8	9	10
Numerical Ability	1	2	3	4	5	**6**	7	8	9	10
Numeric Reasoning	1	2	3	4	5	6	7	**8**	9	10

Occupational Interests

	1	2	3	4	5	6	7	8	9	10
Enterprising	1	2	3	4	5	**6**	7	8	9	10
Financial/Administrative	1	**2**	3	4	5	6	7	8	9	10
People Service	1	2	3	4	5	6	7	**8**	9	10
Technical	1	**2**	3	4	5	6	7	8	9	10
Mechanical	1	2	**3**	4	5	6	7	8	9	10
Creative	1	2	3	4	5	6	7	8	**9**	10

Behavioral Traits

	1	2	3	4	5	6	7	8	9	10
Energy Level	1	2	3	4	5	6	7	8	9	**10**
Assertiveness	1	2	3	4	**5**	6	7	8	9	10
Sociability	1	2	3	4	5	6	7	**8**	9	10
Manageability	1	2	3	4	**5**	6	7	8	9	10
Attitude	1	2	3	4	5	6	7	8	**9**	10
Decisiveness	1	2	3	4	5	**6**	7	8	9	10
Accommodating	1	2	3	4	5	6	**7**	8	9	10
Independence	1	2	3	4	5	6	7	**8**	9	10
Objective Judgment	1	2	3	**4**	5	6	7	8	9	10

Distortion = 10—Distortion scores range from 1 to 10 with the highest scores suggesting the greatest candor.

Paul speaking:

"I was fascinated by how accurately the *Career Coach Report* described my abilities and my job matches. My coach helped me to see that my high job match percentages with sales manager (88%), sales, commissioned (87%), bank manager (84%), inside sales (82%), sales associate (81%) supported my career experiences of superior success as a senior sales manager in the radio broadcasting, television and retail consumer products industries and as an assistant manager in banking.

I also noticed that my job match percentages were lower for head teller (75%), and bank teller (74%); positions that I had held early in my career. My percentage job fit was high though, for similar positions like: trader/stockbroker (88%), financial planner (82%) and senior loan officer (82%). My coach helped me to understand that the analytical skills and data analysis processes involved in these three positions were probably the key matching factors. I know I enjoyed the data and trend analysis functions. But I didn't really care for the day-to-day management functions where I was required to maintain systems that were functioning smoothly.

The Career Coach Report helped me see that I thrive in fast-paced, changing environments that give me the opportunity to engage in responsible risk-taking, multitasking, and complex problem-solving activities. If I were to move into a general manager role in a mature industry, I would die on the vine without opportunities for business process re-engineering, new-product development and change management.

This new information helped me begin to think about some ideal careers for my next position. Working in a people-service role will be essential. I'm also a self-starter and an energetic personal producer; with high energy, endurance and urgency, so I wanted to focus on careers that would be fast-paced, with critical deadlines and timely results.

A sales leadership role that would allow me to manage teams would be ideal. Another good fit would be a trader/stockbroker position if there was an opportunity for advancement into a leadership role. This leadership position could also include business development, staff development, and complex problem-solving around customer service, products and processes.

To begin my job search preparation, my career coach told me that I needed to do some pre-work. Next, I needed to prepare my Personal Career & Education Inventory. He told me that this could take me several hours to complete accurately and comprehensively, but that the investment would reap significant dividends in the end."

Chapter Review

Strategy #10 Uncover Your Natural Gifts and Talents

Strategy #11 Discover Your Gifts
- Search the scriptures
- Ask the Lord for wisdom and direction
- Reflect on your ministry and work experiences
- Carefully attend to your yearnings and sense of calling
- Consider your natural talents and abilities
- Seek confirmation from other believers who know you well

Strategy #12 Discover Your Job Matches
Profiles Career Coach Assessment

Chapter Three:
Your Career and Education History

Strategy #13 Create Your Personal Career & Education Inventory

In preparation for your job search, it is critical that you complete a Personal Career and Education Inventory. By doing so, you will gain several strategic advantages. First, you will restore your confidence by clearly documenting your past accomplishments.

Second, you will be organizing your achievements in preparation for writing your résumés and completing employment applications. Finally, by completing this exercise you will have a concise summary of your professional development. This will assist you in planning your next career steps which may include additional training, education or experience in other areas.

Begin by gathering data about your educational history. The worksheet in the Appendix is designed to accommodate a variety of educational experiences; including high school, trade school, community college, colleges/universities, graduate school and doctoral education. If a section isn't relevant to your personal history, leave it blank.

Strategy #14 Build Your Confidence by Organizing Your Achievements, and Summarizing Your Education & Professional Development

The following section gives you a chance to review Paul Williams' Personal Career & Education Inventory. You can see how it helped him organize his achievements and prepared him for developing his résumés.

Paul Williams' Personal Career & Education Inventory

EDUCATION HISTORY

High School: Fullerton High School

City, State Fullerton, CA   Graduation Date: 06/18/1984

Trade School:

City, State   Graduation Date:

Technical School:

City, State   Graduation Date:

Community College:

City, State

Degree Awarded: Graduation Date: GPA:

College/University (Undergraduate): California State University, San Bernardino

City, State San Bernardino, CA

Major: business administration   Minor:

Degree Awarded: BSBA   Graduation Date: 5/88   GPA: 3.90

College/University (Graduate):

City, State

Major: Minor:

Degree Awarded: Graduation Date: GPA:

EDUCATION HISTORY (Continued)

University (Doctoral):

City, State

Major: Minor:

Degree Awarded: Graduation Date: GPA:

Internships: (dates and descriptions)

University (Post-Doctoral):

City, State

Certification: Graduation Date:

PROFESSIONAL LICENSES, CERTIFICATIONS

Type:

Licensing/Certifying Body:

Original Date of Licensure/Certification:

Type:

Licensing/Certifying Body:

Original Date of Licensure/Certification:

Work History

Now gather and record data about your past employment. This will be a reverse chronological history. Begin with your most recent position and go back to your graduation from high school, college, or trade school. If you attended graduate school after working for a few years, go back as far as your undergraduate college graduation.

WORK HISTORY
Employer: KCMA Radio
City, State Colorado Springs, CO
Start Date: 03/01/2001   Termination Date: 06/30/2004
Industry: Radio Broadcasting   Annual Revenue: $4M   Number of Employees: 45
Job Title: Sales Manager   Direct Reports: 6
Compensation: $65K   Budget Responsibility: $3M   P&L: $ None
Immediate Supervisor: Bill Thompson
Title: Vice President, Sales & Marketing   Phone: (719) 555-1215 ext. 345
Key Functional Skills: sales, business development, sales leadership, C-level CRM, staff training, forecasting, and team management
Duties & Responsibilities: Sold radio advertising. Forged strategic alliances with key customers. Cold calling on potential accounts, contract negotiations, staff training and competitive market analysis. Copy editing and writing.
Reason for Leaving: Company acquired by competitor, my position was eliminated because my position was assumed by an employee of the competitor.

WORK HISTORY (Continued)

Employer: Channel 5 News

City, State Denver, CO

Start Date: 01/03/1997	Termination Date: 08/30/2000

Industry: Television Broadcasting
Annual Revenue: $10M   Number of Employees: 250

Job Title: Regional Sales Associate	Direct Reports: None

Compensation: $55K	Budget Responsibility: $2M	P&L: $ None

Immediate Supervisor: Walter Jones

Title: Vice President, Sales	Phone: (303) 555-1219 ext. 212

Key Functional Skills:

Budget responsibility, business development, strategic alliances, C-level CRM, forecasting and competitive market analysis

Duties & Responsibilities:

Sold television commercial airtime, forged strategic alliances with key customers, captured market share. Grew sales by 20% each quarter over three years.

Reason for Leaving:

Company acquired and position eliminated.

WORK HISTORY (Continued)
Employer: All Sports Outlet
City, State Tustin, CA
Start Date: 06/01/1993   Termination Date: 12/15/1996
Industry: Retail Consumer Products, Sporting Goods   Annual Revenue: $5M   Number of Employees: 175
Job Title: Golf Department Manager / Sales Associate   Direct Reports: 0
Compensation: $45K   Budget Responsibility: $ None   P&L: $ None
Immediate Supervisor: James Cruz
Title: Store Manager   Phone: (71) 555-3131 ext. 12
Key Functional Skills: Cashier, inventory control, stocking, pricing, customer service.
Duties & Responsibilities: Provided retail customer service to store patrons. Assisted with inventory, pricing, stocking, and sales.
Reason for Leaving: Recruited by Channel 5 News to work as Regional Sales Associate in Denver, targeting sporting events companies and retail outlets.

WORK HISTORY (Continued)
Employer: New City Bank & Trust
City, State Omaha, NB
Start Date: 03/12/1989   Termination Date: 05/15/1993
Industry: Financial Services, Retail Banking   Total Assets: $3M   Number of Employees: 30
Job Title: Vice President / Head Teller / Teller   Direct Reports: 15
Compensation: $35K   Budget Responsibility: $None   P&L: $ None
Immediate Supervisor: Kathy French
Title: President   Phone: (308) 555-9393 ext. 14
Key Functional Skills: customer service, staff training, auditing, account reconciliations
Duties & Responsibilities: Managed tellers and loan officers. Financial reporting, customer service.
Reason for Leaving: Recruited by All Sports Outlet to relocate to Tustin.

Military Service

If you served in the military, complete the following section. Record the service branch, your dates of service and your rank at discharge. Next, record a reverse chronological history of your rank and duties, starting with your most recent position. If you completed any special training or received certifications during your military career, record those too.

Service Branch: _____   Service Dates: ___/___/___ to ___/___/___

Rank at Discharge: _____

Reverse Chronological History of Rank and Duties:

Rank	Duties	Dates

Special Military Training, Education & Certifications:

School / Institution	Course / Program Title	Dates

Continuing Education & Professional Development

Review the past ten years and record any continuing education programs, professional development workshops or seminars that you completed.

Provider	Course Name	Dates
Tom Peters	Brand Inside: Brand Outside	2002
Anthony Robbins	Unleash The Power Within	2001
Dale Carnegie Training	Sales Advantage	1998
American Management Association	Customer Service Excellence	1992

Honors, Awards & Professional Recognition

Record any honors, awards, or professional recognition you have received during your high school, college, or university experience and throughout your career. Include honor societies, production or performance awards, biographical sketches in publications like *Who's Who*, community service, and professional association honors or awards.

Conferring Body	Type/Name/Description	Date Awarded
Channel 5 News	Salesman of the Year	2000, 1999
All Sports Outlet	President's Award for Excellence in Customer Service	1996
New City Bank & Trust	Employee of the Year	1992

Community Service

Record community service activities you have participated in over the past 10 years. List the name of the group or activity. Describe your role and the dates you were involved.

Group/Activity	Description	Dates
United Way	Volunteered for annual fundraisings at New City Bank & Trust, raised $10K annually.	1990 to 1993
Habitat for Humanity	Helped build two houses for low income families	1991 to 1992

Charitable Activities

Describe your charitable activities over the past ten years. Record the names of each group or activity/event, describe your role and the dates you participated.

Group/Activity	Description	Dates
First Baptist Church	Volunteer elder board member, Sunday school teacher, and usher	2001 to present

Professional Associations

List any professional associations to which you belonged over the past 10 years. Record the full name, the type of membership you held, e.g., Professional, Regular, Student, Active and the dates of your membership.

Name	Membership Type	Dates

Leisure Activities

Finally, list your leisure activities. Choose those that reflect your achievements whenever possible.

Golf, snow skiing, rock-climbing, and gardening

Strategy # 15 Utilize Your Functional Skills Checklist

Next, Paul reviewed the following checklist and identified his functional skills in each category. He placed a "☑" next to each functional skill, in each category within which he could document performance in his work or educational history. A **Functional Skills Checklist** is in the Appendix for your personal use.

Paul Williams' Functional Skills Checklist

Management Level—Check the area of management at which you see yourself.

- ☐ Executive Level Management
- ☐ Senior Level Management
- ☑ Mid-Level Management

- ☐ Entry-level Management
- ☐ Completed Training
- ☐ Completed Education

Management Skills

- ☑ Budgeting
- ☑ Business Planning
- ☑ Business Re engineering
- ☑ Change Management
- ☐ Consolidations
- ☐ Corporate Finance

- ☑ Cost Control
- ☐ Cross-Functional Teams
- ☑ Decision Making
- ☑ Developing Policies
- ☐ Diversification
- ☐ Divestitures

Management Skills (Continued)

- ☑ Employee Evaluations
- ☐ Financing-Public/Private
- ☐ Government Relations
- ☑ Growth Strategies
- ☑ Hiring/Firing
- ☐ International Management
- ☐ Investor Relations
- ☐ IPO Strategy/Positioning
- ☐ Joint Ventures
- ☐ Labor Relations
- ☐ Manager Development
- ☐ Mergers & Acquisitions
- ☑ Methods & Measures
- ☐ Multi-Site Management

- ☑ Negotiations
- ☐ Officer/Board Member
- ☐ Organizational Development
- ☐ P&L Accountability
- ☑ Project Management
- ☐ Resource Management
- ☐ Restructuring
- ☑ Revenue Growth
- ☑ Staff Development
- ☐ Start-up Situations
- ☑ Strategic Partnerships
- ☑ Strategic Planning
- ☑ Supervision
- ☐ Turnaround Situations

Operations Skills

- ☐ Assembly
- ☐ Automation Engineering
- ☐ Bidding
- ☐ Call Center Operations
- ☐ Configuration
- ☐ Construction
- ☐ Continuous Process Improvements
- ☐ Contract Management
- ☐ Control Systems
- ☐ Distribution/Transportation
- ☐ Document Control Management
- ☐ Environmental Issues
- ☐ Equipment Design
- ☐ Equipment Maintenance & Repair
- ☐ Equipment Management

- ☐ Facility Management/Leases
- ☐ Fleet Management
- ☐ Installation
- ☐ Inventory Control
- ☐ ISO 9000 series
- ☐ JIT (Just In Time Inventory)
- ☐ WIP (Work In Process)
- ☐ MRP (Material Resource Planning)
- ☐ Labor Control
- ☐ Lean Manufacturing (Toyota)
- ☐ Logistics
- ☐ Maintenance
- ☐ Labor Planning/Budgeting
- ☐ Manufacturing Engineering
- ☐ Materials Handling/Management

Operations Skills (Continued)

- ☑ Methods & Standards
- ☐ Multi-Shift Management
- ☐ New Product Development
- ☐ Operations Research
- ☐ Operations Supervision
- ☐ Order Processing
- ☐ Outsourcing
- ☐ Plant Design & Layout
- ☑ Policies & Procedures
- ☐ Process Control Supervision
- ☐ Process Engineering
- ☐ Production Planning
- ☐ Project Coordination
- ☐ Project Management
- ☐ Prototype Operations
- ☐ Purchasing/Procurement
- ☐ Quality Assurance/Control

- ☐ Safety Engineering
- ☐ Service Support
- ☐ Scheduling
- ☐ Shipping & Receiving
- ☐ Start-up Operations
- ☐ Supply Chain Management
- ☐ Theory of Constraints Mfg
- ☐ TQM (Total Quality Management)
- ☐ Traffic Management
- ☐ Troubleshooting
- ☐ Vendor Coordination
- ☐ Warehousing
- ☐ _____
- ☐ _____
- ☐ _____
- ☐ _____

Research & Development Skills

- ☐ Applied Research
- ☐ Basic Research
- ☐ Chemical Engineering
- ☐ Contract Administration
- ☐ Design and Specifications
- ☐ Diagnostics
- ☐ Electrical Engineering
- ☐ Engineering Support
- ☐ Environmental, Health, & Safety
- ☐ Feasibility Studies
- ☐ Field Studies
- ☐ Lab Management

- ☐ Lab/Facility Design & Construction
- ☐ Manufacturing/Engineering Liaison
- ☐ Mechanical Engineering
- ☐ Modeling
- ☐ New Equipment Design
- ☐ Patent Holder
- ☐ Process Engineering
- ☐ Product Applications
- ☐ Product Development
- ☐ Product Engineering
- ☐ Product Re-engineering
- ☐ Product Testing

Research & Development Skills (Continued)

- ☐ Program Development
- ☐ Project Management
- ☐ Prototype Development
- ☐ Quality Control
- ☐ R&D Management
- ☐ Regulatory Compliance
- ☐ Research Publications
- ☐ Security
- ☐ Service Development

- ☐ Simulation Development
- ☐ Software Tools
- ☐ Statistical Analysis
- ☐ Synthesizing
- ☐ Technical Writing
- ☐ Technology Evaluation
- ☐ _____
- ☐ _____
- ☐ _____

Sales and Marketing Skills

- ☑ Account Management
- ☑ Advertising
- ☑ Brand Management
- ☑ Budgeting/Expense Control
- ☑ Business Development
- ☑ Channel Marketing
- ☑ Collateral Development
- ☑ Compensation Plans
- ☑ Competitive Analysis
- ☑ Contract Negotiations
- ☐ Convention Planning
- ☐ Corporate Identity
- ☑ Customer Relations/Service
- ☑ Direct Sales
- ☐ Distribution Channels
- ☑ Distributor Relations
- ☐ Ecommerce/B2B
- ☐ Field Liaison
- ☑ Field Sales (Outside Sales)
- ☑ Forecasting

- ☑ Goal Setting
- ☑ Image Development
- ☐ Import/Export
- ☑ Incentive Programs
- ☐ Inside Sales
- ☐ International Business Development
- ☐ International Expansion
- ☐ Logo Development
- ☐ Market Research & Analysis
- ☐ Market Rollout
- ☐ Marketing Communications
- ☐ Marketing Plans
- ☐ Marketing Promotions
- ☐ Media Buying/Evaluation
- ☐ Media Relations
- ☐ Merchandising
- ☐ Multimedia Presentations
- ☑ New Account Sales
- ☐ New Product Development
- ☐ On-line Marketing & Advertising

Sales and Marketing Skills (Continued)

- ☐ Packaging
- ☐ Pricing
- ☐ Product Demonstrations
- ☐ Product Introduction/Launch
- ☐ Product Line Development
- ☐ Product Management
- ☐ Product Publishing/Sales
- ☐ Product Sourcing
- ☐ Product Specifications
- ☐ Proposal Writing
- ☑ Radio Media
- ☑ Sales Administration
- ☑ Sales Analysis
- ☑ Sales Forecasting
- ☐ Sales Kits
- ☑ Sales Management
- ☑ Sales Presentations
- ☑ Sales Promotions
- ☑ Sales Recruiting

- ☑ Sales Support
- ☑ Sales Training
- ☐ Showrooms
- ☑ Strategic Alliances/Partnerships
- ☑ Strategic Planning
- ☐ Supply Chain Analysis
- ☐ Supply Chain Management
- ☐ Survey Design
- ☐ Technical Sales Support
- ☐ Telemarketing
- ☑ Television Media
- ☑ Territory Development
- ☐ Tradeshows
- ☑ Trend Analysis
- ☐ Video Productions
- ☐ _____
- ☐ _____
- ☐ _____
- ☐ _____

Corporate Communications Skills

- ☑ B to B Communication
- ☐ Community Affairs/Relations
- ☐ Corporate Image
- ☐ Corporate Philanthropy
- ☐ Corporate Publications
- ☐ Corporate Relations
- ☑ Educational Programs
- ☐ Employee Communications
- ☐ Employee Newsletters
- ☐ Event Planning

- ☑ Fund-Raising
- ☐ Government Affairs/Relations
- ☐ Industry/Association Relations
- ☐ Internet Communications
- ☐ Investor Collateral
- ☐ Multimedia Presentations
- ☐ Press Releases
- ☐ Proposal Writing
- ☐ Public Relations
- ☐ Public Speaking

Corporate Communications Skills (Continued)

- ☐ Risk-Management Communication
- ☐ Shareholder Relations
- ☐ Speech Writing
- ☐ Trade Relations

- ☐ Web Site Development—html
- ☐ _____
- ☐ _____
- ☐ _____

Human Resources Skills

- ☐ Affirmative Action
- ☐ Arbitration/Mediation
- ☐ Benefits Vendor Management
- ☑ Career Counseling
- ☐ Career Development
- ☐ Classified Advertisements
- ☐ Company Orientation
- ☐ Compensation & Benefits
- ☐ Computer-Based Training
- ☐ Corporate Culture & Change
- ☑ Cost-Benefit Analysis
- ☐ Course Development
- ☐ Diversity
- ☐ Downsizing
- ☐ EEOC Compliance
- ☑ Employee Coaching
- ☐ Employee Communications
- ☑ Employee Discipline
- ☐ Employee Relations
- ☑ Employee Selection
- ☐ Executive Recruiting
- ☐ Grievances
- ☐ HR Generalist
- ☐ HRIS
- ☐ Human Resources Management
- ☐ Industrial Relations
- ☐ Interactive Training (Internet)

- ☐ International Employees
- ☑ Job Analysis
- ☑ Job Competencies
- ☐ Labor Negotiations
- ☐ Organizational Development
- ☐ Outplacement
- ☑ Performance Measurement
- ☑ Policies & Procedures
- ☐ Psychological Assessment
- ☐ Records Management
- ☑ Recruiting
- ☐ Relocation
- ☐ Salary Administration
- ☑ Succession Planning
- ☑ Team Building
- ☑ Training
- ☐ Training Administration
- ☐ Union Coordination
- ☐ Wage/Rate Analysis
- ☐ Workers' Compensation
- ☑ Workforce Forecasting/Planning
- ☐ Workforce Security
- ☐ _____
- ☐ _____
- ☐ _____
- ☐ _____

Finance Skills

- ☐ Accounting Management
- ☐ Accounts Payable
- ☐ Accounts Receivable
- ☐ Acquisitions & Mergers
- ☐ Actuarial/Rating Analysis
- ☐ Angel Funding
- ☑ Auditing
- ☑ Banking Relations
- ☑ Budget Control
- ☑ Budgeting
- ☐ Capital Budgeting
- ☐ Capital Investment
- ☑ Cash Management
- ☐ Cost Accounting
- ☑ Cost Control
- ☐ Credit/Collections
- ☐ Debt Negotiations
- ☐ Economic Studies
- ☐ Equity/Debt Management
- ☑ Feasibility Studies
- ☑ Financial Analysis
- ☑ Financial Planning
- ☑ Financial Reporting
- ☐ Financial Software Packages
- ☑ Financing
- ☑ Forecasting
- ☐ Foreign Exchange
- ☐ General Ledger

- ☐ Insurance
- ☑ Internal Controls
- ☐ Investor Relations
- ☐ IPOs
- ☐ Lending
- ☐ Lines of Credit
- ☑ Management Reporting
- ☑ New Business Development
- ☐ Operations Research/Analysis
- ☐ Payroll
- ☐ Pension & Fund Management
- ☑ Pricing/Forecast Modeling
- ☐ Private Placements
- ☐ Profit Planning
- ☐ Risk Management
- ☐ Road Shows
- ☐ SEC Reporting
- ☐ Special Reports
- ☐ Stockholder Relations
- ☐ Systems Installation/Training
- ☐ Taxes
- ☐ Treasury
- ☐ VC/Investor Presentations
- ☐ Venture Capital Relations
- ☐ _____
- ☐ _____
- ☐ _____
- ☐ _____

Administrative Skills

- ☐ Concierge
- ☐ Construction
- ☒ Contract Negotiations
- ☐ Credit Transactions
- ☒ Customer Service
- ☐ Equipment Purchasing
- ☐ Facility Management
- ☐ Forms and Methods
- ☐ HVAC
- ☐ Leases
- ☐ Library
- ☐ Logistics
- ☐ Mailroom
- ☐ Office Equipment
- ☐ Office Management

- ☐ Office Relocations
- ☐ Office Staff Training/Supervision
- ☐ Parking
- ☒ Policies & Procedures
- ☐ Project Management
- ☐ Real Estate
- ☐ Reception
- ☐ Records Management
- ☐ Security
- ☐ Space Planning
- ☐ Telecommunications
- ☐ Utilities
- ☐ _____
- ☐ _____
- ☐ _____

Legal Skills

- ☐ Anti-Piracy Investigation
- ☐ Antitrust
- ☐ Board of Director Affairs
- ☐ Case Management
- ☐ City, County, State Issues
- ☐ Contract Administration/Mgmt
- ☐ Copyrights & Trademarks
- ☐ Corporate Secretary
- ☒ Documentation
- ☐ EEO, OSHA, EPA, FDA, etc.
- ☐ Employment Law
- ☐ Federal Issues
- ☒ Financial Regulations
- ☐ Government Contracts

- ☐ Government/Legislative Affairs
- ☐ Incorporation
- ☐ Intellectual Property
- ☐ International Agreements
- ☐ Labor Issues
- ☐ Leases & Records
- ☐ Legislative Affairs
- ☐ Licensing
- ☐ Litigation
- ☐ Lobbying
- ☐ Mergers & Acquisitions
- ☐ Patents
- ☐ Political Relations
- ☐ Purchase Agreements

Legal Skills (Continued)

- ☐ Real Estate Law
- ☒ Regulatory Compliance
- ☐ Safety Regulations
- ☐ Securities Registration
- ☐ Shareholder Proxies
- ☐ Stock Administration
- ☐ Taxes
- ☒ Transactions

Information Systems/Information Technology/Electrical Engineering/Internet Skills

- ☐ Analog Design
- ☐ Algorithm Development
- ☐ Applications Database Admin.
- ☐ Applications Development
- ☐ ASP Applications Systems Provider
- ☐ Broadband Networks
- ☐ Business Systems Planning
- ☐ Cabling
- ☐ Capacity Planning
- ☐ Chip Design
- ☐ CRM-(Client Relationship Mgmt)
- ☐ Computer-Aided Design
- ☐ Computer Architecture
- ☐ Computer Configuration
- ☐ Computer Interface
- ☐ Computer Operations
- ☐ Computer Selection
- ☐ Computer Systems Conversion
- ☐ Data Center Operations
- ☐ Data Mining
- ☐ Data Processing Management
- ☐ Data Security
- ☐ Database Administration
- ☐ Database Development
- ☐ Desktop Publishing
- ☐ Desktop Video Publishing
- ☐ Diagnostics
- ☐ Digital Design
- ☐ Digital Signal Processing
- ☐ Distributed Processing
- ☐ Ecommerce/B2B
- ☐ EDI (Electronic Data Interface)
- ☐ EAP (Enterprise Asset Management)
- ☐ Enterprise Level Applications
- ☐ ERP (Enterprise Resource Planning)
- ☐ Equipment Selection
- ☐ Field Support Engineering
- ☐ Game Design
- ☐ Graphics
- ☐ Hardware Management
- ☐ HTML/XML
- ☐ Information Management
- ☐ IT Administration
- ☐ Integration Software
- ☐ Intranet Development
- ☐ Languages—Java, C++, etc.
- ☐ Linear Programming
- ☐ Linux Operating System
- ☐ Methodology Engineering
- ☐ Microprocessors

Information Systems/Information Technology/Electrical Engineering/Internet Skills (Continued)

- ☐ Modeling
- ☐ Multiplexors
- ☐ Network Engineering
- ☐ Network Operations Management
- ☐ Object-Oriented Development
- ☐ Office Automation
- ☐ Performance Monitoring
- ☐ Peripheral Equipment
- ☐ Portal Design/Development
- ☐ Process Development
- ☐ Programming/Coding
- ☐ Project Management
- ☐ Release Management
- ☐ Software Customization
- ☐ Software Development
- ☐ Software Engineering
- ☐ Spreadsheets
- ☐ Supplier Integration
- ☐ Systems Analysis
- ☐ Systems Applications
- ☐ Systems Development
- ☐ Systems Design
- ☐ Systems Testing

- ☐ Systems/Software Installation
- ☐ Systems/Software Training
- ☐ Technical Evangelism
- ☐ Technical Support/Help Desk
- ☐ Technical Writing
- ☐ Telecommunications
- ☐ Test Engineering
- ☐ Tracking Systems
- ☐ Unix
- ☐ Usability Engineering
- ☐ User Education/Documentation
- ☐ User Interface
- ☐ Vendor Relations
- ☐ Vendor Sourcing
- ☐ Voice & Data Communications
- ☐ Web Development/Graphic Design
- ☐ Web Site Content Writer
- ☐ Web Site Editor
- ☐ Wireless Systems
- ☑ Word Processing
- ☐ _____
- ☐ _____
- ☐ _____

Pastoral & Ministry Skills

- ☐ Preaching
- ☐ Leading Worship
- ☐ Missions
- ☐ Evangelism
- ☐ Church Administration
- ☐ Fund-raising

- ☐ Wedding Ceremonies
- ☐ Funeral Ceremonies
- ☐ Visitation
- ☐ Christian Education
  - ☐ Curriculum Design
  - ☐ Program Director

Pastoral & Ministry Skills (Continued)

Christian Education (Continued)
- □ Children
- □ Youth
- □ Adult
- □ Spiritual Direction

- □ Personal & Spiritual Development
- □ Stewardship
- □ Church Architecture
- □ Church Planting

Ministry Specializations

- □ Death & Dying
- □ Family Life Education
- □ Youth
- □ Singles
- □ Divorce Recovery
- □ Step-families
- □ Single Parents
- □ Children
- □ Adults
- □ Women
- □ Men
- □ Fathers
- □ Seniors
- □ Music
  - □ Choir Director
  - □ Organist
  - □ Pianist
  - □ Singing
  - □ Creative Arts
  - □ Painting
  - □ Drama
  - □ Dance
- □ Pastoral Counseling
  - □ Crisis
  - □ Family
  - □ Pre-marital
  - □ Marital

Pastoral Counseling (Continued)
  - □ Group
  - □ Addictions
- □ Church School
  - □ Administration
  - □ Teaching
  - □ Testing
  - □ Teacher Training
- □ Conference Leadership
- □ Camp Ministry
  - □ Program Director
  - □ Administration
  - □ Recreation
- □ Chaplaincy
  - □ Hospital
  - □ Military
  - □ School
  - □ Corporation
  - □ Correctional Institution
  - □ Hospice
  - □ Camp
- □ Outreach Ministries
  - □ Inner City
  - □ Mothers of Preschoolers
  - □ Campus
  - □ Alzheimer's Day Care
  - □ Pre-school

Strategy # 16 Prepare Your Functional Skills Summary

You can probably divide your functional skills into two general categories. One list would include skills that you are competent at performing, but have no desire to use regularly. The second list would include those that are important to you—the skills that give you a sense of satisfaction and fulfillment when you use them.

Using a highlighter pen, review the functional skills checklist you completed in the previous section. Highlight each functional skill that falls into the second category; those that are important and satisfying to you. These functional skills are key words that are commonly used by hiring managers to sort résumés in their databases. You will want to consistently use these terms in your résumés, cover letters and interviews.

On the worksheet in the Appendix, record the functional skills you highlighted. The following is a summary of Paul Williams' satisfying functional skills.

Budget Accountability	Radio Media	Training
Revenue Growth	Sales Management	Contract Negotiations
Strategic Partnerships	Strategic Alliances/Partnerships	Customer Service
Business Development	Television Media	
Channel Marketing	Territory Development	
Competitive Analysis	Trend Analysis	
Customer Relations/Service	Team Building	

Strategy #17 Compose Compelling CAR Stories

Paul speaking:

"After I had finished the Functional Skills Inventory, my career coach explained the CAR story concept to me. I wrote a story for each of the functional skills I had identified in the inventory that give me a sense of satisfaction and fulfillment when I perform them."

The CAR story concept is the application of storytelling to your job search. You will break down each story into three parts:

C identifies the *challenge* you faced;

A describes the *actions* you took and the skills you employed, and

R summarizes the *results* you accomplished.

Storytelling is a powerful method of communication. Prior to recorded history, key events were passed on from one generation to another orally. Historians were the storytellers. They spoke of community traditions, accomplishments and achievements. Throughout the gospels there are parables—stories illustrating God's will, plan and purpose for all of us.

Reflect back over the past several years on sermons, lectures, speeches and keynote addresses that you have heard. Rarely will you recall the facts, figures, or dates that were shared. Most often your memories are of powerful stories that illustrated the speaker's key points in a clear, concise and compelling manner.

If you've had an opportunity to conduct employment interviews, think back over the candidates that stood out from the group. What made them memorable? How did they create chemistry with you during the interview? Usually you will remember the clear examples they gave you that illustrated their competency, performance and accomplishments.

When examples are shared in a clear, concise and compelling story format; and they are on point with the questions being asked, the interviewer will sense a connection with the candidate. By preparing CAR story examples that support your key functional skills, you can easily create a connection, or "chemistry" in almost every interview.

Many employers are training their supervisors and human resources staff in behavioral-based, structured interviewing techniques. This interviewing style is a structured process designed to assist the interviewer in assessing a candidate's job fit. Questions are developed to uncover specific accomplishments in the midst of challenges, and the steps that were taken to achieve these results.

Developing CAR stories beforehand that clearly, concisely and compelling illustrate your accomplishments will prepare you for any interview. Each CAR story should describe the skills you used to achieve measurable results when you were faced with significant challenges.

Create a CAR story for each functional skill you want to highlight in your job search. This exercise will help you develop your résumés, add value to your job search letters, and prepare you for networking and interviewing. Use the worksheet in Appendix A to develop and record your CAR stories.

When composing your CAR stories, use abbreviated statements. Try to avoid using the passive voice, pronouns, proper nouns and definite articles.

For example, when writing the Challenges section instead of saying:

Paul speaking:

"When I was at KCMA Radio, we were not the market leader. I was challenged by my boss to gain the majority market share in the Denver market.

Shorten it, using the active voice as follows:

Grew annual revenue to $3M from $1M over two-year period. Gained majority market share in metro Denver market. Added twelve additional accounts and $2M in new revenue."

Paul Williams' CAR Story Examples

<u>Functional Skill</u>: Revenue Growth

<u>Employer</u>: KCMA Radio   <u>Position</u>: Sales Manager

*C*hallenges

Did not have majority market share in Denver area

*A*ctions

Retained 98% of current clients. Added twelve additional accounts and $2M revenue. Wrote add copy, part-nered with clients to design marketing strategies targeting key client demographics and market segments.

*R*esults

Grew annual revenue to $3M from $1M over two-year period. Gained majority market share in Denver area. Clients reported average 5% revenue growth annually resulting from radio ad campaigns.

<u>Functional Skill</u>: Sales Management

<u>Employer</u>: KCMA Radio   <u>Position</u>: Sales Manager

*C*hallenges

Sales people did not work as a team, very independent and competitive with one another.

*A*ctions

Led team-building activities. Created team sales goals and performance incentives.

*R*esults

Sales teams exceeded quarterly targets, overall sales increased by 100% annually for two consecutive years.

<u>Functional Skill</u>: Business Development

<u>Employer</u>: Channel 5 News   <u>Position</u>: Regional Sales Associate

*C*hallenges

Company did not have many sporting events, sporting goods and recreation activities market accounts.

*A*ctions

Conducted competitive market analysis and television advertising trend analysis for sporting events, sporting goods and recreation activities market segments in Rocky Mountain region.

*R*esults

Added four major clients ($700K) and grew existing accounts by $300K

Functional *Skill*: Customer Service

Employer: All Sports Outlet   Position: Sales Associate

*C*hallenges
Golf department sales were below revenue targets.

*A*ctions
Created loss leader sales program, set up end caps and designed posters and banners for market blitz. Partnered with representatives from Nike Golf, Calloway and Taylor-Made. Launched three give-away promotions and four sales events. Managed company-sponsored tournament.

*R*esults
Drove 25% sales increase in golf equipment, adding $20K to revenue stream.

Paul speaking:

"After completing my CAR stories, my career coach had me complete a Career History & Goals Worksheet. He emphasized the importance of looking at my job search strategically over the long term. By outlining my career history in terms of job titles, scope of responsibility and company size, I gained a clearer perspective of the scope and breadth of my experience.

In turn, I was able to clearly identify my career goals, beginning with my next position and then progressing through the next two desired promotions. I began to see the importance of long-range planning; it would help me avoid accepting an offered position that could be less than ideal for my long-range goals."

Strategy #18 Create Your Career History & Goals Worksheet

"We ask God to give you a complete understanding of what he wants to do in your lives, and we ask him to make you wise with spiritual wisdom. Then the way you live will always honor and please the Lord, and you will continually do good, kind things for others. All the while, you will learn to know God better and better." Colossians 1:9b-11 (NLT)

List the titles you have held in order of responsibility and seniority. Begin with the highest-level position first. Go back ten years in your work history. (A worksheet is provided for your use in Appendix A.) Here is Paul Williams' job title summary:

Job Titles

1. Sales Manager

2. Regional Sales Associate

3. Sales Associate

4.   <u>Vice President</u>

5.   <u>Head Teller</u>

6.   <u>Teller</u>

Categorize the company sizes you have worked in throughout your career. Record the company name in the chart below under the correct heading.

Small-size Company (Up to $100M revenue)	Medium-size Company ($100M to $1B revenue)	Large-size Company ($1B plus revenue)
KCMA Radio		
Channel 5 News		
All Sports Outlet		
New City Bank & Trust		

Describe your career objective for your next position in one sentence. Some examples include:

To obtain a full-time position as a sales director in a small-size company in the radio or television broadcasting or retail services industry in the Western United States.

To obtain a full-time position as a sales manager of sales/business development in a medium-size company in the radio or television broadcasting or retail services industry in the Southeastern United States.

Outline your short-term, medium-term and long-term position objectives. The company size will influence the title of your position. You may choose to target different positions in different size companies within each objective.

Research various companies within each company size category in the industries you are targeting. Determine the titles used and the career progression within each company to guide your goal setting.

A.   <u>Short-Term Position Objective</u> (Next Position)

1.   Director—Sales/Business Development

2.   Manager—Sales/Business Development

B.   <u>Medium-Term Position Objective</u> (Next promotion in two to three years)

1.   Vice President—Sales/Business Development

2.   Director—Sales/Business Development

C. <u>Long-Term Position Objective</u> (Second promotion in five to seven years)

1.   Chief Executive—Sales/Business Development

2.   Vice President—Sales/Business Development

Paul speaking:

"Now that I had determined what positions would be ideal and what size companies I would most want to work for, I needed to target the various industries that I would enjoy exploring for my next job."

The next section of the Career History & Goals Worksheet presented a comprehensive list of industries. I went through the checklist and marked each one I had experience in; and I highlighted those I wanted to explore further in my job search.

Strategy #19 Use the Industry Checklist to Target Your Search

Place a ☑ next to each industry in the following checklist, within which you have industry experience. Highlight the industries you would like to explore in your search.

Industry Checklist

Aerospace & Defense

- ☐ Aerospace/Defense-Major Diversified
- ☐ Aerospace/Defense-Products
- ☐ Aerospace/Defense-Maintenance & Service

Automotive & Transport Equipment

- ☐ Auto Manufacturers
- ☐ Trucks, Buses & Other Vehicles
- ☐ Auto Parts
- ☐ Recreational Vehicles
- ☐ Motorcycles & Other Small-Engine Vehicles
- ☐ Pleasure Boats
- ☐ Shipbuilding & Related Services
- ☐ Rail & Trucking Equipment

Banking

- ☐ Money Center Banks
- ☐ Banking-Northeast
- ☐ Banking-Mid-Atlantic
- ☐ Banking-Southeast
- þ Banking-Midwest
- ☐ Banking-Southwest
- ☐ Banking-West
- ☐ Banking-US Territories

- ☐ Banking-Canada
- ☐ Banking-Europe
- ☐ Banking-Asia & Australia
- ☐ Banking-Latin America, Middle East & Africa
- ☐ Other Banking Services

Chemicals

- ☐ Diversified Chemicals
- ☐ Basic & Intermediate Chemicals & Petrochemicals
- ☐ Agricultural Chemicals
- ☐ Specialty Chemicals
- ☐ Plastics & Fibers
- ☐ Paints, Coatings & Other Finishing Products

Computer Hardware

- ☐ Diversified Computer Products
- ☐ Large-Scale Computers
- ☐ Personal Computers
- ☐ Miscellaneous Computer-Based Systems
- ☐ Data Storage Devices
- ☐ Networking & Communication Devices
- ☐ Computer Peripherals
- ☐ Electronic Business Equipment

Computer Software & Services

- ☐ Diversified Software
- ☐ Multimedia Production, Graphics & Publishing Software
- ☐ Entertainment & Games Software
- ☐ Educational Software
- ☐ Document Management Software
- ☐ Database & File Management Software
- ☐ Corporate, Professional & Financial Software
- ☐ Manufacturing & Industrial Software
- ☐ Engineering, Scientific & CAD/CAM Software
- ☐ Networking & Connectivity Software
- ☐ Communications Software
- ☐ Internet & Intranet Software & Services
- ☐ Other Application Software
- ☐ Development Tools, Operating Systems & Utility Software
- ☐ Security Software & Services
- ☐ Information Technology Consulting Services
- ☐ Data Processing Software & Services
- ☐ Miscellaneous Computer Services
- ☐ Computer Products Distribution & Support

Conglomerates

- ☐ Conglomerates
- ☐ Trading Companies

Consumer Products-Durables

- ☐ Appliances
- ☐ Home Furnishings
- ☐ Housewares & Accessories
- ☐ Lawn & Garden Equipment & Small Tools & Accessories
- ☐ Office & Business Furniture & Fixtures
- ☐ Consumer Electronics
- ☐ Toys, Games & Other Recreational Goods

☑ Sporting Goods

- ☑ Professional Sports Gear & Apparel
- ☐ Jewelry, Watches & Clocks
- ☐ Photographic Equipment & Supplies
- ☐ Miscellaneous Durable Consumer Goods

Consumer Products-Non-Durables

- ☐ Apparel-Clothing
- ☐ Apparel-Footwear & Accessories
- ☐ Personal Care Products
- ☐ Cleaning Products
- ☐ Business Forms & Other Office Supplies
- ☐ Miscellaneous Non-Durable Consumer Goods
- ☐ Luxury Goods

Diversified Services

- ☐ Advertising
- ☐ Marketing & Public Relations Services
- ☐ Telemarketing, Call Centers & Other Direct Marketing
- ☐ Market & Business Research Services
- ☐ Accounting, Bookkeeping, Collection & Credit Reporting
- ☐ Staffing, Outsourcing & Other Human Resources
- ☐ Management Consulting Services
- ☐ Printing, Photocopying & Graphic Design
- ☐ Building Maintenance & Related Services
- ☐ Miscellaneous Business Services
- ☐ Legal Services
- ☐ Security & Protection Products & Services
- ☐ Car & Truck Rental
- ☐ Personal Services
- ☐ Consumer Services
- ☐ Child Care Services & Elementary & Secondary Schools
- ☐ Education & Training Services

Diversified Services (Continued)

- ☐ Colleges & Universities
- ☐ Technical & Scientific Research Services
- ☐ Charitable Organizations
- ☐ Membership Organizations
- ☐ Foundations & Cultural Institutions

Drugs

- ☐ Drug Manufacturers-Major
- ☐ Drug Manufacturers-Other
- ☐ Drugs—Generic
- ☐ Drug Delivery Systems
- ☐ Vitamins, Nutritionals & Other Health-Related Products
- ☐ Biotechnology-Medicine
- ☐ Biotechnology-Research
- ☐ Diagnostic Substances
- ☐ Drugs & Sundries-Wholesale

Electronics & Miscellaneous Technology

- ☐ Semiconductor-Broad Line
- ☐ Semiconductor-Memory Chips
- ☐ Semiconductor-Specialized
- ☐ Semiconductor-Integrated Circuits
- ☐ Semiconductor Equipment & Materials
- ☐ Diversified Electronics
- ☐ Computer Boards, Cards & Connector Products
- ☐ Miscellaneous Electronics
- ☐ Scientific & Technical Instruments
- ☐ Electronic Test & Measurement Instruments
- ☐ Contract Electronics Manufacturing
- ☐ Electronics Distribution

Energy

- ☐ Integrated Oil & Gas
- ☐ Oil & Gas Exploration & Production
- ☐ Oil & Gas Refining & Marketing
- ☐ Oil & Gas Equipment
- ☐ Oil & Gas Services
- ☐ Oil & Gas Pipelines & Storage
- ☐ Petroleum Product Distribution

Financial Services

- ☐ Investment Banking & Brokerage
- ☐ Asset Management
- ☐ Royalty Trusts
- ☐ Investment Firms
- ☐ Closed-End Investment Funds
- ☐ Venture Capital Firms
- ☐ Consumer Loans
- ☐ Mortgage Banking & Related Services
- ☐ Commercial Lending
- ☐ Leasing
- ☐ Miscellaneous Financial Services
- ☐ Services to Financial Companies

Food, Beverage & Tobacco

- ☐ Diversified Foods-Major
- ☐ Diversified Foods-Other
- ☐ Agricultural Operations & Products
- ☐ Agricultural Services
- ☐ Agriculture-Biotechnology
- ☐ Grains, Breads & Cereals
- ☐ Meat Products
- ☐ Dairy Products
- ☐ Canned & Frozen Foods
- ☐ Other Processed & Packaged Goods
- ☐ Sugar & Confectionery
- ☐ Miscellaneous Food Products
- ☐ Food Wholesale-to Grocers
- ☐ Food Wholesale-to Restaurants
- ☐ Beverages-Brewers
- ☐ Beverages-Wineries

Food, Beverage & Tobacco (Continued)

- ☐ Beverages-Distillers
- ☐ Beverages-Bottlers & Wholesale Distributors
- ☐ Beverages-Soft Drinks
- ☐ Tobacco Products

Health Products & Services

- ☐ Medical Instruments & Supplies
- ☐ Medical Appliances & Equipment
- ☐ Health Care Plans
- ☐ Long-Term Care Facilities
- ☐ Hospitals
- ☐ Specialized Health Services
- ☐ Home Health Care
- ☐ Medical Laboratories & Research
- ☐ Medical Practice Management & Services
- ☐ Medical Products Distribution

Insurance

- ☐ Multi-line Insurance
- ☐ Life Insurance
- ☐ Accident & Health Insurance
- ☐ Property & Casualty Insurance
- ☐ Surety, Title & Miscellaneous Insurance
- ☐ Insurance Brokers
- ☐ Reinsurance

Leisure

- ☐ Lodging
- ☐ Travel Agencies, Tour Operators & Other Travel Services
- ☐ Gambling Resorts & Casinos
- ☐ Gaming Activities
- ☐ Gaming Equipment & Services
- ☐ Sporting Activities
- ☐ Professional Sports Teams & Organizations
- ☐ Restaurants

- ☐ Specialty Eateries & Catering Services
- ☐ Miscellaneous Entertainment

Manufacturing

- ☐ Diversified Machinery
- ☐ Agricultural Machinery
- ☐ Construction, Mining & Other Heavy Machinery
- ☐ Material Handling Machinery
- ☐ Miscellaneous General & Special Machinery
- ☐ Industrial Automation Products & Industrial Controls
- ☐ Machine Tools, Components & Accessories
- ☐ Hardware & Fasteners
- ☐ Metal Fabrication
- ☐ Fluid Control Equipment, Pumps, Seals & Valves
- ☐ Pollution & Treatment Controls & Filtration Products
- ☐ Food Service Equipment
- ☐ Turbines, Transformers & Other Electrical Generation Equipment
- ☐ Wire & Cable
- ☐ Miscellaneous Electrical Products
- ☐ Lighting & Other Fixtures
- ☐ Textile Manufacturing
- ☐ Packaging & Containers
- ☐ Rubber & Plastic Products
- ☐ Glass & Clay Products
- ☐ Paper & Paper Products
- ☐ Miscellaneous & Diversified Industrial Products
- ☐ Industrial Equipment & Products Distribution

Materials & Construction

- ☐ Diversified Building Materials
- ☐ Lumber, Wood Production & Timber Operations
- ☐ Aggregates, Concrete & Cement
- ☐ Plumbing & HVAC Equipment

<u>Materials & Construction</u> (Continued)

☐ Miscellaneous Building Materials

☐ Manufactured Buildings

☐ Engineering & Architectural Services

☐ Heavy Construction

☐ Specialty Contracting & Industrial

<u>Maintenance</u>

☐ Waste Management & Recycling

☐ Environmental Services

<u>Media</u>

☐ Media—Major Diversified

☑ TV Broadcasting

☐ Television Production, Programming & Distribution

☑ Radio Broadcasting & Programming

☐ Motion Picture & Video Production & Distribution

☐ Movie Theaters

☐ Music Production & Publishing

☐ Movie, Television & Music Production Services & Products

☐ Publishing-Newspapers

☐ Publishing-Periodicals

☐ Publishing-Books

☐ Publishing-Other

☐ Information Collection & Delivery Services

☐ Internet & On-line Content Providers

<u>Metals & Mining</u>

☐ Diversified Mining & Metals

☐ Copper

☐ Aluminum

☐ Coal

☐ Gold & Silver & Other Precious Metals

☐ Diamonds & Other Precious Stones

☐ Industrial Minerals & Metals

☐ Steel Production

☐ Miscellaneous Mining & Metals Processing

☐ Metals & Alloys Distribution

<u>Real Estate</u>

☐ REIT-Diversified & Miscellaneous

☐ REIT-Office

☐ REIT-Health Care Facilities

☐ REIT-Hotel/Motel

☐ REIT-Industrial

☐ REIT-Residential

☐ REIT-Retail

☐ REIT-Mortgage Investment

☐ Property Investment & Management

☐ Real Estate Development

☐ Residential Construction

☐ Miscellaneous Real Estate Services

<u>Retail</u>

☐ Clothing, Shoe & Accessory Retailing & Wholesaling

☐ Department Stores

☐ Discount & Variety Retailing

☐ Drug, Health & Beauty Product Retailing

☐ Grocery Retailing

☐ Convenience Stores & Gas Stations

☐ Consumer Electronics & Appliance Retailing

☐ Building Materials & Gardening Supplies Retailing & Wholesale

☐ Home Furnishings & Housewares Retailing

☐ Auto Parts Retailing & Wholesale

☐ Non-Store Retailing

<u>Specialty Retail</u>

☑ Sporting Goods Retailing

☐ Toy & Hobby Retailing & Wholesale

☐ Jewelry Retailing & Wholesale

<u>Specialty Retail</u> (Continued)

☐ Music, Video, Book & Entertainment

☐ Software Retailing & Dist.

☐ Computer & Software Retailing

☐ Office Products Retailing & Distribution

☐ Auto Dealers & Distributors

☐ Miscellaneous Retail

☐ Miscellaneous Wholesale

<u>Telecommunications</u>

☐ Switching & Transmission Equipment

☐ Communications Processing Equipment

☐ Wireless, Satellite & Microwave Communications Equipment

☐ Wireless Communications Services

☐ Long-Distance Carriers

☐ Local Telecom & Private Transmission Services

☐ Diversified Telecom Service Providers

☐ Cable TV & Satellite Systems

☐ Internet & On-line Service Providers

☐ Miscellaneous End-User Communications Services

☐ Miscellaneous Services to Communication Providers

<u>Transportation</u>

☐ Airlines

☐ Air Services, Other

☐ Air Delivery, Freight & Parcel Services

☐ Trucking

☐ Shipping

☐ Railroads

☐ Bus, Taxi & Other Passenger Services

☐ Logistics & Other Transportation Services

<u>Utilities</u>

☐ Diversified Utilities

☐ Electric Utilities

☐ Independent Power Producers & Marketers

☐ Gas Utilities

☐ Water Utilities

☐ Alternative Energy Sources

<u>Ministry Industries</u>

☐ Church, Pastoral

☐ Missions, Field Work

☐ Missions, Board Administration

☐ Denominational Leadership

☐ Schools, Pre-school

☐ Schools, Elementary

☐ Schools, Secondary

☐ College/University/Seminary

☐ Correctional Institutions

☐ Military, Chaplaincy

☐ Parachurch Organizations

☐ Media, Television, Radio, Film

☐ Creative Arts, Singing, Dance, Musician

Strategy #20 Select Your Industry Preferences and Focus Your Search Activity

List your industry preferences for your job search (those highlighted above). The following list is from Paul Williams' summary of preferred industries:

1. TV Broadcasting

2. Radio Broadcasting & Programming

3.   Sporting Goods Retailing

4.   Software Retailing & Distribution

5.   Sporting Goods

Chapter Review

Strategy #13 Create Your Personal Career & Education Inventory

Strategy #14 Build Your Confidence by Organizing Your Achievements, and Summarizing Your Education & Professional Development

Strategy #15 Utilize Your Functional Skills Checklist

Strategy #16 Prepare Your Functional Skills Summary

Strategy #17 Compose Compelling CAR Stories
- Challenges you faced
- Actions you took and skills you employed
- Results you accomplished

Strategy #18 Create Your Career History & Goals Worksheet

Strategy #19 Use the Industry Checklist to Target Your Search

Strategy #20 Select Your Industry Preferences and Focus Your Search Activity

Chapter Four:
SALT—Factors Affecting Your Career Search Length

SALT—Scope, Activity, Liabilities and Timing

Scope, Activity, Liabilities and Timing are the four primary variables in your job search. You can control or influence Scope, Activity and Liabilities. Timing just is—you can't control it.

"I have observed something else in this world of ours. The fastest runner doesn't always win the race, and the strongest warrior doesn't always win the battle. The wise are often poor, and the skillful are not necessarily wealthy. And those who are educated don't always lead successful lives. It is all decided by chance, by being at the right place at the right time." Ecclesiastes 9:11 (NLT)

Scope represents the four realms of your job search. First are your geographic targets. Second are the positions you desire to pursue. Third are the industries you wish to work in. Fourth and last, are the company sizes you perceive as ideal, based on your previous work experience and personal desires.

Activity includes all the actions you engage in during your job search. This is a numbers-driven process. Your effectiveness at creating and maintaining a high activity level and engaging in productive actions will determine your success.

Your activity can be grouped into three job search milestones. The first milestone is getting job interviews, the second is winning job offers and the third is negotiating and accepting a position. Follow-up is a common thread throughout these three milestones.

Liabilities are career search obstacles. You have career obstacles. Everyone has some. The way you manage them during an interview will be a key factor in determining whether you are selected for that specific position. A career obstacle is any issue or event in your personal or employment history that you or a hiring manager could perceive as hindering you from getting a specific job offer.

In the first three realms, Scope, Activity and Liabilities, you can exert some control or influence. You are powerless over influencing or controlling the Timing of hiring managers. Your timing is the present. By increasing your Activity and Scope, you increase the probability of coming into contact with more decision makers who have Timing in alignment with your own.

Strategy #21 Plan the Scope of Your Search

"The LORD will work out his plans for my life—for your faithful love, O LORD, endures forever." Psalm 138:8 (NLT)

The scope of your search encompasses four realms. These are:

- Geographic areas you are willing or able to target for your next position
- Types of positions you are targeting
- Industry segments you are qualified to work in and willing to exploit in your search
- Company size: defined by annual revenue, assets held, or number of employees

The broader your scope in these four realms, the more interest you will generate on behalf of hiring managers and recruiters throughout your search.

Think of scope as a pyramid. The higher you move up the pyramid, the narrower it becomes. As you get more restrictive in defining your scope, you decrease the number of possible companies and positions available to you. This will increase your search time. Expanding your scope will decrease your search time in most circumstances. Give prayerful consideration to planning the scope of your job search. Ask the Lord to make his will clear to you as you plan.

Strategy #22 Identify the Geographic Scope of Your Search

When you limit your search to a small geographic area, it reduces the number of companies and positions you can target. When the numbers are smaller, the search typically takes much longer. Allow for this possible extended time frame in your overall planning and budgeting if you limit your search geographically.

The economic condition in the geographic area you target is also an important factor in determining the possible length of your search. If recent historical growth in your target industries and target positions is high, your search could be quick. If it is declining, your search could be longer.

Strategy #23 Broaden the Position Scope of Your Search

When defining your position scope, you have a range of five options. You may choose to pursue the same *position* in the same or in a different *industry*, seek a different *position* in the same or a different *industry*, or consider self-employment.

1. Same position/same industry
2. Same position/different industry
3. Different position/same industry
4. Different position/different industry
5. Self-employment

By broadening the scope, you increase the potential number of opportunities for exploration. Don't rule out any of the options too quickly. Take your time in exploring each one in each industry segment you target. Your goals for position targeting may be different in different industries.

Strategy #24 Set Your Industry Scope Search Boundaries

Include your current industry in your targeting if you would be satisfied remaining in it. If you are interested in exploring or making an industry change, adding additional industry targets will expand the scope of your search, and increase the number of possible company contacts. (Use the Industry Checklist in the Appendix to identify your industry areas of experience and interest.)

Mature or declining industry targets will probably extend the length of your search. To compensate for this, you may want to expand your geographic targets or expand the scope of your position targets.

Strategy #25 Determine the Size of Your Target Companies

You can focus your job search on company size by categorizing companies in several ways. The most common is to identify a range of annual revenue. Sometimes it makes more sense to categorize companies based on the number of employees, the number of customers served, or a range of assets held.

Company size by annual revenue:
- Small-size company (Up to $100M revenue)
- Medium-size company ($100M to $1B revenue)
- Large-size company ($1B plus revenue)

Company size by number of employees:
- Small-size company (100 to 10,000)
- Medium-size company (10,000 to 25,000)
- Large-size company (25,000 plus)

Company size by number of customers:
- Small-size company (1,000 to 75,000)
- Medium-size company (75,000 to 250,000)
- Large-size company (250,000 plus)

Company size by assets held:
- Small-size company (Up to $100M assets)
- Medium-size company ($100M to $1B assets)
- Large-size company ($1B plus assets)

(Refer back to the Career History & Goals Worksheet you completed in the Appendix to determine the company sizes you want to target.)

Strategy #26 Define Your Search Activities

Activity includes all the actions you engage in during your job search. Some of these include: distributing résumés, responding to job postings, networking, conducting informational interviews, conducting research, contacting recruiters, interviewing, negotiations, offer acceptance and follow-up. Remember the bottom-line: a job search is a numbers-driven activity. Your effectiveness at creating and maintaining a high level of productive activity will determine your success. Activity can be categorized into three job search milestones. They are:

- First milestone—getting job interviews

- Second milestone—winning job offers

- Third milestone—negotiating and accepting a position

These milestones will be described in more detail in the following chapters.

Strategy #27 Identify Your Career Obstacles

> *Career Obstacle: Any issue or event in your personal or employment history that you or a hiring manager could perceive as hindering you from winning a specific job offer.*

You have career obstacles. Everyone has some. The way you manage them during an interview will be a key factor in determining whether you are selected for that position.

A career obstacle is any issue or event in your personal or employment history that you or a hiring manager could perceive as hindering you from getting a specific job offer. The wording of the last sentence is deliberate: What may be perceived as a gateway for one position may be seen as an obstacle for another. Age and maturity may be seen as gateways in a senior management position in a well-established company, and viewed as obstacles in a fast-paced technology start-up.

Career obstacles are inextricably intertwined with who you are as a person. Your life is a unique tapestry of events, emotions, beliefs and relationships. Though you may have regrets about some things in your past, you need not apologize for them during your job search!

> *Career obstacles are inextricably intertwined with who you are as a person. Your life is a unique tapestry of events, emotions, beliefs, and relationships.*

Earlier, you invested significant time praying about, reflecting on, identifying, and inventorying your strengths and accomplishments. Now, it is equally important that you recognize and manage your career obstacles. When you are clear about what you are facing, you can deal with your circumstances purposefully.

Ask yourself the question: *"Is there anything about my background that could hinder me from getting this job offer?"* If you can't think of any specific issues or events, ask your pastor, spouse, a trusted friend or career coach to help you identify them. Remember, everyone has career obstacles.

Common obstacles have been identified and described for you in the following section, along with some specific strategies to effectively manage them in job interviews. In addition, you can think through the following strategy while focusing on each of your personal career obstacles.

Always *acknowledge* a career obstacle when it is raised by a recruiter or hiring manager. Never *agree* with them. For instance, the interviewer may say, "I'm concerned that you don't have project management certification." Your response might be: "I've thought about that in preparing for this interview, and I'm glad we have this opportunity to discuss it." By replying this way, you validate the interviewer's point of view and avoid appearing defensive about the question on the table.

During each interview, you will want to identify the question that's really behind the stated question in the interviewer's mind. For example, lacking a professional certification isn't really about certification at all. A certificate by itself is meaningless. The underlying concern; or question behind the question is whether or not you have the technical competence to perform in this position. Additionally, the interviewer may fear that you will require more training than the current budget allows.

Your response might be: "I can appreciate that this position requires someone who can hit the ground running without a steep learning curve and turn this project around. Is that a correct assessment?" In closing, you can illustrate your strengths or skills that the interviewer may perceive as missing by sharing a relevant CAR story.

I believe that my outstanding track record in project management is exemplified by a recent experience I had at ABC Company. There I was tasked with turning around a major $600K project that was behind schedule thirty days and over budget by 15%.

Immediately I stepped in, reorganized the teams, identified and eliminated unnecessary steps, and got the project back on schedule. In fact, the project finished on time and under budget.

The company awarded me a cash bonus for my contribution. Does that help you see how I can hit the ground running and provide the project leadership you are looking for in this position?

Paul speaking:

"I completed the Career Obstacles Checklist and discussed it with my career coach. I had no idea there were so many things to consider! Here are my results and comments."

CAREER OBSTACLES	YES	UNSURE	NO
No Previous Work History			X
Currently Unemployed		X	
I still have severance, but it may end before I find my next position.			
Discharged From Position	X		
I was terminated as a result of an acquisition when my position was eliminated.			
Disabilities			X
My Gender is nontraditional For My Career			X
Pregnancy			X
Obesity			X
Limited Geographic Constraints			X
I prefer remaining in metro Denver, but will relocate if necessary almost anywhere.			
No College Degree or Graduate Degree			X
No Professional Licenses/Certifications			
I don't have any. Will it limit my search options in other industries?			
Age Concerns			X
Dependent-Care Responsibilities	X		
We have three school-age children and my wife works. Her parents are getting older and need more assistance too.			
Perceived as Lacking Direction or Career Planning			X
Perceived as Specialist in My Field			X
Perceived as Generalist in My Field		X	
Unemployment Gaps			X
Limited Line Experience			X
Limited Staff Experience			X
Lacking Titles That Represent My Scope of Responsibilities			X
Lacking Upward Mobility in My Career			X
Left Short-Term Position			X
Frequently Changed Jobs			X
Left A Company That Was In Financial Difficulty			X
Left A Company That Had A Poor Reputation			X
Adverse Personal Credit Report			X
References Unfavorable			X

Strategy # 28 Manage Your Career Obstacles with the Career Obstacles Checklist

(A worksheet is provided in Appendix A to help you assess your personal career obstacles related to your job search.)

Paul speaking:

"After I had completed the Career Obstacles Checklist my career coach reviewed it with me. I learned that my perceptions about my career obstacles could be just as important as the perceptions of hiring managers and recruiters. By working on changing my perceptions, I can influence the perception others may have of me."

No Previous Work History

> *Whether the economy is strong with low unemployment or weak with high unemployment, you can give yourself an edge over your competition.*

This career obstacle is most common for recent college graduates. Employers will often look at other factors. This may include your GPA, participation in student government, extracurricular activities, volunteer work, athletics, internships, and in some cases, whether or not you held part-time positions while you were studying.

By adding a few phrases in your interview that describe your work ethic, beliefs about work/life balance, organizational culture, organizational and time management skills, etc., you can increase your marketability. It may be helpful to augment this approach with statements that others have made about you, like an employer once said to Paul, "He is a hard worker. I wish I had ten more employees just like him."

A few years ago, when the market for recent college graduates was stronger, an MBA degree from a recognized university was almost always a sure ticket to getting hired. In today's economy, with unemployment hovering around six percent, all other things being equal, your greatest asset will be your ability to stand out in the interview process.

Whether the economy is strong with low unemployment, or weak with high unemployment, you can give yourself an edge over your competition. Developing a strong interviewing presence (supported by clear, concise and compelling CAR stories that make you memorable) is paramount to your success.

Conduct extensive research into any positions and industries you are targeting. When you can speak directly to contemporary industry issues with knowledge and authority, you will be more impressive to an interviewer.

Currently Unemployed

You may be asking, "Is it better to be employed during my job search?" The answer is always an unqualified "Yes!" Being employed gives you a slight advantage, especially with recruiters. However, job seekers who are still employed sometimes find the task of balancing work, family, outside activities, and an intensive job search daunting.

How you use your time during prolonged unemployment periods can be important in the eyes of a hiring manager. They understand that the current market has increased the length between positions for many job seekers. In light of this fact, they may be

> *Perception is everything during interviews.*

inclined to give favor to those who have filled the gap with consulting contracts or have returned to school to gain additional skills.

One thing is certain. If it is 2004, and your last position was in 2002, you are most likely in trouble, at least in the perception game. Perception is everything during interviews. So if you've had a protracted period of unemployment, you might want to include a brief statement about your activities since your last position in your résumé or cover letter. An example would be:

"Following layoff from Frito-Lay, enjoyed an extended family vacation, then pursued ongoing training and engaged in several e-commerce marketing consulting projects with small to medium-size businesses."

Scenario

Steve left his position with a leader in the energy industry in late 2001. Armed with a generous severance package, he and his wife took time during the holidays to visit extended family and enjoy a long, much needed vacation together. When Steve finally ramped up his search, he found it much tougher to land a new opportunity than he had anticipated.

In late 2002, weary of the ongoing frustration and rejection, he and his wife both enrolled in university coursework. Steve took classes in Six Sigma technology. His wife enrolled in project management courses. The academic rigor provided a welcome distraction, and the university environment provided new opportunities for networking.

At one point, Steve became so immersed in his studies that he briefly suspended his job search activities. It was during that time when two solid opportunities surfaced—the fruit of previous activities. Steve joked with his coach, saying, "I didn't find a job until I stopped looking!"

For many years, recruiters have preferred to work with people who are employed but unhappy over those who are currently unemployed. They didn't want to compete with hiring managers. Recruiters are paid by the employer when they find a candidate that accepts a job offer. They don't want to lose out on their fee because you accepted a job with a company they don't represent!

This perception around unemployment is changing rapidly among recruiters. The enormous number of mergers, acquisitions, downsizings, and closures occurring across America in many industries, has led to unemployment for thousands of competent, qualified workers. The recent stereotype—if you're really good at what you do, you shouldn't have any trouble finding a job—is finally being cast aside.

Discharged From Position

Dealing with your emotional baggage as well as the facts surrounding your termination can both be sticky areas. A layoff is the simplest situation to deal with because it's usually created by circumstances beyond your control. A termination for cause is often the most complicated. In either case, describe the circumstances as positively as possible, mentioning no names and assessing no blame. The faster you can get the interviewer to move on to another topic, the better.

In terms of a résumé strategy, it is probably best not to mention it at all. To be consistent, don't mention the details of any job transitions, other than to identify companies into which you were recruited. Make a statement about your ethics and character, and the fact that references will enthusiastically vouch for these personal traits.

Scenario

Don was a successful biotech industry scientist. His career came crashing down when he was accused of sexual harassment by a female co-worker. In exchange for his resignation, the company gave him a generous severance.

Unfortunately, the stock market downturn in 2000—2001 necessitated his return to the marketplace. Here is the statement his coach crafted for him: "I was charged with sexual harassment by a female co-worker.

The allegation was found unproven following the investigation. Nevertheless, the company couldn't afford to have appearances of impropriety jeopardize their start-up funding. In exchange for my resignation, the company gave me with a generous severance." Craft a response that avoids blame and uses no names.

Disabilities

Disabilities can be outwardly noticeable or completely invisible to hiring managers. The Americans with Disabilities Act makes it illegal for employers to discriminate against disabled persons who can perform essential job functions with or without reasonable accommodation.

> *Unfortunately, antidiscrimination laws do not eliminate the practice in all hiring decisions.*

Unfortunately, antidiscrimination laws do not eliminate the practice in all hiring decisions. Many progressive employers approach disabilities directly. They have a question on their employment application that states: "Can you perform all the essential functions of this position with or without reasonable accommodation?" Effectively trained interviewers who are well versed in employment law will ask this question of every applicant.

As with other career obstacles that have protected-class status under the law such as: age, gender, marital status, pregnancy, sexual/relational orientation, and several other categories; it is critical that you frequently and effectively build perceptions of value in the interviewer's mind. Inform the interviewer of the ways you have successfully performed in previous positions using your CAR stories. Make it clear how you can make specific contributions to the company.

My Gender Is Nontraditional For My Career

"Stop judging others, and you will not be judged. For others will treat you as you treat them. Whatever measure you use in judging others, it will be used to measure how you are judged." Matthew 7:1-2 (NLT)

Stereotypes about gender roles in some industries and careers are alive and well. In some cases, they will undermine your search efforts as you pursue positions that may be perceived as non-traditional for your gender. Stereotypes are widely held beliefs about a person formed by assumptions believed to be true about a group within which they are perceived to belong.

> *Stereotypes are widely held beliefs about a person formed by assumptions believed to be true about a group within which they are perceived to belong.*

None of us are exempt from stereotyping. Everyone does it. Some of us are more aware of the tendency to stereotype than others. Challenging your stereotypes when you become aware of them and being open to new perceptions will help you become more inclusive of others who are different from you.

Although stereotypes are based on assumptions and perceptions, they are accepted as truth. As a result, they function as powerful belief systems or filters. They can only be changed by creating awareness and introducing personal examples within the context of personal relationships, to counter them.

How many times have you had encounters similar to these?

Example #1
Karen says to Matrika, "I am really enjoying working with you on this project. When we first teamed up, I have to say I was really nervous about working with you. I am so relieved that you aren't anything like I thought you were going to be!"

Example #2
Jim says, "You know Fred, when Leonardo first came to work here I had heard that he was very outspoken and opinionated about everything. I don't know what you've experienced, but for me that is an understatement, to say the least! He has a classic Italian male temperament if I've ever seen one!"

In the first example, Karen is probably unknowingly admitting that she held some stereotypical beliefs about Matrika. She may have assumed they were true because of her beliefs about women from India. She had never personally known an Indian woman prior to meeting and working with Matrika. Her statement shows her surprise to discover that what she believed to be true about Matrika was in fact unfounded.

> *None of us are exempt from stereotyping. Everyone does it. Some of us are more aware of it than others.*

In the second example, Jim is expressing confirmation of his beliefs about stereotypes he holds true about men of Italian ancestry. He many not personally know anyone else who is an Italian male. Based on his experiences with one person, he is assuming that all other Italian men must be like Leonardo too.

Hiring managers and recruiters aren't exempt from stereotypes either. Their filters or belief systems will effect their hiring decisions. If you have been working in or want to change careers into a position or industry that is non traditional for your gender, you are probably already aware of many prevalent stereotypes. Some examples from our client's stories include women in transportation (trucking) and engineering (mechanical, chemical and electrical), and men in nursing, transportation (airline flight attendants) and administrative assistant positions.

Your primary goal in overcoming gender-based stereotypes is to convert yourself from being perceived as a "male" or a "female" to being seen as a unique individual, with the talent, skills, and abilities to do the job well. Your objective is to break through the hiring manager's assumptions and beliefs about men and women. Persuade him or her to see you as an individual, not a stereotypical member of your gender.

Networking will help you achieve this goal. Study the sections later in this guide on this activity. Building relationships with industry professionals, and obtaining references, endorsements, and referrals will help you open doors that may otherwise remain closed. Most hiring managers first give preference to people they know, then to people who are recommended to them by people they trust, and last to "cold contacts"—résumés and applications received from unknown individuals.

Pregnancy

Pregnancy is another common career liability. Under the law, pregnancy is a disability and a protected-class status for females. You don't have to disclose your pregnancy to a prospective employer. Doing so may decrease your odds of getting hired. Although refusing to hire you on the basis of your pregnancy would be illegal, proving that was the cause for the decision might be difficult.

Once you have accepted a position that could be threatening or dangerous to you or your unborn child, disclosure becomes necessary. Because pregnancy is a protected disability, your employer will be required to provide you with reasonable accommodation during the course of your pregnancy.

Obesity

Obesity is not a protected-class status, nor is it classified as a disability under the law. Discrimination can be more blatant against obese job seekers. If you are obese, there are several things you can do to help offset prevalent stereotypes.

First, be attentive to your career wardrobe. Consider meeting with a fashion consultant to put together your ensembles. This advice is for both men and women! Appearances make strong first impressions. Make yours count!

Second, your communication strategy will need to offset common opposing stereotypes. It is imperative that you emphasize characteristics like: high energy, stamina, endurance, your ability to take things seriously with a balanced sense of humor, disciplined, self-controlled, and strong follow-through on meeting commitments, deadlines, and objectives.

Third, over the long run, you may want to consider medical advice and support for a healthy weight-loss program. Obesity can lead to other serious health conditions, including diabetes, coronary disease and gastrointestinal disorders. These complications increase costs to you and your employer for health care benefits and other expenses.

> *Your self-concept, self-esteem and self-confidence will be your strongest assets. It will be difficult to convince others to believe in you, if you don't believe in yourself and your abilities!*

Finally, but not least in importance—your self-concept, self-esteem and self-confidence will be your strongest assets. If you feel challenged in any of these areas, you might consider working with a coach or a counselor to enhance them. It will be difficult to convince others to believe in you, if you don't believe in yourself and your abilities!

Limited Geographic Constraints

Often job searchers prefer not to relocate. Some would give serious consideration to an offer involving relocation. In a weak economy, you can expand your options if you are willing to relocate. Avoid playing your hand one way or the other with the interviewer. If the question of relocation comes up, it is best to say, "I'm open to relocation," or "for the right opportunity, I'd certainly look at relocation."

Scenario
Carl was a pharmaceutical sales representative based in Tulsa. A recruiter specializing in the high tech industry called him about a director-level sales management position in a technology company with openings in Denver and Dallas.

An avid mountain climber, Carl strongly preferred Denver over Dallas. However, knowing the weakness of the job market, he wisely responded by saying, "I would be open to relocation to either Denver or Dallas for the right opportunity." He was offered the position in Dallas.

The night before he was to travel to Texas to begin orientation for the new job, the vice president of human resources called. She told him that the position in Denver had reopened and asked if he would prefer that location. By staying flexible, Carl got the opportunity he wanted in the geographic area he preferred.

No College Degree or Graduate Degree

When a degree is considered a minimum requirement for a position, hiring managers will often disqualify all applicants who don't have one. In some cases, the absence of a degree will be used when a reason is needed to reject an applicant. In other cases, a strong candidate may get the nod, despite not having a college degree. Equivalent work experience or training may position him or her as the most qualified applicant.

Most hiring managers are primarily concerned with determining your ability to perform the essential job functions required for the position. Prepare CAR stories that highlight similar skills and accomplishments. By doing so you'll most likely put the interviewer at ease about your ability to deliver the results they are seeking.

Scenario

Mike was a leader in his industry, earning upwards of $80K in a highly competitive market. When his lack of a degree was raised Mike would flush, become nervous and get defensive.

His coach created this strategy. Whenever an interviewer says, "Mike, I see you have no degree." Mike would simply reply, "I've thought a lot about that, and I am glad we have the chance to discuss it. From what you have said, it sounds like your biggest priority for the person you hire is two-fold. One aspect is to develop new business and the other is to bring costs in line with revenue projections. If I could show you how I have achieved both in other positions, would that ease your concern about me not having a degree?"

By asking an opened ended question, Mike increased the likelihood of a positive response. "Certainly," his interviewer responded. Mike went on to deliver a CAR story highlighting his strongest example of developing new business and bringing costs into alignment with revenue projections. In the end, the interviewer was highly impressed by Mike's calmness and candor in addressing the issue.

When you are asked a question, you don't always have to give an *answer*—but you must always give a *response*. In the previous example, Mike didn't really answer the question, "I'm concerned that you have no degree." Instead he replied to the interviewer's concern with reassurance that he was capable of performing the job.

If you can respond with poise and confidence in the face of tough questions, your interview outcomes will usually be positive. Be sure to rehearse these tough questions so that you won't be caught off guard when it counts.

No Professional Licenses/Certifications

Sometimes, lack of a license/certification may truly be a deal-breaker, especially if it is a legal requirement for performing essential job functions. In some cases, it is just another level in the sorting and sifting process. In these instances, if you can establish that you have the requisite industry knowledge and skills, the expectation for licensure/certification may be set aside.

Age Concerns

Age is probably one of the most difficult career liability issues. Although age discrimination in employment practices against men and women over forty is illegal under federal law, (unlike many other countries where age is questioned routinely) it happens frequently. Stereotyping is rampant around age and work.

The difficulty arises when the employer has every intention of hiring a younger person. Rarely will they say this directly. There may be a whole host of beliefs and stereotypes at play.

Sometimes hiring managers may be looking for someone who they can "bring up through the ranks" so they can mold them into the company's image. They may hold the belief that hiring an older person would be too costly for the company, both in salary requirements, and in health care costs. Or quite simply, he or she may be threatened by someone who potentially knows more than they do!

Scenario

Greg had a stellar record of success in sales and marketing, working for some of the biggest players in the telecommunications industry. He had an opportunity to interview with the chief operating officer of a start-up wireless networking company.

When the young interviewer showed up in cutoffs and sandals and Greg was wearing a suit, he knew he was in trouble. Though the interview seemed to proceed smoothly, it became apparent that Greg knew more than his interviewer. Later that day, Greg received a brief e-mail expressing admiration for his considerable industry knowledge and expertise. It concluded with: "We don't believe you would be a cultural fit for our organization."

> *Your attitude will be the strongest asset or greatest career obstacle influencing your job search.*

So how do you effectively deal with issues around age? Age discrimination is a marketplace reality everywhere. It will happen. In countries outside the United States, where it is not illegal, questions about age are routine. After you turn fifty, each additional year will probably prolong your search. You must be prepared for the reality that your search may take longer.

Your attitude will be the strongest asset or greatest career obstacle influencing your job search. There are certainly employers out there who will hire you. Are you willing to exert the energy required to stay in the hunt?

How you manage your attitude toward almost certain discouragement will be crucial. Regular exercise, weight control, and maintaining an updated wardrobe consistent with the position you are seeking, are all important strategies.

You may not be comfortable with coloring your hair, especially if you are male. Gray or white hair may increase your older appearance and decrease your chances of serious consideration. This holds especially true in high technology, marketing, advertising, and some consumer products manufacturing and distribution sectors. Conversely, gray highlights add a distinguished look to your appearance and may be perceived as an asset in some industries such as law, financial services and consulting.

Eliminating earlier positions from your résumé (usually beyond the last ten years) can be an effective strategy to control first impressions. It is best not to list the years of your education if it has been more than twenty years since you graduated.

Look for opportunities to communicate perceived value to the interviewer early in the screening process. Be prepared to answer interview questions with CAR stories that show how you can provide value immediately to the organization.

Your willingness to take a lesser title or to start a new position in a contract or part-time role may provide an attractive option for the employer. Senior management gets the benefit of seeing your experience in action without making a long-term commitment. You get an opportunity to begin employment again. Many of our clients have seen this kind of arrangement turn into a mutually beneficial, long-term relationship.

Dependent-Care Responsibilities

Many job searchers, especially baby boomers, find themselves in the "sandwich" generation. They are faced with responsibilities for dependent children and for parents who are rapidly approaching dependency status.

Avoid revealing these issues during an interview. Let the interviewer develop an interest in you first. Help them see you as the best-qualified candidate. Then if dependent-care issues must be raised because of travel responsibilities, routine overtime, or the need for a flexible work schedule; bring them up during your final negotiations. Once the hiring manager is sold on you, he or she will be much more likely to make accommodations during the negotiations stage.

Scenario
Carmen was a single parent in her mid-thirties. She had immigrated to the United States from Latin America. Very vibrant and engaging, her favorite topic of conversation was her five-year-old son. She frequently referred to him as: "The light of my life."

Noticing that she did not wear a wedding ring, her coach cautioned her about mentioning her son during interviews. She asked, "Why not?" The coach replied, "The first thing an interviewer may think is—hmmm…no wedding ring and a five-year-old son. Every time the child is ill, she will be taking sick days because she has no backup at home." Or "With day care restrictions, she may not be available for overtime." Carmen made a concerted effort not to mention her son in her interviews.

Perceived as Lacking Direction or Career Planning

Most people don't plan their careers. For many, their careers "just happen to them." Sometimes they have moved from job to job, either in the same company, or with different employers, without gaining significant increases in scope of responsibility or title.

> *Most people don't plan their careers. For many, careers "just happen to them."*

If this is your experience and you are determined to make a major change in your career trajectory, be prepared for how some potential employers will perceive your past record. They may view your lateral job shifts as a lack of ambition or talent.

It is never too late to start moving upward. Your lateral job shifts may indicate that you simply met the expectations for the job, and spent little time in self-promotion for advancement. There isn't necessarily a relationship between your lack of advancement and your ambition to make a more significant contribution.

Today, you can decide to start making contributions at a higher level. With determination and the willingness to do whatever it takes, you will eventually be given new opportunities. This may occur with your current employer or in a new company.

Right now you have the sum total of all your talents, abilities and strengths. You have developed them throughout your career. Now you can apply them with renewed vigor to the problems and challenges of companies in this new economy.

Perceived as Specialist in My Field

You may have chosen to highlight a particular skill or technical discipline as a way to win promotions or favor in your current or most recent position. While this is good, it has the disadvantage of suggesting to others that you may have limited appeal.

Take the time to identify your experience and skills across a range of functional areas. Although you may have chosen to emphasize one or two of these skills over others, when facing interviews, you want to focus on what the company needs done, and your ability to do it. Downplay the fact that you are a specialist in one particular area.

Scenario

When Trent came for coaching, he expressed concern that his specialty in telecommunications as a software developer was particularly unmarketable in the local area and in the current economy. In subsequent coaching sessions, he identified numerous functional skills that could be applied broadly across multiple industries. These included project management, software development in other sectors, coding and programming skills, and technical support skills.

Trent researched companies and industries where these skills might be valued. Then he worked with his coach to tailor a communication strategy that emphasized his value across many industries. He highlighted his ability to rapidly develop new skills. This new perspective increased Trent's self-confidence and gave him added leverage in conversations with hiring managers and recruiters.

Perceived as Generalist in My Field

You may be concerned that recruiters or hiring managers will perceive you as a generalist in your field. This may arise if you have extensive experience in one function across a diverse background of companies and industries. It could also result from broad consulting experience across multiple industries or from several years in a general management or operations role in a small company.

When you have diverse skills and/or a broad range of experience, tailor your emphasis to your targeted positions. You don't have to include all your skills and experience within your résumé. Doing so can actually detract from your positioning and weaken your case.

Let's look at Paul Williams' experience and skills.

Paul speaking:

I told my coach I had extensive experience in recruiting, sales training and team development, but I didn't want to seek a position that would emphasize these skills. Additionally, my banking experience included accounting, internal controls, financial reporting and risk management, but I didn't want to pursue a banking or finance career either.

Together, we selected some functional skills like budget accountability, team leadership, and customer relations. Then we positioned these as foundational to my successes in sales and business development.

We transformed my background from a generalist into a specialist. Now I could position myself as bringing a unique combination of budget accountability, team leadership and sales achievements to the table. I am someone who grasps bottom-line drivers and the value of strategic relationships.

Unemployment Gaps

Gaps of unemployment may appear in your career history for several reasons. Sometimes new parents choose to leave a corporate career for several years. They make raising their child or children a full-time job. At times it may be necessary to take several months or even years off from work because of an extended illness or short-term disability. Regardless of the reason, a gap occurs in your employment history.

Most job seekers decide to use a letter résumé in these circumstances. This approach gives you more flexibility around describing your functional skills and experiences in an appealing and marketable manner. This résumé style is explained in detail in the next chapter.

If your circumstances include an extended gap and you were involved in community or volunteer activities, write up these activities in your Personal Career & Education Inventory. Use the Functional Skills Checklist to identify the skills you learned and used in your community-service or volunteer activities. Then write CAR stories illustrating your accomplishments.

Scenario
Carol took sixteen years off from her career as a registered nurse to raise her daughter. When she was ready to go back to work, she realized that nursing had changed dramatically during her absence. She didn't want to take extended refresher courses and start at the bottom of the pay scale again. She began exploring other career options. While raising her daughter, Carol served for three years as the PTA president of the elementary school. During her tenure, she planned, organized, and managed six district-wide fund-raisers.

Each one raised more money than the previous event. All set historic district records. Carol's coach helped her write CAR stories that captured her talents and accomplishments in budgeting, financial planning and reporting, fund raising, team leadership, volunteer recruitment and project management.

Carol also volunteered her time as a board member of her homeowner's association. She wrote the monthly newsletter. Weekly, she conducted neighborhood compliance inspections based on the covenants and regulations governing the subdivision. These accomplishments were captured in CAR stories that illustrated her skills in graphic design, word processing, editing, journalism, policy and procedure, compliance, quality control and administration.

If your personal circumstances include a long-term illness or injury, then you may wish to consider creating a communication strategy that speaks to this crisply, confidently and unemotionally. Consider Chris's approach below.

Scenario
Chris had been out of work for three years following a series of grand mal seizures. For the first six months doctors had trouble isolating the cause. He lost his driver's license. Because of the potential risks, he could not operate equipment or machinery.

After determining that he had a non-malignant brain growth that periodically bled causing the seizures, routine brain surgery was performed to remove it. When he had been seizure-free for two years, his doctors said he was medically cleared to drive and work again.

Chris's communication strategy was this: "For the past three years, I had a short-term disability that made it impossible for me to work. My doctors have agreed that I am fully recovered and able to return to work without any complications or limitations. You can see from my employment record that I was a dependable employee who received frequent promotions throughout my career. I am confident that I will be able to do the same in my next position."

Employers are required by law to reasonably accommodate persons with disabilities who are able to perform essential job functions, with or without reasonable accommodation. Hiring managers are not allowed to question prospective employees about their medical history, or the nature of past illnesses, injuries or disabilities.

Pre-employment physicals may be required. Disclosure of your personal disability to the physician may be necessary to protect your health and safety. However, it is never anybody else's business during the hiring process.

Limited Line Experience

Often hiring managers seeking to fill a management position expect candidates to have a track record working their way up the line. They want to see a history of learning to lead people, functions, departments, or operations within a company or business unit. Ideally, they want to see increasing levels of responsibility for profit and loss—managing the bottom line—in a business unit, division or an entire organization.

Many employees fill staff positions where their talents are leveraged over an entire organization. In these roles, they build a solid record of achievements without acquiring the line experience expected for many attractive, competitive positions.

Some common staff positions in small companies include: controller, sales manager, human resources manager, training manager, marketing manager, IT manager, MIS manager and loss prevention manager. Each of these roles carries significant responsibilities. In small companies, individuals in these roles may not have any direct reports.

If you have the staff label, and cannot identify significant line experience, you may find that some employers will have reservations about your ability to lead and manage people. Devise a communication strategy to effectively address their concerns.

Determine what skills the employer is looking for in the position. Do they need someone who can rapidly contribute to the turnaround of a business unit? If so, then you'll want to emphasize situations through your CAR stories where you've successfully turned around an operation.

When you approach the interview this way, the hiring manager will probably lose sight of your limited line experience as they hear you describe solutions to some of their current business problems. Hiring managers are ultimately interested in learning if you can provide solutions for their current problems. Do this, and you will ace the interview.

Limited Staff Experience

This career obstacle is the opposite of the one previously presented. Sometimes you will be interviewed for a line position where your significant staff experience will be held as suspect. In those situations, emphasize how you have been accountable for P&L responsibilities on a broader scale.

In addition, you'll want to emphasize your broader leadership responsibilities, regardless of the title you held. Remember, employers are most interested in the "steak," not the "sizzle." They will be interested in the ways you have contributed to the management and growth of the organization, rather than the titles you have held.

Lacking Titles That Represent My Scope of Responsibilities

Companies do not always use standard titles. Although the titles are known and recognized within the company, they may not adequately communicate the scope of your duties and responsibilities to outside hiring managers.

When you are writing your résumé, use titles that are generally accepted across industries to describe the positions you held. For example, one client held the title unit manager, for a Fortune 100 company. This was the highest position in that business unit. He was fully accountable for $300M in profit and loss and had five direct reports, with over 400 employees in the organization beneath them. The generally accepted title for this role would be general manager.

Keep in mind that your résumé is a powerful marketing tool. Use it to communicate who you are, what you have accomplished, and how you can contribute in your next position. Don't exaggerate or lie. Avoid misrepresenting or "stretching the truth." And, don't sell yourself short! Communicate persuasively and convincingly. Tell your story with clarity, conciseness, and convincing CAR story illustrations.

An employer's primary interest in you is twofold: Do you have the essential skills to perform the job, and secondly, will you be the best fit for the position? If you are able to communicate the accomplishments you have achieved, the challenges you faced, and the executions you undertook, you will successfully focus the interviewer's attention on your job skills and fit.

Lacking Upward Mobility in My Career

Self-perception will always be your biggest challenge or your greatest strength regarding career obstacles. Do you see yourself as damaged goods because you haven't moved up in your career? If so, then hiring managers will perceive that too.

Many job seekers have been significant corporate contributors without receiving promotions. There are many factors that may lead to these circumstances.

Some companies simply don't promote often. Others reward exceptional performance with raises or with stock options, rather than with promotions. In some cases, employees have no desire to move up. They enjoy being individual contributors. Personal satisfaction and fulfillment comes from a job done well and a job well done. They take great personal pride in their work.

Other companies have no room for upward mobility. You may have been employed by a family-owned business, a highly matrixed organization, or a company that is "flattened" with few senior managers. In each instance, opportunities for advancement can be severely limited. Your résumé can be structured to highlight the many positive contributions you have made in each of your positions. These matter most.

Scenario
Rick had been an exceptional performer in a Fortune 500 company division. His personnel file contained many exceptional performance reviews. He had recently earned an MBA from the University of Chicago.

Despite these achievements, he had failed to win promotions. In his own words, Rick highlighted his problem: "I've just been notoriously bad at self-promotion. That's what promotions were all about in my company. It was never about what you knew; it was who knew you, and who knew what you did. I just didn't feel comfortable in the spotlight."

As a result of several factors including coaching, his diligence, and persistence, Rick obtained a new position. He was hired as a director. He had previously held a senior manager title. In addition, the position was with a Japanese technology company, requiring relocation to Japan—a demand that Rick was eager to meet.

Left Short-Term Position

This can happen for several reasons. You may have accepted a position without fully understanding what it involved. Sometimes hiring managers can be misleading when zealously recruiting a talented applicant. Another common scenario can occur when you have joined a company that went through a change of ownership, or lost funding and had to shut down unexpectedly.

If you accepted a new position only to discover early on that it wasn't the right fit, it is important to grapple with how that occurred. Sometimes, it's a matter of internal politics, or conflicting personalities. Other times, it is because the job was misrepresented. Finally, it could be an honest misunderstanding of the position's duties.

Discuss these circumstances in detail with your coach. Use your coach as a sounding board to work through any negative emotions you may be experiencing. Work hard to identify what you could have done differently to avoid it. Let go of the things you were powerless to change. Apply your learning to your current job search.

You will need to develop a communication strategy for your interviews if the second scenario is closer to your circumstances. This message should be designed to explain your unfortunate turn of events. Avoid casting blame or responsibility for your misfortune on anyone in particular.

When you begin interviewing for your next position, expect that the short time in your most recent or present job will be a concern to many potential employers. The focus will immediately be upon you. Be prepared to proactively speak to these circumstances.

Hiring managers may be thinking to themselves: "Were you able to contribute? Was your personality difficult?" If they sense that you are resentful toward your current or most recent employer, they may be concerned that you would be a liability to future employers too.

> *What really matters is whether or not you are the person best qualified to fill this employer's current job opening.*

What really matters is whether or not you are the person best qualified to fill this employer's current job opening. You can persuasively sell yourself by identifying the skills, talents and abilities that you bring to the job through clear, concise and compelling CAR stories.

Many other job seekers have left short-term positions. The interviewer may have had a similar experience. Or he or she may have hired others who did, who turned out to be highly productive and valued employees.

Job seekers in similar circumstances have often chosen to leave their present or most recent position off their résumé. They chose instead to address the matter in a cover letter. Others decided to discuss it face-to-face in each interview. This strategy gave them an opportunity to present it in a favorable light with an explanation of the circumstances involved. Some have positioned their short-term experience as a temporary consulting role, with a possibility of becoming a permanent position later on.

You will want to use a positioning summary at the top of your résumé that briefly highlights your accomplishments and contributions. This will immediately offset a hiring manager's tendency to place much significance on your recent short-term experience.

Frequently Changed Jobs

Research shows that job turnover is frequent at all levels in organizations. Fortune magazine reported recently that the average tenure for a CEO within the Fortune 500 is three and one-half years. This means that there are an average of 500 CEO openings every forty-two months or nearly twelve openings monthly at the very top of the pyramid!

Additionally, the U.S. Department of Labor reports that the average person will work in 3.5 careers during a lifetime with ten different employers. Each position will last an aver age of 3.5 years. The National Association of Colleges and Employers Journal of Career Planning (1995) reported that "The average American beginning his or her career in the 1990s will probably work in ten or more jobs for five or more employers before retiring." This statistic remains true across most industries and functions. One exception is the high technology sector. The average employee in this industry stays in a company between eighteen and twenty-four months before moving on to the next opportunity.

Job stability was a norm in past generations. Most people found secure jobs with employers and the loyalty was mutual. Forty years ago you could accept an entry-level position in utilities, telecommunications, steel, gas & oil, manufacturing, state or federal government, military service, financial services, or retail services and be assured of job security. You could realistically plan to put in your twenty to thirty years and retire comfortably.

If you changed jobs every three to five years a generation ago, you would have been labeled as unstable, high risk and virtually unemployable. Today, if you have been with the same company more than ten years, many recruiters and hiring managers will view you as a hiring risk! They are fearful that you will expect long-term job security and loyalty from your next employer. There are no guarantees anymore!

Job seekers who have changed jobs every two to five years are within the norm. Positioning each move as a promotion, a strategic change to gain new skills or experience, or a planned move for some other business reason reduces the impact of most perceived liabilities around frequent job changes.

Left A Company That Was in Financial Difficulty

Your decision to leave a company may have been made because the organization hit rough economic seas. This is not an uncommon event. There have been many others in your situation recently. The primary issues are twofold. First, did you have a direct hand in its downfall? And secondly, could you have had a material impact on either its decline or its turnaround? A sharp interviewer will press these issues for answers.

> *You will appeal to employers most if the talents, strengths and abilities you bring to a position are a close match.*

You will appeal to employers most if the talents, strengths and abilities you bring to a position are a close match. These can be tailored to the challenges facing them in the immediate future. If you can describe your accomplishments in your department or function, they are not likely to place much significance on the fact that the company you worked for failed despite your strong contributions.

Most employers realize that in today's fast-paced, competitive environment, a company can do many things well and still fail. If you were responsible for functional areas that excelled, highlight your contributions and emphasize your achievements in each area. Delivering clear, concise, and compelling CAR stories has made a difference with hundreds of job seekers!

Left A Company That Had A Poor Reputation

In this situation, you may need to differentiate yourself from the company you left. For instance, how did former Enron executives or employees from Arthur Andersen, Safety-Kleen, Worldcom or Firestone do when they entered the job market?

Generally speaking, those who left with good reputations and stellar references did fine. Many achieved successes by emphasizing their key accomplishments, with verification by their references. Some employers do not conduct thorough reference checks. You shouldn't risk losing an opportunity though by failing to follow-up with your references and preparing them to support you in your search.

Adverse Personal Credit Report

Recent research seems to indicate that a correlation exists between how an individual manages their personal credit, and how they would manage a company's budget and finances. More and more companies are including credit reporting in their background investigations and pre-employment screenings.

Countless advertisements can be found by companies claiming to be able to "clean your credit report" or "wipe out derogatory records" from your credit file. Don't be fooled by these claims. If accurate information is present, it cannot be removed until a certain period of time has elapsed.

Public record items, if they exist, will remain on your record as follows:

- Tax liens (reported for seven years after the lien is filed)
- Judgments (reported for seven years after the judgment is entered)
- Chapter 7 bankruptcies (reported for 10 years following the bankruptcy)
- Chapter 13 bankruptcies (reported for seven years following the bankruptcy)
- Collection items (if they exist) and their status
- Up to seven years of credit history
- A list of companies making inquiries into your individual credit file
- A list of member companies (creditors) and their phone numbers

You may wish to contact one of the credit reporting companies and request a copy of your personal credit report to verify the accuracy of the data it contains. If you discover inaccurate reporting, contact the agency for instructions on how to correct it.

Credit Reporting Agencies:

- Equifax
  800-525-6285
  www.equifax.com
- Experian
  888-397-3742
  www.experian.com

- TransUnion
  800-680-7289
  www.tuc.com

On occasion, you may be asked to sign a release-of-information form allowing a prospective employer to access your credit file to conduct a pre-employment screening check. If you have accurate, derogatory information in your credit file, consider attaching a brief letter of explanation to the signed release.

When you or an immediate family member has had a catastrophic illness, a disability resulting in long-term unemployment and large medical expenses, or some other reasonable event that caused your financial problems, an explanation may help offset the unfavorable report.

References Unfavorable

During reference checks, job seekers often lose opportunities because their references didn't offer a strong endorsement. In this day and age, the likelihood is high that references will be checked. Regardless of your level, if you have poor references, it can become a career obstacle.

Fearful of unfavorable references, many job seekers have gone back to previous managers and explained that they were searching for a job. They have asked for a positive reference and obtained it. Most people like to think they have helped others along the way rather than intentionally seeking to hurt them.

Strategy #29 Understand Timing's Influence on Your Job Search

Timing has two important considerations. On the one hand, your timing is now; you are seeking a position today. On the other hand, timing for prospective employers is an unknown variable. By increasing your scope and activity, you can increase the probability of matching your timing with the timing of hiring managers. They don't know you exist and you don't know they exist!

> **Prayer of St. Francis**
>
> *"God, grant me the serenity to accept the things I cannot change, the courage to change the things I can, and the wisdom to know the difference…"*
>
> Reinhold Niebuhr

You can influence being discovered as a strong candidate for desirable positions by persistence, consistency and follow-up. Don't give up. Stay focused. Remain determined. Courageously press forward. Your success will come in its own time. Often it happens when you are least expecting it.

Chapter Review

SALT-Scope, Activity, Liabilities and Timing

Strategy #21 Plan the Scope of Your Search
- Geographic target areas
- Positions you desire
- Industry segments you prefer
- Company size

Strategy #22 Identify the Geographic Scope of Your Search

Strategy #23 Broaden the Position Scope of Your Search
- Same position/same industry
- Same position/different industry
- Different position/same industry
- Different position/different industry
- Self-employment

Strategy #24 Set your Industry Scope Search Boundaries

Strategy #25 Determine the Size of Your Target Companies

Strategy #26 Define Your Search Activities

Strategy #27 Identify Your Career Obstacles

Strategy #28 Manage Your Career Obstacles with the Career Obstacles Checklist

Strategy #29 Understand Timing's Influence on Your Job Search

Chapter Five:
Creating Your Career Search Activity &
Scope Action Plan (ASAP)

Strategy #30 Develop Your Activity & Scope Action Plan (ASAP)

"How can we understand the road we travel? It is the Lord who directs our steps." Proverbs 20:24 (NLT)

Paul speaking:

"My coach told me that my Activity & Scope Action Plan (ASAP) was critical to my success. He helped me understand that the job search process is not rocket science, but it is filled with distractions that could prolong my search. By planning my work and working my plan, I can avoid many of these mistakes.

Together, we reviewed my planned job search activity, scope and targets. This gave me a clear picture of which companies, recruiters, investment firms, and networking contacts I wanted to reach; which industries I wanted to focus on, and the geographic range I preferred for my next employment opportunity. We set goals that were specific, measurable, activity-oriented, results-driven and time-oriented."

The Bureau of Labor Statistics reported that in August, 2003 unemployment was at 6.1 percent. There were 8.9 million unemployed people and an additional 503 thousand who were unemployed but no longer looking for jobs. Conversely, there were 137.6 million employed persons n the United States.

Paul speaking:

"I learned that most people will seek the path of least resistance and most comfort. Spending most of my time searching Internet job boards was comfortable and seemed quite productive. It was easy to stay busy responding to advertised positions that I thought were ideal for me. In many instances, I just knew I was the most qualified and the phone would start ringing within days! By replying to hundreds of job postings that sounded exactly like my résumé, I felt so productive.

When my coach told me that this strategy was ineffective, I was frustrated. He told me recent research shows the average employer fills less than eight percent of its current openings with candidates sourced on-line, and only five percent of its openings from candidates who apply through the company's own Web site.

It makes sense that there are millions of résumés on the Internet at any given time. After all, each of the major on-line job boards boast millions of résumés posted and thousands of jobs to be filled. CareerBuilder.com recently advertised to employers: 'Reach 9 million job seekers with your ad!'"

Strategy #31 Create Your Activity & Scope Targets & Goals

Job search activities and success rates have remained constant over time despite changes in the economy and unemployment rates. Many different organizations have tracked statistics on the percentage of successes job seekers have had using different job search strategies.

The chart below was created by adapting some of the statistics published by *Fast Company* in its article, "*What Happened To Your Parachute?*" It can be viewed on-line at: http://pf.fastcompany.com/magazine/27/bolles.html (October 2, 2003).

Activity	Success Rate
Randomly mail out your résumé	7%
Respond to classified advertisements in trade journals	7%
Respond to classified ads in newspapers or on-line	10%
Networking	33%
Letter Résumé Style (get a job created)	47%
Networking influential industry contacts	69%
Use a job match assessment; target strong fits; use Letter Résumé	86%

Targets

There are eight target areas you can consider. Remember the impact of scope as you set the parameters for each target.

Target One: Industries

Refer to your Industry Checklist. Identify the industries you want to include in your job search. Research each one and learn about:

- Current trends
- Industry leaders (companies)
- New products/services
- How market share is distributed
- Projections for the future
- Leading publications
- Key players (individuals)

Strategy #32 Access Internet Search Engines & Career Portals

As a job searcher, you have vast on-line resources available at your fingertips. Some of the best are found at major search engines like:

Google.com Yahoo.com Infoseek.com   LookSmart.com Dogpile.com

HotBot.com AltaVista.com Lycos.com   Metacrawler.com

These resources provide job-search services of various kinds and degrees of usefulness. Unquestionably, the most popular during recent years were: Yahoo.com and Google.com.

Paul speaking:

"First I visited the Google home page (www.google.com) and clicked 'Business,' in the 'Directory.' Then I chose 'Employment,' and, under that, 'Job Search,' where I was presented with numerous choices. These included: Executive Search, Industries, Interview Advice, Recruiters, Résumé Advice and Worldwide. On the same page were links to 100 or so job-search companies.

I clicked the 'By Industry' option. Here I was able to select from twelve industry sources, as well as sixty-five company Web sites (on that particular day.) Other options given included choosing among five research tools (Salaries, Companies, Industries, Occupations and Relocations), and a "Browse Jobs" option. Since I was interested in IT, I found numerous IT positions under subcategories like: engineering; information technology, media, arts and design."

Target Two: Geographic Locations

Determine your geographic preferences. Visit the execunet.com Web site and review the "Executive Talent Demand Index" for the current quarter. Summary data is provided comparing the percentage change between the present quarter and previous year's quarter in four segments: Function, Region, Industry and Salary.

Paul speaking:

"When I reviewed the 'Executive Talent Demand Index' with my career coach, I learned the following information about talent demand under the Region section. Comparing last quarter to the previous year's quarter, demand increased to sixteen percent in the New York metro area. The Midwest and Mid-Atlantic showed gains of seven percent and five percent respectively. Growth was zero percent throughout the Mountain states region and it showed a decrease of eighteen percent in New England/Northeast, three percent in the Southwest and West Coast.

This data helped me realize that if I limited my search to the Rocky Mountain region where the demand was at zero percent my search would probably be longer. My career coach encouraged me to include the Midwest and the Mid-Atlantic regions where growth was the highest.

Ideally, I wanted to stay in Colorado. On Google.com, I found profiles of leading companies headquartered in Denver. The 'Companies' option under 'Information Technology,' for example, featured in-depth company profiles through a link to www.WetFeet.com. 'Relocation,' a little farther down the page, allowed me to compare United States cities by: 'Cost of Living,' 'Real Estate Value,' and 'Quality of Life,' among other subjects. Salary comparisons were also available at Salary.com."

Your geographic targets can range from specific metropolitan areas, to states, to regions, to countries. Write down the specific areas you want to target and prioritize them. You may wish to divide them into stages. Starting first in one or two areas, and then after a specified time frame, expanding into additional areas.

Target Three: Employers

Refer back to your Career History & Goals Worksheet. Decide what size employers you want to target (small, medium or large). Determine employer sizes for each geographic and industry target.

Paul speaking:

"I wanted to follow my coach's advice, so I created a list of twenty-five to fifty companies that I thought would be ideal employers. My coach gave me this overview of some on-line resources; places where I could find companies to put on my list."

Good places to start:

Hoover's Online (www.hoovers.com)

Hoover's Online is a premier on-line information resource. Some of its services are free. Premium features can be accessed for a modest monthly fee. At the core of Hoover's is a database of some 85,000 public and private companies worldwide, and the industries in which they operate.

Bizjournals.com (www.bizjournals.com)

If you have decided to target companies in large U.S. cities, this site is a must. Bizjournals.com offers complete, up-to-date business news. A subscription buys you the paper edition, as well as that city's *Book of Lists*. This resource provides essential information on the leading buyers, businesses and employers in over sixty of the country's most dynamic markets. It's a snapshot of local economies, with a perspective you can't get anywhere else. On-line job listings and a place to post your résumé are also available.

Business.com (www.business.com)

Developed by a team of industry experts and library scientists, the Business.com directory contains more than 400,000 listings within 25,000 industry, product, and service subcategories. It is a great place to find the leading companies nationwide, in a broad variety of industries. It also has a listing of industry associations for each industry represented. These industry associations offer their members additional services, among them career counseling, special clinics for selected stages of a job search, and on-line job listings.

Public Library Resources

Many public libraries have excellent research capabilities. Some, particularly those in metropolitan areas, are available by remote access from your home computer. For example, at Mergent Online you can obtain information on 28,000 domestic and international public companies. This data includes a detailed corporate history, annual reports, and live news feeds. You can search by yellow page category, SIC code, geography, and other parameters.

Paul speaking:

"After I developed my list, I wanted to learn more about the companies I had selected. My coach suggested that I visit their company Web sites as a beginning point. It was clear that this would give me relatively thorough information about goods, services, mission statements, corporate culture and key officers.

Another good source he recommended was EDGAR (Electronic Data Gathering, Analysis and Retrieval system.) All public companies, foreign and domestic, are required to file registration statements, periodic reports, and other forms electronically through EDGAR. Anyone can access and download this information for free, at www.sec.gov/edgar.shtml.

As I compiled research about my target companies, I looked carefully for information about new developments like mergers and acquisitions, new product launches, declining sales, retiring or newly hired executives and other strategic business issues. These developments could be used in conjunction with my Letter Résumé to make my initial company contacts, and to prepare for informational interviews.

Next, I decided who to approach within each company. This contact information was often readily available on the company's Web site. I simultaneously sent my Letter Résumé to several key people within the same company. My credentials were more likely to be passed around among decision makers within my target companies if I made more than one internal contact."

Target Four: Positions & Functions

Decide what positions you wish to target in each employer and industry. Remember to refer back to your Career History & Goals Worksheet.

Target Five: Recruiters

On-line recruiting ($780 million business in 2001) is expected to grow to $2.3 billion by 2005, according to Forrester Research. The array of choices on the Web is dizzying. Literally hundreds of sites specialize in job search, recruitment, career changes and vocational counseling.

The following Internet addresses include sites in all four of these categories. Familiarize yourself with them. Use those you find helpful. Register with any sites that provide the kind of information and services you need.

If you don't want to go to the trouble to post your own résumé, there are a number of services that will post it on multiple job banks automatically. Be sure to use the Internet Résumé for this purpose. RésuméRabbit (www.resumerabbit.com) is an example. Others can be located on search engines such as Google.com, Yahoo.com, DogPile.com, and AltaVista.com.

Internet Job Boards and Recruiter Web sites

www.hotjobs.com

www.6figurejobs.com

www.jobs.internet.com

www.theworksite.com

www.wetfeet.com

www.kforce.com

www.careermosaic.com

www.vault.com

www.craiglist.com

www.jobsonline.com

www.careerbuilder.com

www.nettemps.com

www.jobtrack.com

www.monster.com

www.flipdog.com

www.dice.com

www.brassring.com

www.directemployers.com

www.chiefmonster.com

www.cfo.com

www.yahoo.com

www.cio.com

www.usajobs.com

www.collegegrad.com

In addition to the above, there are a number of job search sites that cater specifically to Christian job seekers. Some are oriented to Christians seeking jobs in ministry. Others are with organizations that have a Christian world-view.

Christian-oriented Job Search Sites & Resource Web Sites

www.christianet.com/christianjobs

www.christiancareercenter.com

www.ministryemployment.com/

www.ministrysearch.com

www.jobsearchmonitor.com

www.jobleads.org

www.christianemployments.com

www.christian-careers.com

www.gospelcom.net

www.churchstaffing.com

www.christianplacements.com

www.goshen.net

www.christianitytoday.com

www.christianjobsmall.com

www.intercristo.com

www.crosssearch.com

www.churchjobsonline.com

www.teaching-jobs.org

www.ministryemployment.ca

www.christianjobs.com.au

www.christianjobs.com

www.christianet.com

Target Six: Key Industry Leaders

Strategy #33 Conduct Informational Interviews—They Are Your Most Powerful Search Tool

> *Research shows that informational interviews have a 69 percent success rate for leading to new jobs.*

Research shows that sixty-nine percent of successful job seekers reported that an informational interview led to getting a job created just for them! Informational interviews are a vastly under-used tool for getting your message out. Every conversation will not be helpful to you. But every conversation should generate names—and names will lead you to conversations that *will* help you.

It is a universal law—the law of numbers. Conversations will lead to other conversations. These will lead to other names. By contacting these individuals, you will uncover new opportunities. As you build your network, you will find people who know things about your target companies. Or they will know others who do, and you need to be talking to them.

Who are potential contacts for informational interviews? Start with people you know. Use your "warm" market. This includes anyone you have something in common with inside your circle of acquaintances. They can give you names of people you don't know. Then you'll be able to make the bridge to the "cold" market—people you don't yet know—with greater ease (less fear?)

When setting up informational interviews, don't mention that you're looking for a job. You are just seeking information. This should be truthful, presuming they will get something out of the information exchange as well.

Maybe you haven't been the greatest networker. But you can change that, even at this point in the game. Think of it this way, you are building a life team. With the contacts you are making, you'll always have a network to go back to in the future. Perhaps they will call you a few months down the road to ask a return favor. That's the way an interpersonal network functions.

Always leave your informational interview with more names of prospective contacts. Set a goal to get two names from every conversation. Soon, you'll have more people to talk to than you have hours in the day!

Ask each person you interview if you can use their name when you make contact with someone they have recommended. Or ask if they would be willing to make a call or send an e-mail of introduction, prior to your first contact. By adding these extra steps, you will maximize the value of each informational interview.

Whenever you are communicating with a networking contact, emphasize that you are not asking them for a job! Clarify that you are working to expand your contacts in a specific industry by getting to know key leaders.

If you are successful at getting informational interviews, you will see a pattern develop. Some will be short and uneventful. Others will result in chemistry, and go in directions you never would have expected! Some of these unexpected events can include:

1. Telling you about a colleague looking to fill a position that may be a fit for you

2. Describing a vision they have for their company/division/department that you could help make a reality

3. Deciding to explore creating a position uniquely for you that would combine your talent with their current business needs

Be prepared to talk intelligently about the company, its products/services, key leaders, industry challenges and major customers. By demonstrating that you have done your homework, you will win more confidence and trust on behalf of the interviewee. You want these influential industry leaders to tell you who they know, who you need to know, and what they know about the state of the industry, major competitors, key customers and leading products.

Prepare a list of open-ended questions and use them to keep on track.

1. *What do you see as the biggest challenge facing the (industry name) industry in the next few years?*

2. *Today, the (industry name) industry is a ($XXB) market, where do you see it in five years? In ten years?*

3. *If you had your career to do over again, what would you do differently?*

4. *What is the best advice you would have for someone looking to enter this industry?*

5. *In your opinion, who are the most important leaders in the (industry name) industry today? How did they achieve this recognition in your mind?*

6. *If you could change three things in your industry, what would they be and why?*

7. *What is the single most important factor for success in the (industry name) industry?*

8. *Who do you know who I should be talking to in the (industry name) industry?*

9. *What gives you the most pride in your career in the (industry name) industry?*

10. *How do you express your passion for work in the (industry name) industry?*

11. *Where do you see growth/change occurring?*

12. *Who do you know who is making this change occur?*

13. *What are some of the key trends in the industry, as you see them?*

14. *What would you do if you were me?*

15. *Whom do you know at XYZ Company who I could talk to?*

Industry Influential Introduction Letters will open many new doors. Ask influential leaders in your targeted industries to allow you to draft a letter of introduction. Forward it to them electronically for reproduction on corporate letterhead with their signature. Review the sample provided earlier for a suggested format. By offering to do the work for them, you will greatly increase your chances of getting such letters.

Don't be discouraged if it takes a number of informational interviews to produce your first job interview. This strategy will produce dividends—be persistent!

Target Seven: Investment Firms

Some candidates are highly sought after by venture capital firms and private equity investors. Typically, these companies prefer candidates with six to ten years of in-depth leadership experience in the industry they specialize in funding. If this target area interests you, spend some time researching these firms on-line. PriceWaterhouseCoopers has a site called MoneyTree.com at: http://www.pwcmoneytree.com/moneytree/index.jsp

Here, you can research the market by: region, industry, stage of development, financing sequence, VC firm, investee company or summary report. Study the companies that have received funding. Learn about their products, services and executive team members. If you think you could make a contribution, use your Letter Résumé to make contact. Refer to their company Web site and aggressively follow-up.

> *Despite the proliferation of on-line recruiting, significantly more people are still hired through networking than through any other job search strategy.*

Typically, opportunities in this market segment will be high risk / high reward. They will be operating on limited budgets, and compensation may be tied heavily to an equity position. If the company succeeds, this can be quite lucrative. If it fails, it can be disastrous for you financially and emotionally.

Target Eight: People in Your Network

Despite the proliferation of on-line recruiting, significantly more people are still hired through networking than by any other job search activity. There's no way around it. Finding a job in the "old/new /old again" economy is a function of how many people you talk to, and how many people hear your "story."

Merely mentioning the word "networking," strikes terror in most people's hearts. It shouldn't. You've worked hard. You have a good story to tell with nothing to hide. If you find your new employer, rather than the other way around, they don't have to pay recruiters' fees. This is an added bonus for them.

Strategy #34 Compose Your 30-Second Commercial

Telling your story to others helps them remember you. Create a thirty-second "commercial" or "elevator speech." This clear, concise story will summarize your background, achievements and career goals. You can share it with anyone who is in a position to help you. Make it memorable and make it sizzle. Practice it in front of a mirror, with your dog, and in your car. Run it by someone who knows you well, to make sure it sounds like "you."

Paul speaking:

"I worked hard on my thirty-second commercial for networking opportunities:

> *I have a career foundation of progressively responsible roles in finance and accounting. This gave me the skills I needed to achieve outstanding sales and drive revenue growth over ten years as a business development executive. I have a proven record of accomplishments leading sales teams and forging strategic alliances with C-level customers in the financial services, technology, manufacturing, and retail services industries. I am looking for a position as a director or manager of sales and business development in the metro Denver area. Who do you know who I should be talking to today?*

I sat down with my spouse and later with several long-time, trusted colleagues. We simply brainstormed names of people I knew. As the names came up, I didn't qualify them. My coach emphasized that it didn't matter if I knew how to find them, or if they could ultimately help me. I just needed to write the names down."

Everyone should make your list. Don't forget other parents of children on your child's sports teams. Even include competitors, customers, vendors and suppliers. Add your lawyer, CPA, and people from your house of worship. They may know nothing about you or your industry, but they do know other people.

Go to your class reunions. Attend trade fairs, conventions and association meetings in your field. Keep a supply of business cards (just your name and contact info if you are unemployed) and résumés available to pass along whenever the occasion presents itself to network.

Paul speaking:

"I was worried about how I could find some of the people I had written down. My coach helped me find tremendous free resources on the Web for finding people. Among the many were: peoplefind.com, whowhere.com, questdex.com, whitepages.com, reversedirectory.net, anywho.com and peoplespot.com. Using these resources, I was able to locate almost everyone on my list. Sometimes I only had a shred of information.

I divided my name list into categories to make it easier to use. They included:

1. Family members

2. Friends & acquaintances

3. Co-workers & colleagues

4. Former employers & supervisors

5. Alumni (college, graduate school, trade school)

6. Community service activity contacts

7. Professional associations (members & officers)

8. Clubs (members &officers)

9. Religious leaders and members

10. References."

Strategy #35 Set SMART Goals for Your Job Search Activity

"Our goal is to stay within the boundaries of God's plan for us, and this plan includes our working there with you."
II Corinthians 10:13b (NLT)

SMART Goals are: Specific, Measurable, Activity-oriented, Results-driven and Time-limited. Remember the impact of activity as you set goals. Remember the percentage success rates for each activity. Some have a much higher probability of resulting in a job than others. This number follows each target in parentheses.

Paul speaking:

"With my coach's assistance, I completed my ASAP Goals & Tracking Worksheet. My goals were aggressive because I was able to devote an average of five hours daily to my job search. I would do more on weekends."

ASAP Goals & Tracking Worksheet

Target Activity & Daily Goals	Weekly Goals	Monthly Goals
Résumé Distribution Services (Electronic) (7%)		
1. I will distribute my résumé to targeted employers on a <u>monthly</u> basis.	N.A.	1,000
2. I will distribute my résumé to targeted recruiters on a <u>monthly</u> basis.	N.A.	1,000
Résumé Distributions (First-Class Mail) (7%)		
1. I will distribute my résumé to <u>48</u> targeted employers.	12	48
2. I will spend <u>15</u> minutes daily in follow-up activities.		
Responding to Job Openings in Trade Journal (7%)		
1. I will spend <u>10</u> minutes daily researching and applying to openings.	5	20
2. I will spend <u>5</u> minutes daily following up on openings applied to earlier.	5	20
Applying via On-line Job Boards (10%)		
1. I will spend <u>10</u> minutes daily researching and applying to openings	10	40
2. I will spend <u>5</u> minutes daily following up on openings applied to earlier.	10	40

Target Activity & Daily Goals	Weekly Goals	Monthly Goals
Applying to Company Web site Job Boards (10%)		
1. I will spend <u>10</u> minutes daily researching and applying to openings.	10	40
2. I will spend <u>5</u> minutes daily following up on openings applied to earlier.	10	40
Contacting Recruiters (15%)		
1. I will spend <u>10</u> minutes daily researching & applying to recruiter Web sites.	10	40
2. I will spend <u>5</u> minutes daily sending e-mails with my résumé to recruiters.	5	20
3. I will spend <u>10</u> minutes daily calling recruiters to follow-up on Web site applications and e-mails.	5	20
Contacting Investment Firms (15%)		
1. I will spend <u>15</u> minutes daily researching investment firms on-line and making contact via e-mail, mail or phone.	3	12
2. I will spend <u>5</u> minutes daily in follow-up activities (e-mail, mail, or phone).	3	12
Networking Family Members (33%)		
1. I will spend <u>10</u> minutes daily contacting family members via e-mail, mail or phone.	3	12
2. I will spend <u>5</u> minutes daily in follow-up activities via e-mail, mail or phone.	3	12
Networking Friends & Acquaintances (33%)		
1. I will spend <u>10</u> minutes daily contacting friends & acquaintances via e-mail, mail or phone.	3	12
2. I will spend <u>5</u> minutes daily in follow-up activities via e-mail, mail or phone.	3	12
Networking Co-workers & Colleagues (33%)		
1. I will spend <u>10</u> minutes daily contacting co-workers and colleagues via e-mail, mail or phone.	3	12
2. I will spend <u>5</u> minutes daily in follow-up activities via e-mail, mail or phone.	3	12

Target Activity & Daily Goals	Weekly Goals	Monthly Goals
Networking Former Employers & Supervisors (33%)		
1. I will spend <u>10</u> minutes daily contacting former employers & supervisors via e-mail, mail or phone.	3	12
2. I will spend <u>5</u> minutes daily in follow-up activities via e-mail, mail or phone.	3	12
Networking Alumni (33%)		
1. I will spend <u>5</u> minutes daily contacting alumni via e-mail, mail or phone.	3	12
2. I will spend <u>5</u> minutes daily in follow-up activities via e-mail, mail or phone.	3	12
Networking Professional Associations (33%)		
1. I will spend <u>5</u> minutes daily contacting professional members via e-mail, mail or phone.	3	12
2. I will spend <u>5</u> minutes daily in follow-up activities via e-mail, mail or phone.	3	12
Networking Clubs (33%)		
1. I will spend <u>10</u> minutes daily contacting networking members via e-mail, mail or phone.	5	20
2. I will spend <u>10</u> minutes daily in follow-up activities via e-mail, mail or phone.	5	20
Networking Religious Affiliations (33%)		
1. I will spend <u>5</u> minutes daily contacting members of my religious group via e-mail, mail, or phone.	2	8
2. I will spend <u>5</u> minutes daily in follow-up activities via e-mail, mail or phone.	2	8
Direct Mail to Employers (Letter Résumé, Value-Proposition Letter & Industry Influential Introduction Letter) (47%)		
1. I will spend <u>20</u> minutes daily researching target companies in my targeted industries and geographic regions.	5	20
2. I will spend <u>20</u> minutes daily writing letters based on my research, to target companies in my targeted industries and geographic regions.	5	20
3. I will spend <u>20</u> minutes daily in follow-up activities via e-mail, mail or phone.	10	40

Target Activity & Daily Goals	Weekly Goals	Monthly Goals
Informational Interviewing (60%)		
1. I will spend <u>20</u> minutes daily researching influential leaders and executives in my targeted industries and geographic regions.	5	20
2. I will conduct informational interviews via e-mail, telephone or in-person.	2	8
3. I will spend <u>20</u> minutes daily in follow-up activities via e-mail, mail or phone.	2	8

Strategy #36 Participate in a Network Group

By participating in a network group, you expand your circle of influence. Many groups feature guest speakers who provide valuable information on industry trends, economic forecasts, strategies to work with recruiters, and other helpful job search information. You will also have an opportunity to meet local industry leaders. These people can help you expand your contacts for informational interviewing opportunities and job offers through networking.

Two on-line companies provide postings for networking opportunities in many major metropolitan areas across the United States. These are: **Execunet.com** and **Netshare.com**. Visit their Web sites for additional information. Both companies offer a wide range of services if you choose to become a subscriber. Some of the content is free.

Strategy #37 Join a Job Seeker's Group

Many job seekers enjoy the support and fellowship among others who are also looking for employment opportunities. You will discover that several opportunities will come to your attention that won't be a good match for you. But they could be ideal for someone you know in your job-seekers' group. Exchanging leads is a powerful way of expanding your contacts and reaching your goal: a new job!

Check your local newspaper or the weekly bulletin at your place of worship. Many communities and worship centers offer job seekers' groups for local community members in need.

If one isn't available in your area, you may find an on-line group you can participate in via the Internet. Use one of the major search engines such as Google or Yahoo! to locate one that meets your needs.

Chapter Review

Strategy #30 Develop Your Activity & Scope Action Plan (ASAP)

Strategy #31 Create Your Activity & Scope Targets and Goals

Strategy #32 Access Internet Search Engines & Career Portals

Strategy #33 Conduct Informational Interviews-They Are Your Most Powerful Search Tool

Strategy #34 Compose Your Thirty-Second Commercial

Strategy #35 Set SMART Goals for Your Job Search Activity
- Specific
- Measurable
- Activity-oriented
- Results-driven
- Time-limited

Strategy #36 Participate in a Network Group

Strategy #37 Join a Job Seekers' Group

Chapter Six:
Milestone One—Getting Job Interviews

Milestone One Tools

Strategy #38 Get Job Interviews with Persuasive Resumes

"Don't be impatient for the LORD to act! Travel steadily along his path." Psalm 37:34 (NLT)

Getting interviews is the first objective in any job search. In a competitive market, this becomes even more challenging. You must have an opportunity to talk with hiring managers before you will have a chance at winning job offers. Persuasive résumés will increase your odds of getting interviews for desirable positions.

A résumé has one primary purpose: to pique interest and arouse curiosity among hiring managers, compelling them to interview you. Rarely will a résumé get you a job!

> *A résumé has one primary purpose: To pique interest and arouse curiosity among hiring managers, compelling them to interview you. A résumé will rarely get you a job!*

More frequently, a résumé will be used to exclude someone from potential consideration. Seldom will it be used to include an individual in a candidate pool. Most résumés tell too much about the individual, giving the reviewer multiple reasons to disqualify them. The objective is to tell enough of your story to compel the reader to want to talk to you. Hopefully this will result in an interview.

Creating an effective résumé requires several critical ingredients:

(1) Job titles sought

(2) Industry or function

(3) Positioning paragraph

(4) Career history

(5) Key achievements & skills

(6) Education summary

(7) Professional development

(8) Awards, professional associations, community service

Titles

Tell the reader immediately what you are looking for by placing the job title or titles that you are seeking at the top of the résumé. If you are searching outside your industry, research common position titles to determine the correct ones to use. You may search on-line job boards for current postings, or you may visit several employer Web sites to see how they name their positions.

Industry/Function

Some position titles also span industries like: C-level positions (chief executive officer, chief financial officer, chief operating officer, chief information officer, chief technology officer, or chief marketing officer) and director or manager-level positions (business development, finance, human resources, marketing, operations, sales, or IT).

Sharpen your focus by combining a position and industry. Capitalize the titles when inserting them in your résumé. For example: Business Development Director—Manufacturing; Sales Manager—Consumer Products; Technology Director—Secondary Schools; or Controller—Automotive Parts & Supplies.

If you are targeting a function that spans multiple industries, insert this function following the title(s). Capitalize the function. Some functional targets include: Accounting, Business Development, Finance, Human Resources, Marketing and Sales. For example: Director—Accounting; Manager—Business Development; Vice President—Finance, Director—Human Resources, or Vice President—Sales and Marketing.

Positioning Paragraph

Communicate your experience and achievements in a clear, concise and compelling way. Tell the reader what you have done in previous positions. Identify what you can do for them. Poorly written positioning statements focus on what the applicant wants. Effective positioning statements address what the hiring manager can expect from you. Remember your audience!

Hiring managers prefer candidates who have spent all or the majority of their career in the function they are seeking to fill. Not many job seekers fit this ideal profile. Most people entering the workforce will make five to seven job changes and two or three career changes before retirement.

If you are like the majority, you have experience in more than one function. Lead with your functional skills that support your positioning. For example, Paul used this positioning statement:

Paul speaking:

"Sales executive with more than ten years experience in retail, radio and television broadcasting business development. Proven record of accomplishments in progressively responsible leadership roles driving 100% revenue growth, capturing market share, and forging strategic alliances with key client accounts such as Nike Golf, Calloway and Taylor-Made."

Paul's positioning statement shows that his earlier experience in finance and accounting has given him a deeper understanding of the sales and business development process. He understands the importance of bottom-line costs and return on investments.

Career History

Include key achievements in your résumé's career history section. List your skills beneath each position in reverse chronological order. Emphasize the past ten years of your work history. Most recruiters and hiring managers are primarily interested in this time frame. You can summarize earlier work experience by listing the company name, your titles, and the years worked in reverse chronological order. Put this under the heading: "Earlier Career History."

Key Achievements & Skills

You will use the information you entered in your Career History & Education Inventory to develop the "Career History and Key Achievements" section of your résumé. Include CAR stories that support your job title, function and industry targeting. Create a logical flow from the positioning paragraph statement. Summarize your skills for each position. For example: Skills: accounting, budgeting, finance, project management, financial reporting, forecasting and trend analysis.

Education Summary

Summarize your education directly beneath the "Career History and Key Achievements" section. Begin with your most recent degree, followed by the university's name and the year you graduated. For example: MBA, University of Chicago, 1998.

If you had a major or concentration relevant to the position you are seeking, include that following the degree. For example: BSBA, (accounting) University of Southern California, 1995. If age is a concern, leave off the graduation year.

Professional Development

Highlighting your professional development, continuing education and professional licenses/certificates is also beneficial when they are relevant to your positioning. Only include professional development activities within the past ten years. If you have completed a well-known executive level certificate program, be sure to include it. For example: Executive Development Program, the Wharton School, 1994.

Awards, Professional Associations and Community Service

Be sure to include any awards you may have received within the past then years. If you are seeking a sales position and you have been recognized as a top producer, this will add credibility to your résumé. Serving as a committee member or board member of a professional association is another valuable addition to include along with any community service activities you have been involved in such as: March of Dimes, United Way, Red Cross, Habitat for Humanity, etc. If you raised funds or served in some formal capacity, include this information.

Résumé Formatting

For best results with scanning technology, you should use eight and one-half-inch by eleven-inch white paper. Set one-inch margins all around, and use Courier, Times New Roman or Arial fonts. Do not use fonts smaller than 11 pts. Avoid using italics, underlining, highlighting, graphics or borders. Use black printing, either ink jet or laser.

If you use bullets:

- Use solid squares
- Keep bolding to a minimum

Sample résumés for a variety of applications are provided for your use as a guide in developing your own set of résumés. Each style is explained in detail.

Strategy #39 Use Different Résumé Styles for Optimum Success

Résumé Styles

Introductory Résumé

The Introductory Résumé is designed for your initial contact with a recruiter or hiring manager. This résumé style should be used whenever you mail a résumé, or personally deliver a résumé to a decision maker. Always include a personalized cover letter. Sample cover letters are provided later in this guide.

You may create numerous versions of your Introductory Résumé throughout your job search. Changing your title, function and industry positioning will lead to changes in your positioning paragraph. Write at least ten to twelve CAR stories covering all your functional skills. Choose CAR stories for each version that best support your positioning and your understanding of the position's essential job functions.

If the Introductory Résumé functions well and your targeting is accurate, you should get an interview. Timing is an important factor that always influences your search. It there are no openings, the best résumé in the world won't lead to an interview.

Paul speaking:

"My career coach went through my original résumé with me. He helped me understand potential career obstacles and weaknesses that could be strengthened. Then, he gave me a list of items to consider as I created my new Introductory Résumé."

Paul Williams' Original Resume

Paul Williams

365 Sky Ridge Lane
Colorado Springs, CO 80505

Telephone: (719) 555-1212   **E-Mail Address:** williams@email.com

Career Objective:

I want to find a fulltime position that will enable me to fully utilize my education, skills and experience as a sales and marketing leader in a growing company.

Work History:

KCMA Radio
4328 Broadcast Parkway, Colorado Springs, CO

From: March, 1st, 2001 **To:** June, 30th 2004
Title: *Sales Manager*
Duties Performed: I managed all the radio advertising salesmen for the company. I was also the key person that was responsible for hiring new staff. I did lots of training and I taught new people how to sell. I was also responsible to make sure that we met our sales targets each quarter as a team.

- *Managed the sales teams*
- *Found new business for the company*
- *Met all my target sales goals each quarter*

Channel 5 News
1618 Broadway, Denver, Colorado 80001

From: January 3rd, 1997 **To:** August 30th, 2000
Title: *Regional Sales Associate*
Duties Performed: Responsible for the Front Range territory. Selling television commercial spots to key accounts, providing customer service, following-up and supporting clients. Developed new accounts and grew existing client accounts. I was also the Salesman of the Year in 1999 and 2000.

- *Grew new sales by 25% each quarter each year*
- *Achieved sales quotas quarterly every time*
- *Developed new business in existing accounts*

Paul Williams   **Page Two**

Work History: (Continued)

All Sports Outlet
56872 Recreation Court, Tustin, CA 92982

From: June 1st, 1993 **To:** December 15th, 1996

From: April 1st, 1994 **To:** December 15th, 1996
Title: Golf Department Manager
Duties Performed: I managed the golf department, set up displays, demonstrated equipment for customers, did custom club fittings and stocked merchandise.

♦   *Managed company golf tournament*
♦   *Sold golf equipment and clothing*

From: June 1st 1993 **To:** March 30th, 1994
Title: Sales Associate
Duties Performed: I was 1 of the cashiers. I stocked items from the storeroom when inventory got low. I did some of the pricing and I helped customers find what they were looking for.

♦   *Kept inventory in my department current*
♦   *Made sure prices were consistent with sales promotions*

New City Bank & Trust
1428 Center Street, Omaha, Nebraska 68102

From: March 12th, 1989 **To:** May 15th, 1993

Title: *Vice President* (01/01/1992 to 05/15/1993)
Duties Performed: I managed 12 tellers for the retail and business accounts section of the bank. I trained new employees on banking procedures. I also did the auditing of the cash drawers and deposits and withdrawals transaction records.

♦   *Managed tellers*
♦   *Performed spot audits*
♦   *Trained new employees in bank procedures*

Paul Williams   Page Three

Work History: (Continued)

Title: *Head Teller* (02/01/1991 to 12/31/1991)
Duties Performed: I was the head teller, responsible for scheduling breaks, covering the customer service desks and drive up window and serving customers.

♦ *Scheduled teller breaks*
♦ *Provided customer service to banking customers*
♦ *Assisted wit drive up window transactions*

Title: *Teller* (03/12/1990 to 01/31/1991)
Duties Performed: I served banking customers at the walk up and drive through teller windows. I reconciled cash and check deposits and withdrawals, balanced accounts.

Education:

Bachelors in Business Administration from California State University at San Bernardino in 1988

Seminars:

Tom Peter's course in branding in 2002
Anthony Robbins course in selling in 2001
Dale Carnegie's Sales Training in 1998
Customer Service Excellence in 1992

Community Service:

I am a member of the First Baptist Church and I serve on the Elders board and I have taught Sunday school classes since 2001

I helped build 2 houses for Habitat for Humanity in 1991 and 1992 in Denver

I volunteered for the United Way annual fundraisings at New City Bank each year from 1990 to 1993

Paul Williams   Page Four

Professional Associations

Association of Christians in Broadcasting, 1997 to present

References:

Bill Thompson, Vice President Sales & Marketing, KCMA Radio (719) 555-1215
Walter Jones, Vice President Sales, Channel 5 News (303) 555-1219
Rev. Charles Truman, Pastor, Fist Baptist Church (719) 555-1519

Personal:

I am a U.S. Citizen. I was born on April 13th, 1966 and I have been married 10 years. We have three children, 8, 6, and 4 years old. I am a Republican and I enjoy reading, swimming and backpacking in my spare time.

Paul Williams' original résumé contains several red flags. The following summary identifies key things to think about changing.

1. The Career Objective is directed at what will benefit Paul. It should address potential benefits to the prospective employer.

2. Represent state names by their abbreviation or full name; choose one style.

3. Indicate dates in the same format, for example, January 1st, 2003 or 01/01/2003.

4. Identifying numerical values, best practice—spell out the number if it is between one and nine and use numerals for two digit numbers.

5. Edit for grammatical errors. Paul has misused apostrophes, switched tense several times, misspelled words (e.g., fulltime is full-time) and included run-on sentences.

6. Avoid using several different fonts, italics and underlining; it causes the document to look chaotic and it can interfere with scanning.

7. Paul is targeting a director of sales position but he puts a lot of emphasis on his finance and accounting experience. This can confuse the reader regarding his sales and business development experience—his positioning objective.

8. When stating leisure activities, by emphasizing high energy activities you can minimize stereotypes around age concerns. For example, if a hiring manager thinks you are over forty; concerns around your energy level

may arise. Listing things like: reading, theatre and gardening may support this stereotype. Listing activities like: hiking, cycling, skiing, and sailing help to minimize it.

9. When listing community activities, consider avoiding anything that could be perceived as controversial like religious and political affiliations. If your connections to these groups are such an integral part of who you are and what you do that you would be uncomfortable working in an environment that did not support them, then by all means put them in your résumé.

10. Degree titles should be represented accurately, for example, "Bachelor of Science in Business Administration."

11. Correct course titles should be used for continuing education experience.

12. Identify each previous employer's size (annual revenue or number of employees).

13. Indicate scope of responsibilities by stating dollar amounts of budgets managed or P&L responsibility and number of direct reports.

14. Don't put references in your résumé. Create a separate page of references with complete names, titles, and contact information. Supply this list when it is requested by a hiring manager or recruiter.

15. Leave personal information out of your résumé like birthdates, political affiliation, number of children or your marital status. Many of these are protected classes and employers who are careful to avoid discrimination don't want to know this information prior to making a hiring decision. Those who may discriminate can use this information inappropriately in their hiring decisions.

16. This résumé is four pages long. Reduce it to two pages for clarity and conciseness.

Paul Williams' Introductory Résumé, on the following page, illustrates all the ingredients of an effective résumé described in this chapter. Use it as a model for creating your own Introductory Résumé.

Paul Williams
365 Sky Ridge Lane, Colorado Springs, CO 80505

Telephone: (719) 555-1212   e-mail address: williams@email.com

Director—Sales/Business Development

Sales executive with more than ten years experience in retail, radio and television broadcasting business development. Proven record of accomplishments in progressively responsible leadership roles: driving 100% revenue growth, capturing market share, and forging strategic alliances with key client accounts such as Nike Golf, Calloway and Taylor-Made.

- **Grew annual revenue to $3M from $1M over two-year period**

- **Captured additional 40% of market share, adding $1M to annual revenue in first year**

- **Drove 25% sales increase in golf equipment, adding $20K to revenue stream**

CAREER HISTORY & KEY ACHIEVEMENTS

KCMA Radio ($4M revenue, 45 employees, radio broadcasting), 2001 to 2003
Sales Manager; $3M budget responsibility, 6 direct reports

Skills: budget accountability, sales team leadership, business development, customer service, strategic alliances, contract negotiations, training, territory development, trend analysis, competitive analysis, and channel marketing

- **Grew annual revenue to $3M from $1M over two-year period.** Gained majority market share in metro Denver market. Retained 98% of current clients and added twelve additional accounts and $2M revenue. Wrote ad copy, partnered with clients to design marketing strategies targeting key client demographics and market segments. Clients reported average 15% revenue growth annually resulting from radio ad campaigns.

- **Increased revenue by $1M in first year.** Won four key accounts in metro Denver market from leading competitor. Forged strategic alliances with customer stakeholders. Designed sales promotions with themes and supporting copy. Each customer's business grew by at least 20% over twelve-month period as a result of radio advertising campaigns.

Channel 5 News ($10M revenue, 250 employees, television broadcasting) 1997 to 2000.
Regional Sales Associate; $2M budget responsibility

Skills: budget accountability, business development, territory development, customer service, trend analysis, competitive analysis, contract negotiations and strategic partnerships

- **Captured additional 40% of market share, adding $1M to annual revenue in first year.** Conducted competitive market analysis and television advertising trend analysis for sporting events, sporting goods and recreation activities market segments in Rocky Mountain region. Added four major clients ($700K) and grew existing accounts by $300K.

Paul Williams   Page Two

All Sports Outlet ($5M revenue, 175 employees, consumer products, retail), 1993 to 1996
Golf Department Manager / Sales Associate

Skills: customer relations, inventory control, pricing, cashiering, and loss prevention

- **Drove 25% sales increase in golf equipment, adding $20K to revenue stream.** Created loss leader sales program, set up end caps and designed posters and banners for market blitz. Partnered with representatives from Nike Golf, Calloway, and Taylor-Made. Launched three give-away promotions and four sales events. Managed company-sponsored golf tournament.

- **Led $5K golf sales promotion.** Spearheaded golf department revitalization. Partnered with department manager to add new product line—Wilson Kids Clubs. Designed children's golf promotion and give away program. Success led to promotion to Golf Department Manager and promotion of previous manager to store's assistant manager position.

Early Career: New City Bank & Trust, 1989 to 1993, Vice President / Head Teller / Teller

EDUCATION & TRAINING

BSBA, California State University at San Bernardino, 1988

Brand Inside: Brand Outside, Tom Peters, 2002
Unleash the Power Within, Anthony Robbins, 2001
Sales Advantage, Dale Carnegie Training, 1998
Customer Service Excellence, American Management Association, 1992

PROFESSIONAL ASSOCIATIONS / AWARDS / COMMUNITY SERVICE

Association of Christians in Broadcasting, Individual Member, 1997 to present

Salesman of the Year, Channel 5 News, 2000, 1999
President's Award for Excellence in Customer Service, All Sports Outlet, 1996
Employee of the Year, New City Bank & Trust, 1992

United Way, volunteered for annual fundraisings, raised $10K annually, 1990 to 1993
Habitat for Humanity, helped build two houses for low income families, 1991 to 1992

Internet Résumé

The Internet Résumé is specifically designed for electronic distribution. It has several unique formatting characteristics compared to the Introductory Résumé, but the content is the same.

Instructions for reformatting the Introductory Résumé into an Internet Résumé:

1. Set your page margins to: Left Side: one-inch, Right Side: three and one-half-inches, and Top & Bottom: one-inch.

2. Select all text in the document.

3. Reformat font size to 11 points, and set all fonts to "Normal" (no bold, italics or underlining).

4. Remove any borders.

5. Delete any bullets and substitute with a dash or hyphen "—."

6. Save file under new name (Internet Résumé) and Save As a text (txt) file or rich text file (rtf) file.

7. Double check your document after saving the file to make sure the résumé looks proper without formatting.

How to use your Internet Résumé:

1. Open the file.

2. Select all the text.

3. Copy and paste it into your e-mail browser or into the frame on a Web site.

The three and one-half-inch, Right Side margin is important. It ensures that your message opens and reads like you intended, without random breaks in sentences and paragraphs.

When you e-mail your résumé to a decision maker, always cut and paste it into the body of the e-mail. Then attach your Introductory Résumé and cover letter as Word files. If they are unable or unwilling to open unsolicited attachments, they will still get your résumé in the body of the e-mail message.

Write a personalized cover letter, using the samples later in this guide. Format the cover letter the same way you format the Internet Résumé. Cut and paste the cover letter into your e-mail browser or Web site frame. On Web sites, the cover letter is usually an option with its own designated space. When e-mailing a cover letter, put it first in the message body, followed by your Internet Résumé.

Internet Résumé Sample

Paul Williams
365 Sky Ridge Lane, Colorado Springs, CO 80505
(719) 555-1212 /williams@email.com

Director—Sales/Business Development

Sales executive with more than ten years experience in retail, radio and television broadcasting business development. Proven record of accomplishments in progressively responsible leadership roles: driving 100% revenue growth, capturing market share, and forging strategic alliances with key client accounts such as Nike, Calloway and Taylor-Made.

*Grew annual revenue to $3M from $1M over two-year period
*Captured additional 40% of market share, adding $1M to annual revenue in first year
*Drove 25% sales increase in golf equipment, adding $20K to revenue stream

CAREER HISTORY & KEY ACHIEVEMENTS

KCMA Radio ($4M revenue, 45 employees, radio broadcasting), 2001 to 2003
Sales Manager; $3M budget responsibility, 6 direct reports

Skills: budget accountability, sales team leadership, business development, customer service, strategic alliances, contract negotiations, training, territory development, trend analysis, competitive analysis, and channel marketing

Grew annual revenue to $3M from $1M over two-year period. Gained majority market share in metro Denver market. Retained 98% of current clients and added twelve additional accounts and $2M revenue. Wrote ad copy, partnered with clients to design marketing strategies targeting key client demographics and market segments.

Clients reported average 15% revenue growth annually resulting from radio ad campaigns.

Increased revenue by $1M in first year. Won four key accounts in metro Denver market from leading competitor. Forged strategic alliances with customer stakeholders. Designed sales promotions with themes and supporting copy. Each customer's business grew by at least 20% over twelve-month period as a result of radio advertising campaigns.

Channel 5 News ($10M revenue, 250 employees, television broadcasting) 1997 to 2000.
Regional Sales Associate; $2M budget responsibility

Skills: budget accountability, business development, territory development, customer service, trend analysis, competitive analysis, contract negotiations and strategic partnerships

Captured additional 40% of market share, adding $1M to annual revenue in first year. Conducted competitive market analysis and television advertising trend analysis for sporting events, sporting goods and recreation activities market segments in Rocky Mountain region. Added four major clients ($700K) and grew existing accounts by $300K.

All Sports Outlet ($5M revenue, 175 employees, consumer products, retail), 1993 to 1996
Golf Department Manager / Sales Associate

Skills: customer relations, inventory control, pricing, cashiering, and loss prevention

Drove 25% sales increase in golf equipment, adding $20K to revenue stream. Created loss leader sales program, set up end caps and designed posters and banners for market blitz. Partnered with representatives from Nike Golf, Calloway, and Taylor-Made. Launched three give-away promotions and four sales events. Managed company-sponsored golf tournament.

Led $5K golf sales promotion. Spearheaded golf department revitalization. Partnered with department manager to add new product line—Wilson Kids Clubs. Designed children's golf promotion and give away program. Success led to promotion to Golf Department Manager and promotion of previous manager to store's assistant manager position.

Early Career: New City Bank & Trust, 1989 to 1993, Vice President / Head Teller / Teller

EDUCATION & TRAINING

BSBA, California State University at San Bernardino, 1988

Brand Inside: Brand Outside, Tom Peters, 2002
Unleash the Power Within, Anthony Robbins, 2001
Sales Advantage, Dale Carnegie Training, 1998
Customer Service Excellence, American Management Association, 1992

PROFESSIONAL ASSOCIATIONS /
AWARDS / COMMUNITY SERVICE

Association of Christians in Broadcasting,
Individual Member, 1997 to present

Salesman of the Year, Channel 5 News,
2000, 1999
President's Award for Excellence in
Customer Service, All Sports Outlet,
1996
Employee of the Year, New City Bank &
Trust, 1992

United Way, volunteered for annual
fundraisings, raised $10K annually, 1990
to 1993
Habitat for Humanity, helped build two
houses for low income families, 1991 to
1992

Letter Résumé

On occasion, you may choose to send a Letter Résumé in place of the Introductory Résumé and cover letter. The Letter Résumé may be more effective for reaching decision makers when there is not a current position opening. It is always used as a standalone document.

If you were to send an Introductory Résumé and cover letter, it would probably be re-routed to human resources or to the company's internal recruiter, without ever reaching the decision maker. A personal letter is more likely to reach its intended recipient than a traditional résumé.

Look for a current article, such as a press release or news item that mentions your targeted decision maker. Enclose a copy with your Letter Résumé. Highlight a few key points. Write a note in the margin identifying how you can help. Here are a few examples:

Congratulations on your new product approval! At (name company), I've successfully launched new products in new markets. Let's talk about how I could do the same for you!

I saw your press release announcing a second quarter of sales decline. I've successfully turned around under-performing sales and driven 100% revenue growth. Let's talk about how I can do the same for your sales!

I heard your keynote at the (name of organization's) annual conference last week where you announced your upcoming corporate move. I've led corporate relocations without losing any key staff or revenue. Let's talk!

I saw your promotion announcement in Tuesday's (business journal, newspaper, etc.) Congratulations! I imagine you'll be forming your team soon. At (company name) I drove record sales growth and captured market share. Let's talk about how I could do the same for you.

The Letter Résumé has several style differences compared with the Introductory Résumé. Don't include a positioning section with title, function or industry targets. Instead, write two strong opening paragraphs, followed by supporting CAR bullets. Then close with a call to action and your commitment to follow-up.

Begin your opening paragraph with an attention-getting statement. Persuasively express your business savvy, and/or industry knowledge about a current challenge. Communicate how your talents, skills, abilities and accomplishments have addressed this challenge in other businesses. Your CAR stories will give your claims additional support.

In closing, ask the decision maker to contact you. Let them know you will be calling them if you don't hear from them sooner.

Letter Résumé Style Sample

Paul Williams
365 Sky Ridge Lane, Colorado Springs, CO 80505

Telephone: (719) 555-1212   e-mail address: williams@email.com

Date

Decision Maker
Company Name
Address
City, State ZIP Code

Dear Decision Maker:

Key challenges for most companies include creating and maintaining customer loyalty, capturing market share in a competitive, demanding economic climate, and growing revenue streams in existing client accounts. I am a sales executive with more than ten years experience in retail, radio and television broadcasting business development.

I have a proven record of accomplishments in progressively responsible leadership roles driving 100% revenue growth, capturing market share, and forging strategic alliances with key accounts such as Nike Golf, Calloway and Taylor-Made. Some of my key achievements include:

- **Grew annual revenue to $3M from $1M over two-year period.** Gained majority market share in metro Denver market. Retained 98% of current clients and added twelve additional accounts and $2M revenue. Wrote ad copy, partnered with clients to design marketing strategies targeting key client demographics and market segments. Clients reported average 125% revenue growth annually resulting from radio ad campaigns.

- **Captured additional 40% of market share, adding $1M to annual revenue in first year.** Conducted competitive market analysis and television advertising trend analysis for sporting events, sporting goods and recreation activities market segments in Rocky Mountain region. Added four major clients ($700K) and grew existing accounts by $300K.

- **Drove 25% sales increase in golf equipment, adding $20K to revenue stream.** Created loss leader sales program, set up end caps and designed posters and banners for market blitz. Partnered with representatives from Nike Golf, Calloway, and Taylor-Made. Launched three give-away promotions and four sales events. Managed company-sponsored golf tournament.

I am confident that I can help (*company name*) grow in their new (*city name*) metro market by capturing market share (*or, expand their market penetration*) through new business development, customer loyalty and superior customer service strategies. If I don't hear from you, I will call you next week to follow-up.

Sincerely,
Paul Williams

Value—Proposition Letter

Many clients have successfully negotiated with prospective employers to create a new position that was not advertised. These jobs are uniquely tailored to match individual skills, talents and abilities to the company's current needs. This method of obtaining employment is initiated with the Value—Proposition Letter.

Prior to submitting a Value—Proposition Letter, several steps should be completed. First, you need to identify companies located within your industry, company size and geographic targets. Second, identify key decision-makers within each company.

Third, schedule Informational Interviews with key decision-makers. If you are unsuccessful at getting Informational Interviews on your own, work through your network to obtain an introduction and appointment.

Fourth, prior to your Informational Interview, carefully research the company. Review the company Web site. Search for press releases on the Internet or at your local library. Talk to people in your network familiar with this industry segment. Learn the company's reputation "on the street."

Finally, compose your Value—Proposition Letter. Carefully match your talents, skills and abilities with the company's needs. Successful job seekers produce between thirty and forty of these letters during the course of a search.

Constructing the Value—Proposition Letter

Grab the reader's attention by identifying a need and proposing a solution in the opening paragraph. If you found a recent news article about the company, its products or services, or its key executives, reference this in a complementary style.

Your positioning paragraph is second. It will be similar to what you have composed for your Introductory Résumé or your Letter Résumé. Lead with a statement like Paul used.

> I am a sales executive with more than ten years experience in retail, radio and television broadcasting business development. I have a proven record of accomplishments in progressively responsible leadership roles driving 100% revenue growth, capturing market share, and forging strategic alliances with key client accounts such as Nike Golf, Calloway and Taylor-Made.

Include a minimum of three, and a maximum of five CAR stories in the next section. Each one should support your claims in the first paragraph. Choose CAR stories that closely align with the company's needs identified in your opening paragraph.

Write a concise summary of what you can do for the company. Follow this with a call to action in the closing paragraph. Tell the reader that you will be contacting them in the next few days to arrange a meeting if you don't hear from him or her beforehand.

Value—Proposition Letter Sample

Paul Williams

365 Sky Ridge Lane, Colorado Springs, CO 80505

Telephone: (719) 555-1212   e-mail address: williams@email.com

Date

Mr. James Walton
Vice President, Sales & Marketing
KPRZ Christian Radio
4325 Main Street
Tustin, CA 92804

Dear Mr. Walton:

Congratulations! I saw your press release in the *Denver Business Journal* last week announcing your expansion plans into the metro Denver market.

I am a sales executive with more than ten years experience in retail, radio and television broadcasting business development. I have a proven record of accomplishments in progressively responsible leadership roles driving 100% revenue growth, capturing market share, and forging strategic alliances with key client accounts such as Nike Golf, Calloway and Taylor-Made.

- **Increased revenue by $1M in first year.** Won four key accounts in metro Denver market from leading competitor. Forged strategic alliances with customer stakeholders. Designed sales promotions with themes and supporting copy. Each customer's business grew by at least 20% over twelve-month period as a result of radios advertising campaigns.

- **Grew annual revenue to $3M from $1M over two-year period.** Gained majority market share in metro Denver market. Retained 98% of current clients and added twelve additional accounts and $2M revenue. Wrote ad copy, partnered with clients to design marketing strategies targeting key client demographics and market segments. Clients reported average 125% revenue growth annually resulting from radio ad campaigns.

- **Captured additional 40% of market share, adding $1M to annual revenue in first year.** Conducted competitive market analysis and television advertising trend analysis for sporting events, sporting goods and recreation activities market segments in Rocky Mountain region. Added four major clients ($700K) and grew existing accounts by $300K.

I am confident that I can help KPRZ Radio grow in their new Denver metro market by capturing market share, especially from Christian businesses, through new business development, customer loyalty and superior customer service strategies. If I don't hear from you, I will call you next week to follow-up.

Sincerely,
Paul Williams

Chapter Review

Milestone One Tools-Getting Job Interviews

Strategy #38 Get Job Interviews with Persuasive Resumes

Strategy #39 Use Different Résumé Styles for Optimum Success
- Introductory Résumé
- Internet Résumé
- Letter Résumé
- Value-Proposition Letter

Chapter Seven:
Writing Compelling Job Search Letters

Throughout your job search you will be sending correspondence. Many hiring managers and recruiters give as much weight to your letters as they do to your résumé in their decision making. Write clearly, concisely and convincingly. Follow accepted style, grammar and formatting principles.

Take the time to gather some resources if you are not confident in your writing abilities. You can find style guides on-line at various university Web sites. A dictionary and thesaurus are also two more important references.

Strategy #40 Write Compelling, Persuasive Job-Search Letters

Twelve Letter Writing Essentials

1. *Limit the body to five paragraphs, two-thirds of a page maximum.*

2. *Paragraphs should be a minimum of two and a maximum of five sentences long.*

3. *Shorter sentences are more effective than longer ones.*

4. *Write in the active voice and in the first person.*

5. *Make "I" statements, avoid "we," "they," "our," etc.*

6. *Use action-oriented and results-oriented words.*

7. *Never exceed one page.*

8. *Use 8½ X 11 inch white paper and set margins at one inch all around.*

9. *Mail-merge programs help personalize letters to each company and decision maker.*

10. *Open with a strong statement or question that compels the reader to continue reading.*

11. *Clearly state in the body how the reader will benefit by taking action.*

12. *Close by calling the decision-maker to action with a time frame.*

Cover Letter—Direct Mail

Opinions among experts seem to vary about fifty-fifty on whether or not to use a cover letter with your résumé. Those against them say they don't get read by the decision maker. They believe that often cover letters are tossed out by human resources staff. Some decision makers expect to find everything they need to know in the résumé and view a cover letter as redundant.

Those in favor say you must avoid generic cover letters at all costs! If you are going to take the time to include one, make it personal. Tailor it to the company and address it to the proper contact person. Spell names and titles correctly. If you can't write a personal cover letter, don't send one!

Direct Mail Cover Letter Sample

Paul Williams
365 Sky Ridge Lane, Colorado Springs, CO 80505

Telephone: (719) 555-1212   e-mail address: williams@email.com

Date

Decision Maker, Title
Company Name
Address
City, State ZIP

Dear Name of Decision Maker:

In today's economy, it has become increasingly important to identify top talent to remain competitive in this volatile business climate. While researching target companies in your area, I identified *(company's name)* as one that might be seeking talented people you could bring on board. If so, my letter may interest you.

I am a sales executive with more than ten years experience in retail, radio and television broadcasting business development. I have a proven record of accomplishments in progressively responsible leadership roles driving 100% revenue growth, capturing market share, and forging strategic alliances with key client accounts such as Nike Golf, Calloway and Taylor-Made.

I would be interested in talking with you to discuss how I could contribute to *(company's name)* growth and profitability. I will call you in a few days to schedule a convenient time to meet if I don't hear from you sooner. I look forward to visiting with you.

Sincerely,
Paul Williams
Enclosure

Cover Letter—Classified Advertisement

When you are responding to a classified advertisement, always consider a cover letter. Many will ask for one. Your opening should state what position you are writing about and where you saw it advertised.

The body should include your positioning paragraph. You can include two or three bulleted CAR stories following your positioning paragraph. This is a great strategy when you have several skills directly related to the position. Highlight two or three in your cover letter. Underline an additional two or three in your Introductory Résumé.

Classified Advertisement Cover Letter Sample

Paul Williams
365 Sky Ridge Lane, Colorado Springs, CO 80505

Telephone: (719) 555-1212   e-mail address: williams@email.com

Date

Decision Maker, Title
Company Name
Address
City, State ZIP

Dear Name of Decision Maker:

Please accept this letter as my application for the *(position title)* position currently available with *(company's name)* as listed in the *(newspaper/journal)* or posted on *(job board)*.

I am a sales executive with more than ten years experience in retail, radio and television broadcasting business development. I have a proven record of accomplishments in progressively responsible leadership roles driving 100% revenue growth, capturing market share, and forging strategic alliances with key client accounts such as Nike Golf, Calloway and Taylor-Made.

<u>*Suggested Phrase for Salary Requests*</u>: *I will submit a salary history and other personal information when you indicate a serious interest in my qualifications. Or respond with a range that includes an entire compensation package, i.e. benefits, retirement, etc. Over the past couple of years, my total package has been in the high five-figure range.*

I look forward to hearing from you! I would like to schedule a meeting to learn more about this position and *(company's name)* plans and goals. I'm confident I could contribute to the continued success of your organization.

Sincerely,
Paul Williams
Enclosure

Cover Letter—Recruiting Firm

Let recruiters know that you have done your homework. Make it apparent that you have sought them out because of their expertise within specific industry segments. Keep it short, direct and specific for best results.

Recruiting Firm Cover Letter Sample

Paul Williams

365 Sky Ridge Lane, Colorado Springs, CO 80505

Telephone: (719) 555-1212   e-mail address: williams@email.com

Date

Decision Maker, Title
Company Name
Address
City, State ZIP

Dear Name of Decision Maker:

I have learned that your firm has an excellent reputation for placing executives with top organizations in the (*industry name*). After reviewing my experience and skills, I am confident you will agree that I would be a strong candidate for a Director/Manager—Sales/Business Development position for one of your clients. I have included a résumé for your review. The following briefly highlights my record of accomplishments.

I am a sales executive with more than ten years experience in retail, radio and television broadcasting business development. I have a proven record of accomplishments in progressively responsible leadership roles driving 100% revenue growth, capturing market share, and forging strategic alliances with key client accounts such as Nike Golf, Calloway and Taylor-Made.

My demonstrated ability to achieve improved profitability and performance by implementing cost controls, streamlining operations and enhancing process flow would likely be valued by a leading *(industry)* organization desiring a competitive advantage. I look forward to hearing from you.

Sincerely,
Paul Williams
Enclosure

Networking Letter—Industry Influential

Surveys among successful job seekers indicate that between thirty-three percent and sixty-nine percent found their next position through networking and informational interviews. They contacted influential industry leaders by phone, mail or e-mail. Then they conducted informational interviews that led to additional contacts and custom-tailored offers.

Industry Influential Networking Letter Sample #1

Paul Williams
365 Sky Ridge Lane, Colorado Springs, CO 80505

Telephone: (719) 555-1212   e-mail address: williams@email.com

Date

Decision Maker, Title
Company Name
Address
City, State ZIP

Dear Name of Decision Maker:

I received your name from *(name of referring party)* last week. I spoke to *(him/her)* regarding career opportunities within the *(industry)* and *(he/she)* suggested I contact you. While I am looking for a new position, I am not seeking employment from you. I am hoping to schedule a brief meeting or phone call to exchange information and ideas.

I am a sales executive with more than ten years experience in retail, radio and television broadcasting business development. I have a proven record of accomplishments in progressively responsible leadership roles driving 100% revenue growth, capturing market share, and forging strategic alliances with key client accounts such as Nike Golf, Calloway and Taylor-Made.

As I seek a new career direction, I want to contact a few professionals in target industries to get their advice. Perhaps you might be willing to meet or talk with me over the phone for ten to fifteen minutes. I am confident that our shared backgrounds will lead to a mutually interesting and informative conversation.

Changes are occurring daily in American business. Getting to know professionals like you will help me obtain current information about your industry and how to focus my career strategy. The opportunity to exchange ideas with you and develop contacts with other professionals would be extremely helpful to me. I will be calling you in the next few days to introduce myself and schedule a brief meeting or phone call. Thank you in advance for any advice you might be able to provide me.

Sincerely,
Paul Williams

Industry Influential Networking Letter Sample #2

Paul Williams

365 Sky Ridge Lane, Colorado Springs, CO 80505

Telephone: (719) 555-1212   e-mail address: williams@email.com

Date

Decision Maker, Title
Company Name
Address
City, State ZIP

Dear Name of Decision Maker:

Because you are a leader in the (*industry name*) industry, I am writing to seek your opinion and insights. I would like to meet with you, (or talk with you on the phone) briefly at your convenience to learn more about the (*industry name*) industry and share my experiences with you.

I am a sales executive with more than ten years experience in retail, radio and television broadcasting business development. I have a proven record of accomplishments in progressively responsible leadership roles driving 100% revenue growth, capturing market share, and forging strategic alliances with key client accounts such as Nike Golf, Calloway and Taylor-Made.

I am currently transitioning between careers. In my pursuit of a new future direction, I am contacting a few professionals. I would like to obtain your insights and update myself on current business activities in a variety of industries. When we meet, I am confident our shared backgrounds will provide a mutually beneficial connection.

I will call you in a few days to introduce myself and to set up a brief meeting or phone call. Thank you in advance for your valuable time and advice.

Sincerely,
Paul Williams

Industry Influential Introduction Letter Sample (Fictitious—not actual correspondence)

Trinity Broadcasting Network

James Cole
Vice President, Sales & Marketing

2442 Michelle Drive ♦ Tustin ♦ CA 92780 ♦ (714) 555-1414

Date

Decision Maker, Title
Company Name
Address
City, State ZIP

Dear Name of Decision Maker:

I am pleased to introduce Mr. Paul Williams. He is a sales executive with more than ten years experience in retail, radio and television broadcasting business development.

Mr. Williams has a proven record of accomplishments in progressively responsible leadership roles driving 100% revenue growth, capturing market share, and forging strategic alliances with key client accounts such as Nike Golf, Calloway and Taylor-Made.

He would be interested in talking with you to discuss how he could contribute to your organization's growth and profitability. Mr. Williams will call you in a few days to schedule a convenient time to meet, if he doesn't hear from you sooner. Please don't hesitate to contact me directly if you have any questions I may be able to answer.

Sincerely,
James Cole

Networking Letter—Colleagues, Friends, Acquaintances

Don't be nervous about contacting colleagues, friends and acquaintances. You are not asking them for a job! You want to find out who they know who you should be talking to during your job search. If you are clear in what you are asking for, it will be easy for them to be helpful.

Tell them why you are writing in the first paragraph. In the body of your letter explain how they can be of assistance. In closing, thank them in advance. Let them know you will be making contact if you don't hear from them beforehand.

Colleagues, Friends, Acquaintances Networking Letter Sample

Paul Williams
365 Sky Ridge Lane, Colorado Springs, CO 80505

Telephone: (719) 555-1212   e-mail address: williams@email.com

Date

Name
Address
City, State ZIP

Dear Name of Friend or Acquaintance:

I know you don't often receive letters from me. I wanted to let you know that I am changing careers. As part of this process, I am asking for your advice and suggestions. Part of my strategy includes contacting a few friends to seek their thoughts and ideas about what steps I should take, or which companies I could contact.

I am hoping you might take a moment to review my résumé. As you can see, I would like to find a position as a Director/Manager—Sales/Business Development. I would be open to exploring other opportunities too. I am confident my strengths are applicable in a variety of industries. Your suggestions and ideas of organizations to contact would be very encouraging. I am open to any suggestions you may have for me.

I am also interested in expanding my circle of acquaintances. You may be able to provide me with a few people to contact. Anyone who might be able to assist me, or refer me to others, would be greatly appreciated. The more contacts I make, the more opportunities I can uncover.

I will contact you in a week or so to discuss your ideas if I don't hear from you beforehand. Thank you in advance for your help.

Sincerely,
Paul Williams
Enclosure

Reference Contact Letter

Hiring managers and recruiters usually request three references:

1.   Your current employer/immediate supervisor

2.   Previous employer/immediate supervisor

3.   Personal reference (customer/vendor/colleague/co-worker/friend/professor)

Make a list of your references on a separate sheet of paper. Include their:

- Full name

- Title

- Company name

- Address

- Telephone

- e-mail address

Contact each person. Verify their willingness to serve as your reference. Let them know you will be sending them a letter and a current résumé.

Sometimes it is helpful to match references with the positions you are seeking, or with questions a hiring manager may have regarding your experience. For example, if an interviewer wants to know about your specific experience in business development, key account management or new product launches, you can use a reference with specific knowledge of your skills in these areas.

Whenever you give a person's name out for a reference, contact them right away. Let them know the details. For example, tell them who you interviewed with, the company's name, and the title of the position you are seeking. If you need them to emphasize anything particular in your background, describe it. Ask them to contact you when they are contacted. Thank them again for their support of your job search.

Sometimes recruiters and hiring managers will ask your references for additional references. You might want to send a copy of your reference list to each person on it. Then they can recommend one another if this question ever arises. Be sure to get permission to do this from each reference beforehand. Ask your references to tell you whenever they give out a name that is not on your list. Then you can make contact with that person as well.

Reference Contact Letter Sample

Paul Williams
365 Sky Ridge Lane, Colorado Springs, CO 80505

Telephone: (719) 555-1212   e-mail address: williams@email.com

Date

Name
Title
Company Name
Address
City, State ZIP

Dear (name of reference):

Thank you for your willingness to serve as a reference during my job search.

As my search gains momentum, you will undoubtedly receive calls from potential employers who are interested in evaluating me for a current opening. I thought it would be helpful if you had my current résumé. You are probably familiar with most of my background, but hopefully it will assist you in answering any questions.

As we discussed over the phone, I am also enclosing my reference list. Sometimes potential employers may ask references for additional names. You may wish to consider one or more of my references if you are asked to refer prospective employers to someone else.

Thank you very much for your support. I will let you know whenever I give your name and contact information to a recruiter or prospective employer. I would appreciate it if you would contact me when you receive inquiries. I will keep you updated on my progress.

Sincerely,
Paul Williams
Enclosure

Alumni Executive Letter

Alumni Executive Letter Sample

Paul Williams
365 Sky Ridge Lane, Colorado Springs, CO 80505

Telephone: (719) 555-1212   e-mail address: williams@email.com

Date

Decision Maker, Title
Company Name
Address
City, State ZIP

Dear (Name of Alumnus):

As fellow alumni of Southern University, we share some life perspectives that have benefited us over the years. I am hoping you might be willing to meet with me or have a brief phone conversation to share information, opinions and suggestions. I'm confident I could benefit from your advice and insights.

My experience spans more than ten years in retail, radio and television broadcasting business development. I have a proven record of accomplishments in progressively responsible leadership roles driving 100% revenue growth, capturing market share, and forging strategic alliances with key client accounts such as Nike Golf, Calloway and Taylor-Made.

The purpose of our meeting will be to exchange information and discuss your perspectives on your industry. I am transitioning between careers. Connecting with professionals like you is a crucial and enjoyable part of my search.

I will call you in a few days to introduce myself and determine a time when we might meet or speak over the phone. Thank you in advance for advice and valuable time.

Sincerely,
Paul Williams

Follow-up Letters

Follow-up Letter Sample #1

Paul Williams
365 Sky Ridge Lane, Colorado Springs, CO 80505

Telephone: (719) 555-1212   e-mail address: williams@email.com

Date

Decision Maker, Title
Company Name
Address
City, State ZIP

Dear Name of Decision Maker:

I can imagine how busy you are running *(company's name)*. Your company's products and services are of particular interest to me. I believe a meeting would be mutually profitable so I am taking the risk of contacting you again.

As I indicated previously, I am a sales executive with more than ten years experience in retail, radio and television broadcasting business development. I have a proven record of accomplishments in progressively responsible leadership roles driving 100% revenue growth, capturing market share, and forging strategic alliances with key client accounts such as Nike Golf, Calloway and Taylor-Made.

I am hoping we will have an opportunity to meet. Regardless of our difficulty in connecting, my initial interest in your company is still strong. I am firmly convinced my skills and experience would make me an asset to your firm. I think you will agree my qualifications and accomplishments are worth discussing.

Let's meet for a few minutes to discuss how I might best contribute to *(company name's)* continued success and profitability. I will call you within the next several days to discuss your requirements if I don't hear from you beforehand.

Sincerely,
Paul Williams

Paul Williams

365 Sky Ridge Lane, Colorado Springs, CO 80505

Telephone: (719) 555-1212   e-mail address: williams@email.com

Date

Decision Maker, Title
Company Name
Address
City, State ZIP

Dear Name of Decision Maker:

Because I am convinced we share common goals and interests, I am contacting you a third time. I am sincerely interested in assisting you in growing your business to the next level of success. I suspect you are approached frequently by others with similar claims. In my case, however, my record of achievement speaks to my ability to excel in driving revenue growth and leading sales teams. Some of my key achievements include:

- **Grew annual revenue to $3M from $1M over two-year period.** Gained majority market share in metro Denver market. Retained 98% of current clients and added twelve additional accounts and $2M revenue. Wrote ad copy, partnered with clients to design marketing strategies targeting key client demographics and market segments. Clients reported average 125% revenue growth annually resulting from radio ad campaigns.

- **Captured additional 40% of market share, adding $1M to annual revenue in first year.** Conducted competitive market analysis and television advertising trend analysis for sporting events, sporting goods and recreation activities market segments in Rocky Mountain region. Added four major clients ($700K) and grew existing accounts by $300K.

- **Drove 25% sales increase in golf equipment, adding $20K to revenue stream.** Created loss leader sales program, set up end caps and designed posters and banners for market blitz. Partnered with representatives from Nike Golf, Calloway, and Taylor-Made. Launched three give-away promotions and four sales events. Managed company-sponsored golf tournament.

While I can appreciate how difficult it is to cope with urgent demands on your time, I urge you to consider briefly meeting with me to discuss how my abilities could be of value to your company. Please call me at your convenience. I will also attempt to reach you by phone. I look forward to speaking with you.

Sincerely,
Paul Williams

Follow-up Letter Sample #3

Paul Williams
365 Sky Ridge Lane, Colorado Springs, CO 80505

Telephone: (719) 555-1212   e-mail address: williams@email.com

Date

Decision Maker, Title
Company Name
Address
City, State ZIP

Dear Name of Decision Maker:

I wrote you a letter recently seeking an opportunity to briefly meet with you. I have tried to reach you several times by phone and have come to the conclusion that you are a very busy person!

I am contacting you again because I want to learn more about opportunities within the (*industry name*). Although you may or may not be seeking key people to help your organization grow, I hope to learn more about your company's new (*expansion/product/services*).

I have been unable to reach you directly so I will enclose a résumé for your brief review. If you have any advice or ideas please let me know. Feel free to forward my résumé on to anyone you know who may have a need for someone with my skills.

Thank you very much for your time and consideration. Please feel free to contact me if you have advice or insights for me.

Sincerely,
Paul Williams
Enclosure

Follow-up Letter Sample #4

Paul Williams
365 Sky Ridge Lane, Colorado Springs, CO 80505

Telephone: (719) 555-1212   e-mail address: williams@email.com

Date

Decision Maker, Title
Company Name
Address
City, State ZIP

Dear Name of Decision Maker:

Thank you very much for speaking with me on the phone yesterday (*meeting with me in person*). Enclosed as you requested is a copy of my résumé. I am grateful for your willingness to review my background and experience and give me any feedback you may have—practical input is always welcome!

Thank you for keeping my job search in mind. If you think of any organizations or key individuals I should contact, please let me know.

Thanks again for your time and personal interest. I will keep you updated on my job search progress.

Sincerely,
Paul Williams
Enclosure

Thank You Letters

Many hiring managers and recruiters have given the same reason for not moving forward with a candidate. They didn't receive a thank-you note or letter following an interview. This oversight was believed to be an example of the job seeker's degree of conscientiousness and manners, and a reflection of his or her potential behavioral style with important customers!

Thank You Letter—Interview

Paul Williams
365 Sky Ridge Lane, Colorado Springs, CO 80505

Telephone: (719) 555-1212   e-mail address: williams@email.com

Date

Decision Maker, Title
Company Name
Address
City, State ZIP

Dear Name of Decision Maker:

I am excited about the possibility of joining your team! Thank you very much for meeting with me (*yesterday, last Tuesday, etc.*). I enjoyed getting to know you and learning more about (*company name's*) mission and goals. The (*position title/job opening*) position you are trying to fill sounds exciting and rewarding.

While I was returning home, I gave more thought to our discussion about (*list specific job functions you talked about*) and my fit for your needs and future growth. I wanted to take a moment to tell you about some of my key accomplishments in these areas.

- **Captured additional 40% of market share, adding $1M to annual revenue in first year.** Conducted competitive market analysis and television advertising trend analysis for sporting events, sporting goods and recreation activities market segments in Rocky Mountain region. Added four major clients ($700K) and grew existing accounts by $300K.

- **Drove 25% sales increase in golf equipment, adding $20K to revenue stream.** Created loss leader sales program, set up end caps and designed posters and banners for market blitz. Partnered with representatives from Nike Golf, Calloway, and Taylor-Made. Launched three give-away promotions and four sales events. Managed company-sponsored golf tournament.

I look forward to your call next week (*or whenever they said they would contact you*). I would be honored to work at (*company name*). It would be a pleasure to serve under your leadership. My unique background qualifies me in many ways to make significant contributions to (*company name's*) bottom line and future growth.

Sincerely,
Paul Williams

Paul Williams
365 Sky Ridge Lane, Colorado Springs, CO 80505

Telephone: (719) 555-1212   e-mail address: williams@email.com

Date

Decision Maker, Title
Company Name
Address
City, State ZIP

Dear Name of Decision Maker:

Thank you very much for referring me to (*contact name*). I had an opportunity to meet with (him/her) last (*day of week*) and learn more about (*company name*) and the (*industry name*) industry in the (*city name*) metro area.

Our conversation was very productive. I was able to share some valuable information with (*him/her*) and (*he/she*) gave me several great suggestions. I am grateful for the opportunity you have provided me to expand my network of colleagues in the (*city name*) metro area. Please let me know how I can return the favor any time you think I could be of help to you.

Sincerely,
Paul Williams

Thank You Letter—Informational Interview

Paul Williams

365 Sky Ridge Lane, Colorado Springs, CO 80505

Telephone: (719) 555-1212   e-mail address: williams@email.com

Date

Decision Maker, Title
Company Name
Address
City, State ZIP

Dear Name of Decision Maker:

Thank you very much for meeting with me last (*day of week*). I know your time is valuable and your schedule is quite full. I am grateful for your opinions and advice. As a result of our time together, I think I am much better equipped to focus my job search in the (*city name*) metro area in the (*industry name*) industry. Thank you, too, for the list of introductions you provided me. I will be calling them this week.

I feel privileged to add you to my new network of colleagues. Please let me know how I can return the favor any time you think I could be of help to you.

Sincerely,
Paul Williams

Thank You Letter—Reference

Paul Williams
365 Sky Ridge Lane, Colorado Springs, CO 80505

Telephone: (719) 555-1212   e-mail address: williams@email.com

Date

Decision Maker, Title
Company Name
Address
City, State ZIP

Dear Name of Decision Maker:

Thank you very much for serving as a reference for me during my job search. I am grateful for the time you invested reviewing my credentials and speaking to various hiring managers when they called you. Your support has benefited me immeasurably.

I accepted an offer last (*day of week*) from (*company name*) for the position of (**position title**). I will be starting on (**start date**). I will e-mail you my contact information when I begin my new job!

Sincerely,
Paul Williams

Strategy #41 Obtain Essential Job-Search Equipment

You may need to make an equipment investment if you don't already have these tools. You will need a:

- Telephone with voicemail

- Fax machine

- Complete computer system (CPU, monitor, keyboard, mouse, printer, modem and Internet access)

- Dedicated e-mail account

Strategy # 42 Dedicate an e-mail Account & Phone to Your Job Search

Dedicate an e-mail account and a phone line with voicemail to your job search. Use this e-mail address and phone number on all your résumés, correspondence and e-mail messages. You will have several versions of your résumé in circulation, along with numerous letters and messages.

> *Dedicate an e-mail account and phone with voicemail to your job search.*

When choosing your e-mail address, avoid "cute" sounding names like: soccerdaddy@email.com, weluvducks@email.com, me4u4$@email.com, or anything else humorous. Attempt to keep it simple. Use your first initial and last name, or your first and middle initial and last name. Additionally, try to avoid using a lowercase "l" because it can be misread for a number "1." Often an e-mail program will suggest alternate accounts like Paul111 or Paul123, try to avoid these too.

Avoid using free e-mail accounts (Yahoo, Lycos, Hotmail, etc.) for your job search. Even if you've purchased additional storage on one of these accounts, many servers have spam-blocking software that excludes e-mail from these providers. Most clients find that high speed Internet access is best, if available in their area.

> *Your voicemail greeting should be business-like and professional.*

Some clients have been successful using their cellphones with voicemail. If cellular service is good in your area and you have caller ID, this may work for you. Others have leased pagers with voicemail and used this dedicated number.

Your voicemail greeting should be business-like and professional. If you are using a home line, be sure you check your greeting. If in doubt, stay conservative with something like: "You have reached the Williams residence at (303) 555-1212. Your call is important to us. Please leave your name, telephone number including Area Code, and the nature of your call at the tone. We will call you back promptly. Thank you."

If it is not possible to use a dedicated phone, use your home phone with voicemail or an answering machine. Whenever possible, resist the temptation to answer the phone during your job search. Let all calls go to voice mail. After you have listened to the message, you can take the time you need to refer to your notes before calling them back. This gives you control over the calls and it allows you to mentally prepare for each conversation.

Return all calls promptly. When you must answer the phone and a caller attempts to interview you on the spot, be prepared to re-schedule the interview. Ask if it is possible to reschedule a call later in the day. Inform them that you are on your way out to an appointment. Or, tell them that you have another previously scheduled call in the next few minutes and you need to keep your line open. This strategy will give you time to focus your attention, gather your thoughts and notes, and fully prepare for the upcoming interview.

Paul speaking:

"I was only two weeks into my job search. While I was taking a nap one afternoon, I answered the phone. It was a recruiter who had noticed my résumé on a job board. He conducted an interview with me for about thirty minutes. At the end of the interview he said, 'Well Paul, you are highly skilled and you certainly have the right experience, but your energy level just isn't high enough for my client's needs.'"

Chapter Review

Strategy #40 Write Compelling, Persuasive Job-Search Letters

- Twelve Letter Writing Essentials
- Cover Letter-Direct Mail
- Cover Letter-Classified Advertisement
- Cover Letter-Recruiting Firm
- Networking Letter-Industry Influential
- Networking Letter-Colleagues, Friends & Acquaintances
- Reference Contact Letter
- Alumni Executive Letter
- Follow-up Letters
- Thank You Letters

Strategy #41 Obtain Essential Job-Search Equipment

- Telephone with voicemail
- Fax machine
- Complete computer system
- Internet access
- Dedicated e-mail account

Strategy #42 Dedicate an e-mail Account & Phone to Your Job Search

Chapter Eight:
Milestone Two—Winning Job Offers

Milestone Two Tools

After you get interviews, the next step in your journey is to win job offers. Your résumés, letters, networking, research and follow-up activities secured these interviews. Now, successful interviewing will generate competitive job offers for the positions you want, desire and fit.

Flawless interviewing requires diligent preparation. Using proven techniques will enhance your success in winning desirable job offers. Become intimately familiar with the Interview Preparation Checklist. This tool will help you get fully prepared for each interview. Follow each step carefully. By preparing in advance, you will increase your confidence and enhance your presentation. Practice and preparation will lead to success.

Strategy #43 Practice for all Your Interviews

Paul speaking:

"My coach took me through the interview preparation process and introduced me to the Interview Preparation Checklist. As I completed each action item, I checked it off."

Strategy #44 Utilize Your Interview Preparation Checklist

☑ 1. <u>Reviewed research</u>

   ☑ Company history (revenue growth/decline, expansions, mergers/acquisitions)

   ☑ Company culture (mission, vision, values, dress code)

   ☑ Products/services (new launches, market leaders)

   ☑ Key executives (bios, titles)

   ☑ Media releases

   ☑ Major customers

☑   2. <u>Reviewed position description</u>

      ☑ Chose CAR stories supporting fit for each essential skill

      ☑ Identified potential career obstacles

☑   3. <u>Prepared list of anticipated questions</u>

      ☑ Practiced answering questions using CAR stories

      ☑ Prepared to respond to career obstacles with examples of similar skills or accomplishments which are highly transferable

☑   4. <u>Practiced thirty-second commercial</u>

      ☑ Focused on strengths relevant to position

      ☑ Tailored positioning statements to position

☑   5. Role-played interview with coach or family member/friend

      ☑ Videotaped or audiotape recorded role-play

      ☑ Debriefed the recording

      ☑ Repeated role-play, incorporating feedback from debriefing

Strategy #45 Respond to Interview Questions with CAR Stories to Win Job Offers

If you have carefully prepared for the interview by matching your CAR stories with the essential skills required for the position, you will be thoroughly prepared for most interview questions. You will be giving clear, concise examples of challenges you faced, the actions you took and the results you achieved. Your CAR story answers can be expanded in any area whenever you are asked probing questions for more detail.

Keep in mind that your answers should never be more than one and one-half to two minutes long. Let the interviewer go in the direction he or she desires. These are your stories. You can speak about them at length. Guard against talking too much about any one question.

When interviewers want more details, they will ask a follow-up question. Don't second guess. Keep your answers focused on what they ask you. If you aren't clear about the question, ask for clarification before you reply.

Common Interview Questions and Suggested Replies

Hiring managers have three concerns in every interview. These are:

- *What can you do for our company?*

- *Will you be a strong match for the position?*

- *Will you be a good fit for our company's culture?*

By tailoring your replies to these three areas of concern, you can position yourself head-and-shoulders above your competition every time!

Tell me about yourself

Use your thirty-second commercial to reply to the question, "Tell me about yourself." Tailor your CAR stories to the essential duties required for the position, if you know them. If this is an introductory interview, focus on your strongest key achievements.

Your reply should be a clear, concise and compelling overview of your professional skills, talents and abilities. By sharing information relevant to the position for which you are being interviewed, you will assist the interviewer in concluding that you are a strong match for the position. For example:

"I have a career foundation of progressively responsible roles in finance and accounting. This gave me the skills I needed to achieve outstanding sales and drive revenue growth over ten years, as a business development executive.

I have a proven record of accomplishments leading sales teams and forging strategic alliances with C-level customers in the financial services, technology, manufacturing and retail services industries."

What are your short-term career goals?

Focus your answer on the position under consideration. Think a moment about your knowledge of the company, its growth and promotion patterns. You want your goals to be realistic, based on your company knowledge and the position's key duties. Don't focus on your needs, or what the company can do for you. Instead, focus on contributions you can make to the company!

Hiring managers want to know if you plan to stay on board once you are hired. They may wonder if you are using this opportunity as a stepping stone to get into another company. Additionally, they may wonder if you are seeking a position with growth potential, or a job that you may keep for a long time.

What are your long-term career goals?

Be flexible. Refer to your desire to move up quickly based on your record of achievements and contributions. If you have the opportunity, consider asking the interviewer for his or her perspective on potential promotion opportunities within the company down the road. For example:

"Where would you see someone like me five years down the road, with your company?"

Or

"Does your company have a policy of promoting from within, or do you routinely recruit talent from the outside?"

What do you look for in an ideal position?

Speak about your key functional skills and achievements. Relate these to a position that allows you to make similar contributions on a larger or broader scale. Completing the *Career Coach*, Functional Skills Inventory, and writing your CAR stories will prepare you to answer this question clearly and concisely. For example:

"An ideal position would be one in which I can develop new business relationships with senior level executives in key accounts, drive revenue growth by launching new products and improve performance by delivering exemplary cus-

tomer service. I have a proven record of accomplishments driving double-digit revenue growth through new product launches in new territories, and I enjoy these aspects of a position."

Why are you (did you) leaving (leave) your current (last) position?

Always answer this question in a positive manner. Don't make negative or judgmental comments about previous employers, supervisors or products. Be careful to avoid disclosure of confidential or proprietary information. Positive replies can be something like:

"I was in the same position for a few years. Upward mobility was not an option because the company was an extremely flat organization."

"The company had reached a plateau. Promotions were severely limited."

"The company is planning to relocate and I would like to remain in this area."

"The company was recently acquired and the new owners are taking the business in a different direction. There was no longer a fit for me in my previous role."

What can you do for our company that makes you the most qualified person for the position?

The company research you have conducted will prepare you to answer this question on target. Identify two or three of your top functional skills that relate to the position. Use the CAR story method to illustrate your past record of accomplishments. Close your answer with a statement like:

"I'm confident that I could deliver similar results in this position."

Why should I offer you this position?

The hiring manager is always looking for a strong match. Focus on your past record of accomplishments. Talk about your ability to achieve similar results in this role. For example:

"In my previous role as a business development manager, I successfully led three new product launches, opened two new regional territories with record sales, and captured market share by winning over three key accounts from the competition. I understand that your company is planning to launch two new products in a new region. Given the opportunity, I'm confident I could achieve similar results for you."

How would you describe your energy level?

Sometimes hiring managers will ask this question when they have concerns about your ability to work long hours, keep up a fast pace, or exhibit enthusiasm and excitement. They may be basing their concerns on stereotypes they believe to be true about you based of your physical appearance.

Speak to your ability to work tirelessly and effectively, doing whatever it takes to get the job done well. Use a CAR story that illustrates working long hours over an extended period of time to complete a project. Refer to your active lifestyle or leisure activities such as: rock climbing, mountain biking, snow or water skiing, hiking, jogging and weight training. Avoid speaking about low energy activities like reading, attending the theater, and stamp or coin collecting.

How well do you work under pressure and tight deadlines?

Be prepared with two or three CAR stories that illustrate your abilities to work under pressure and tight deadlines. For example:

"I was able to retain all our key managers while recruiting and deploying fifty-three staff during a seamless, cross-country corporate relocation. Our European parent company moved us from CA to NJ. I developed a relocation strategy and successfully moved the subsidiary over a ninety-day period, on time and on budget, without any disruption to our operations or revenue."

Tell me about your personal management philosophy

Develop an answer that accurately describes your personal management philosophy. You may be tempted to tailor your answer to what you think this hiring manager is looking for, but this approach can backfire. If you aren't a good match based on a shared management philosophy, you won't be happy or effective in the position. For example:

"I believe that when you put the right people in the right positions; and give them the support, resources, and tools to do the job; you will have a profitable, productive, and high-performing organization. As a leader, it's my responsibility to know my people, match their skills to the jobs needed, and provide them with the coaching, support, and resources necessary to excel."

Describe your most significant accomplishments in your present or last position

Select past accomplishments supported by CAR stories that are similar to the company's needs. Paint a picture for the hiring manager in which he or she can see you achieving similar results for their company.

What is your greatest strength?

Emphasize your personal strengths that are related to the position. For example, strong customer service skills, careful attention to detail, or the ability to work independently with minimal supervision and direction. Illustrate one or two of these skills by sharing a CAR story.

What is your greatest weakness?

Choose something that was a weakness early in your career that you have successfully overcome. Your example should be something neutral and relevant to most managers. Usually it's safe to talk about delegation. For example:

"In my first management position, I learned that I had difficulty delegating. I believed that if you wanted a job done right, you should just do it yourself. When I was responsible for leading a team project, I discovered that it was no longer possible to do it all myself. As I learned to delegate, I also learned the importance of follow-up and accountability. For many years now, I have experienced successes leading diverse teams that have achieved results I could never have attained as an individual contributor."

If I were to hire you, how long would it take for you to make a measurable contribution to the company?

Demonstrate your abilities to hit the ground with your feet already moving. Use one or two CAR stories to illustrate your abilities around getting up to speed quickly and making a rapid contribution. For example:

"I drove an $8M revenue stream in a start-up over a one year period by cold calling C-level executives, establishing a new embedded engineering vertical, and expanding business services within existing client accounts. I developed key client accounts with companies like ABC Services, Credit Services, Franklin-Jones Engineering, Cloud Computer Engineering Services, the Department of Energy and the US Army. I'm confident I could achieve similar results in this position."

If I were to hire you, how long would you plan to stay with our company?

Speak to what you bring to the table and what you expect from your next employer. For example:

"I believe that employer—employee relationships are two-way. I am committed to giving 100% of my effort to my next position.

Based on my research of your company, I've learned that you have a reputation for supporting your employees, and providing an environment that is challenging and rewarding. As long as we have a mutually beneficial relationship, I would probably have no reason to consider making a move."

If you could begin you career over, what would you do differently this time?

Don't use this as an opportunity to "bare your soul" with the hiring manager! Although your intentions may be honorable, you have no control over the unintended impact your reply may have on the interviewer. Consider something like:

"Hindsight is always twenty-twenty. Most everyone would probably make some changes if it were possible. Overall, though, I am quite proud of my accomplishments and my career growth to this point."

How do you evaluate your role as an employee?

Use objective criteria with measurable results. For example:

"I think past performance is the best predictor of future behavior. In my opinion, tangible results of being a top producer in a sales and business development role include: exceeding quotas, setting new sales records and winning awards. I have a proven record of accomplishments in each of these areas. I think I am a high achiever and a superior performer in sales and business development roles."

Tell me about how you would describe your most recent superior to your replacement if given the opportunity?

Always focus on the positive. Never comment negatively or judgmentally about a previous employer or supervisor. Doing so will make you appear to be a person who has conflict with authority figures. You will be perceived as someone who can't accept constructive feedback, or as an employee who is not supportive of upper management.

Even if you had compelling reasons for leaving your last position because of your previous employer's unethical or inappropriate behavior, the interview is not the time or place to address it. Find something positive to say and leave out any criticism or negativity. For example:

"I would tell him or her that Mr. Jones is a dependable, reliable manager. He will support you in all your efforts. I would describe him as loyal to the company and the customers. He is willing to go the extra mile to get the job done."

Why haven't you already found a new position?

Remain positive and optimistic. Don't fall into the trap of trying to justify your unemployment, no matter how long or short it has been. For example:

"I am not just looking for another job. My next position will be one that matches my strengths, skills and abilities with a career that gives me the support and resources to make contributions to the company's growth and success. It will be a leadership role that challenges me to expand the scope of my responsibilities and my achievements."

What have you disliked the most about your previous positions?

Adapt your reply to the position and company under consideration. For example, if you are interviewing with a large size company you might say:

"I disliked working for small-size companies because they lacked the resources and staff to support rapid growth in a competitive market."

Emphasize your desire to fill a narrow, specialized role as a subject matter expert in a specific function or market segment.

Alternatively, if you are interviewing with a small-size company you might say:

"I disliked working for a large-size company because the bureaucracy made it difficult to get things done in a timely and efficient manner."

Emphasize that you enjoy wearing multiple hats and taking a hands-on approach, versus filling a narrow role as a subject matter expert in a specific market segment.

Tell me about an instance in which your work was criticized

Focus on a lesson learned from your early career. Describe a situation in which you were criticized for a decision you made or for actions you took. Talk about how you acknowledged your growth area and learned to perform differently. For example:

"Early in my career, I was criticized for being a perfectionist and holding others to impossible standards. I realized that others don't always have a similar drive. By learning to accept performance from others that was at or above the expected performance level for the position, I was able to win employee loyalty and trust."

Do you usually initiate conversations with others before they speak to you?

Be yourself. Don't try to be someone different than you really are in a social situation. You might say something like:

"It depends on the circumstances. I am a very outgoing person. Interactions with others are enjoyable for me in a variety of settings. I'm not hesitant to introduce myself or invite others to join me in a conversation. Establishing rapport quickly, and encouraging others to feel comfortable, both come easily for me in one-on-one and group situations."

What was the best book you've read, most entertaining movie you've seen, or most recent sports event you have attended?

These questions are designed to give the interviewer some insights into your personality, interests and leisure activities. Avoid naming controversial books, movies or events. Be prepared to answer follow-up questions if you name a specific book, movie or event because the hiring manager may be familiar with what you mention!

Consider investing time and effort into staying abreast of current best-selling books related to the industries or fields you are targeting. When you can reference these works, your credibility will be enhanced.

What do you find most appealing about the position we are seeking to fill?…The least appealing?

Speak about the job functions that benefit the employer, not you. For example, you might say:

"I am excited about the challenges of launching new products, penetrating new markets, and capturing market share from the competition by winning over key accounts, and delivering excellent customer service."

If you are asked the second question, you might say something like:

"Based on my understanding of the position, I can't identify any aspect that I would find undesirable."

Don't you think you might be a better fit in a (smaller/larger) organization?

When this question arises, it is usually an indirect way of stating a concern regarding a career obstacle. The interviewer may wonder if you have enough direct experience with a company the same size, or with similar products or services.

For example, if you are interviewing with a large size company you might say:

"Although the majority of my experience is with small size companies, I disliked working in them because they lacked the resources and staff to support rapid growth in a competitive market."

Alternatively, if you are interviewing with a small-size company you might say:

"Although the majority of my experience is with large-size companies, I disliked working for them because the bureaucracy made it difficult to get things done in a timely and efficient manner."

Emphasize your enjoyment wearing multiple hats and taking a hands-on approach versus a narrow role, with limited variety in a specific functional area.

Why isn't your salary history higher at your age and experience level?

If you have been working in an industry that historically pays lower wages, make sure to indicate that to the interviewer. Emphasize that you were awarded performance bonuses and raises because of your superior performance. You may wish to say that you are seeking a position in a new industry that offers more competitive compensation.

Are you a competitive employee, with an eye out for your supervisor's position at the first opportunity?

Balance your reply to this question. You want to communicate that you are a hard-working, ambitious employee, and that you are also a team player who supports his or her upper management.

You might say something like:

"I would always view opportunities to get ahead as favorable. Being offered my supervisor's job would certainly be a plus. The way I would see that coming about is by doing my very best in my current position. In this way, my strengths would get noticed, and I would hope to be considered for a variety of promotions as they became available. All my previous promotions have come about in part because of my support and commitment to my supervisor's objectives."

Do you see yourself as flexible?…Adaptable?…Creative?…Analytical?…A problem-solver?

Always keep your answer affirmative. Support it with one or two CAR stories that illustrate your claim. If possible, link your reply regarding one aspect with other similar adjectives to the one asked of you.

For example if you were asked about seeing yourself as adaptable, you might reply:

"I turned around a stalled client project and generated more than $12M in new revenue over two years. I adapted my approach to the client's needs by analyzing the obstacles stalling the project, and creatively adopting solutions that solved the problem. I forged strong, strategic alliances with the customer's management team members, and won the main project management engagement role as a result."

How would your direct reports describe you?

Choose two or three strengths that support your ability to perform functions key to the position. For example:

"My direct reports would describe me as consistent, dependable and appreciative of their contributions. In my last position, I was honored with a plaque for being the 'Best Boss of the Year.' Several of my staff told me that they really appreciated how I would follow-through on my commitments to them, and to their clients. They valued my leadership abilities, and frequently told others I was a great mentor and coach."

Have you ever terminated an employee?

Balance your compassion and sensitivity with your willingness and ability to do the right thing, even when it's a tough decision. For example you might say:

"Terminating an employee is always a last resort. I believe in seeking out ways to improve an employee's performance first. If this fails, then I look for another position within the organization that may be a better fit before considering termination.

I want to know that I have exhausted all other possibilities, or that the employee really has no desire to improve his or her performance before I make a termination decision. It nearly always costs the company more to terminate someone than it does to salvage an under-performing employee who desires to remain with the company."

Have you ever hired a new employee? How did you make your hiring decisions?

Demonstrate your knowledge and experience with recruiting and hiring employees. You might say something like:

"Throughout my career, I have hired several people for a variety of positions. In each instance I worked with human resources to develop a detailed job description.

Next, I created a list of skills needed to perform the job's essential functions. Then I created interview questions to identify these skills. After posting the position, I screened the résumés I received, selected several promising candidates and conducted interviews.

After narrowing down the list further, I presented my semi-finalists for team interviews. These teams were made up of the supervising manager and one or two peers with some time and grade in the same or a similar position. Finally, a hiring decision was made based on the results of these activities."

Why do you want to join our company?

Show your knowledge of the company, its products and services, and its reputation in the community. You might say something like:

"I've learned from my research that your company has achieved impressive results with its previous product releases over the past three years. Because of this growth, I think my background in successfully launching new products and capturing market share in new territories would be an ideal match. I love a competitive environment where I can excel. I see your company as being all of this, and more."

If you could work for anyone in any position, what would your position be and what company would you choose?

Don't name a specific position or an individual company. You don't want to alienate the hiring manager by creating a belief that another company would be your first choice. Instead, say something like:

"I am looking for an opportunity to increase my ability to contribute to a successful company's growth and profitability. An ideal position would give me increased responsibilities. These could include selling a larger range of products and services, or being assigned a broader geographic territory to develop new business and key accounts. I believe the quickest way for me to get ahead is to help my employer succeed."

Behavioral-Based, Structured Interview Questions

More and more hiring managers are getting trained in behavioral-based, structured-interviewing techniques. This interview style is designed to assist the interviewer in evaluating a candidate's job fit based on past experience.

First, a position description is written that identifies essential skill sets. Second, structured interview questions with sample answers are developed to measure each skill. Last, a ranking system is created to score each answer and rank candidates based on their individual answers.

The core of behavioral-based, structured interviewing is the questioning style. Each question is designed to probe the candidate for specific examples of skill mastery. Here are some sample questions to illustrate this technique:

> *Overcoming stalls and objections from C-level executives is a critical skill set for the director of business development in our firm. Tell me about a situation in which you were able to overcome an executive level client's objection to purchasing your product or services. What were the specific objections and what did you say or do to overcome them?*

> *Leading new-product launches is a critical skill set for the director of new business development & sales in our company. Describe a situation for me in which you had the opportunity to launch a new product. What did you do and why did you choose those priorities? What was the result?*

> *Leading cross-functional teams in a matrixed organization is a critical skill for the manager of sales/business development at our company. Give me an example of how you formed and led a new team. How did you select the team members? How did you establish team norms and create shared vision and ownership when team members were your peers?*

The following section includes behavioral-based questions related to each major functional skill. Review your Functional Skills Checklist and practice using CAR stories to answer the questions. With practice, you can be thoroughly prepared for your interviews that include behavioral based, structured interview questions.

Operations Function

Tell me about a situation that shows how you reorganized an operational process that resulted in improved efficiency or improved production. How did you assess the problem? How did you determine the best changes? What steps did you take?

Describe your experience in managing the day-to-day operations of a department. What were your duties? How many direct reports did you have? How large was your budget? What were your reporting responsibilities?

Tell me about your experience in managing multiple functions within an operation like accounting, sales, marketing, and human resources.

Research & Development Function

Describe a research project you managed. What was the scope of the project? How did you plan the data collection and analysis? How did you design the project? What was the outcome? How were the results used?

Tell me about your experience in developing new products. What steps did you take? How did you prioritize your activities? What were the results?

Sales & Marketing Function

Describe a situation in which you managed a large account. How did you build relationships with the key decision-makers? How did you resolve customer complaints? How did you grow sales revenue?

Tell me about your experience in marketing a new product or service. How did you determine your market segment and targets? How large was your budget? How did you develop marketing collateral? Who else was involved? What was the outcome?

Corporate Communications Function

Describe a situation in which you designed a corporate communication strategy. What methods did you use to share information? Who were your target audiences? How did you create your message? What was the outcome?

Tell me about your experience communicating with other businesses. What were your strategies? What mediums did you utilize? How did you measure your effectiveness?

Human Resources Function

Describe a situation in which you had to coach an employee for poor performance. What did you document? What steps did you take? Who else was involved? How did you measure the outcomes? What was the result?

Tell me about your experience in recruiting new employees. How did you target your recruiting? How did you structure your interviews? What criteria did you develop for determining essential job skills and competencies? How did you rank candidates?

Accounting & Finance Function

Describe a situation in which you managed the accounting function or department. What software did you use? How large was the budget? How many departments were involved in reporting? What was your role in terms of strategic planning, financial reporting, and budget planning?

Tell me about your experience in managing budget compliance across multiple departments. How did you hold department managers accountable? What methods did you use to communicate expectations? How did you manage noncompliance issues?

Legal Function

Describe a situation in which you managed contracts or documents. What system did you use? How were documents logged or retrieved? When did you interact with other departments and what was your role?

Tell me about your experience in copyrights, trademarks and intellectual property. What is your knowledge of the law in these areas? What role did you play in these areas?" How well did you work with the legal department and with other divisions?

IS/IT Function

Describe a situation in which you set up a new company-wide intranet. How did you plan it? Who else was involved? What steps did you take from beginning to end?

Tell me about your experience in managing a technical help desk department. How did you schedule your staff? How did you measure performance? How were shifts managed? How did you measure customer satisfaction?

Chapter Review

Milestone Two Tools-Winning Job Offers

Strategy #43 Practice for all Your Interviews

Strategy #44 Utilize Your Interview Preparation Checklist

Strategy #45 Respond to Interview Questions with CAR Stories to Win Job Offers

Chapter Nine:
Milestone Three—Negotiating & Accepting a Position

Milestone Three Tools

The final job search milestone along your journey is negotiating and accepting a position. One with a strong personal fit, in a company and industry you desire. Many times candidates often jump at the first offer they get, especially if their search has been long and frustrating. Take the time to strategically negotiate your best package. It will often benefit you the rest of your career.

Job seekers have frequently failed to negotiate the best offer simply because they didn't ask for what they wanted! An executive with a large municipality in the Denver suburbs reported that in more than ten years of hiring clerical and administrative employees, only three had ever attempted to negotiate their salary packages.

When asked how many could have benefited from negotiations had they initiated them, her response was "All of them. There was always something they could have asked for, even if I couldn't budge on salary—a hiring bonus, additional training, more vacation, flex hours, or partial telecommuting. But they didn't get them because they didn't ask!"

> *Job seekers have frequently failed to negotiate the best offer simply because they didn't ask for what they wanted!*

Several principles apply to all successful negotiations. First, be prepared. Take the time to review your homework. Second, have a set of goals in mind. Decide beforehand what you are willing to negotiate, and what will cause you to decline the offer.

Finally, get your offers in writing. Ask for a copy of the employer's bonus plan and benefits package. An offer is not an offer until it is committed to paper. Employers, especially those from smaller companies, may resist your request. It is crucial that you insist on it. Once you've accepted the new position, it is too late to go back and negotiate. Getting the offer in writing buys you some time. It allows you to take a step back and be more objective during the negotiations process.

Paul speaking:

"I had received an offer letter from KPRZ Christian Radio in Tustin, California. After faxing it to my career coach, I called to schedule a phone consultation to review it. My coach suggested that I call the human resources department and see if I could obtain a copy of the bonus plan and the employee benefits package.

My offer letter follows outlining their offer of employment to me for a Business Development Manager position."

KPRZ Christian Radio

4325 Main Street, Tustin, CA 92804

November 15th, 2004

Mr. Paul Williams
365 Sky Ridge Lane
Colorado Springs, CO 80505

Dear Mr. Williams:

We are delighted to make you this offer of employment to join our team as a business development manager. The essential duties are outlined in the job description we provided you during your last interview. You have come to us with exemplary references and a proven record of impressive achievements in the high tech arena.

We are pleased to offer you a base salary of $65K with a competitive bonus package. The complete bonus program will be given to you by our human resources director. Historically, bonuses related to the company's overall performance have been paid ranging from 20% to 40% of the base salary. Additionally, you will be eligible for our personal-performance bonus plan. This plan is tiered, based on achieving or exceeding individual and team revenue targets on a quarterly basis.

We are confident you will find our employee benefits package quite competitive. We offer a choice of indemnity and HMO/PPO plans for family medical, dental and vision coverage. Your entire premium is paid by the company and in addition we will credit you up to $300 per month toward family coverage, so your actual out-of-pocket cost will vary depending on the coverage plans you choose.

You will receive two weeks of paid vacation annually and you will be eligible for one week after your first six months of continuous employment with KPRZ Christian Radio. Additionally, you will receive 11 paid holidays annually. These holidays are published by Human Resources at the beginning of each calendar year.

Time is of the essence so we are hoping you will find this offer acceptable and begin your employment with us on January 3rd, 2005. This offer expires at midnight, Friday, December 3rd, 2004 unless extended in writing by an authorized agent.

Please feel free to contact me to discuss this offer or to clarify any items it contains.

Very truly,
Mr. James Walton
Vice President, Sales & Marketing

Paul speaking:

"After I obtained the details of the bonus program and the company's benefits package, I completed the Negotiations Worksheet with my career coach. I identified the items that were non-negotiable and negotiable so I could prepare my counter offer letter."

Strategy #46 Prepare Your Negotiations Worksheet

"The LORD says, 'I will guide you along the best pathway for your life. I will advise you and watch over you.'"
Psalm 32:8 (NLT)

Negotiations Worksheet (Example)

Non-negotiable items

1. $70K minimum base salary requirement

2. I need a minimum of 21 days vacation or personal paid leave annually

3. I have a family vacation planned and paid for in June for two weeks, so I will need this time off with pay.

Negotiable items

1. I would prefer a director of business development title

2. Signing bonus

3. Start date, I would prefer starting on January 10th, 2005

4. Stock options

5. Waive the 30-day waiting period on the benefits package

Strategy #47 Use Your Negotiations Preparation Checklist

Negotiations Preparation Checklist Example

☑ 1. Company history

  ☑ (1) Revenue growth or decline?

  ☑ (2) History of layoffs or acquisitions?

☑ (3) Business structure

(a) Family-owned and operated

(b) Closely held private corporation

(c) Publicly traded company

☑ 2. <u>Industry history</u>

☑ (1) Growth, stable, declining?

☑ (2) Future projections?

☑ 3. <u>Salary ranges for position being offered</u>

☑ (1) Salary.com reports

☑ (2) Salaryexpert.com reports

☑ 4. <u>Cost-of-living factors if relocating</u>

☑ (1) Moving.com reports

☑ 5. <u>Relocation-assistance package</u>

☑ 6. <u>Growth potential for me in the company</u>

☑ (1) Career-path planning

☑ (2) Professional-development resources

☑ 7. <u>Employee benefits</u>

☑ (1) Family coverage for medical/dental/vision/disability insurance

☑ (2) Vacation/personal paid leave

☑ (3) Stock options

☑ (4) Bonus program

☑ (5) Paid holidays

☑ (6) Employee assistance program

☑ (7) Medical spending accounts

☑ (8) Retirement plan, vesting period, employer matching funds

☑ (9) Family-leave policy

☑ (10)Bereavement-leave policy

☑ (11)Health and wellness program or benefits

☑ 8. <u>Employee expense-reimbursement policy</u>

☑ (1) Corporate credit card

☑ (2) Corporate calling card

☑ (3) Cellphone provided

☑ (4) Laptop provided

☑ 9. <u>Travel required? What percentage? How long is average trip?</u>

☑ 10. <u>Title—Is it negotiable?</u>

☑ 11. <u>Executive Benefits</u>

    ☑ (1) Stock grants

    ☑ (2) Country club membership

    ☑ (2) Car

    ☑ (3) Airline club memberships

    ☑ (4) Limousine service

    ☑ (5) Business-class airline travel overseas

    ☑ (6) Use of corporate jet

Strategy # 48 Write Down Your Negotiations Questions

<u>Sample Negotiations Questions</u>

1. It is important to me not to take a pay cut. I would require a minimum base salary of $70K to accept your employment offer. Would you consider changing the title to director, business development, and increasing my scope of responsibilities to support the new title and increased base salary?

2. I have a pre-paid family vacation scheduled for two weeks in June. Will I be able to take this time off with pay?

3. I am accustomed to 21 days of annual paid vacation. Is this negotiable?

4. What percentage of travel is expected for the position?

5. Does the company provide a cellphone, corporate calling card, or laptop?

6. May I have a copy of the bonus plan for review, prior to accepting your offer?

7. Am I eligible for a stock option plan?

8. What resources are available to me for career planning and growth?

9. A start date of January 10th, 2005 would be ideal for me. Is this acceptable?

10. Could the 30-day waiting period for benefits coverage be waived?

Strategy #49 Put Every Counter Offer in Writing

Paul speaking:

"Based on advice from my coach, I drafted a counter offer letter to KPRZ Christian Radio. Being careful to avoid a demanding tone I expressed my wishes in the context of beginning a new long-term relationship that would be a win/win for both of us. I was careful to omit "negotiations" style language because I wanted to communicate discussion points rather than make specific demands.

Before e-mailing my reply, I called Mr. Walton to alert him that it would soon be on its way. I told him that I had a few points I wished to discuss with him and asked that he call me after he had time to review my e-mail.

Here is my counter offer letter."

Paul Williams

365 Sky Ridge Lane, Colorado Springs, CO 80505 (719) 555-1212/williams@email.com

November 19th, 2004

Mr. James Walton
Vice President, Sales & Marketing
KPRZ Christian Radio
4325 Main Street
Tustin, CA 92804

Dear Mr. Walton:

Thank you for your offer of employment that you sent me on November 15th, 2004. I am excited about this opportunity and am looking forward to joining the KPRZ Christian Radio team. Based on the details we discussed during my two interviews, I am convinced that this is the right fit for both of us.

In thinking through your letter, I identified a few items I would like to discuss with you. Thank you for your invitation to dialogue about any questions.

From my perspective, I see our discussions as the first of many business development conversations. It is also our first opportunity to agree on a "win-win" decision together. It is in this spirit that I would like to reach a mutually fair and attractive agreement.

The following thoughts and suggestions came to mind as I reviewed your offer:

1. **Title and Base Salary:** I have researched current salaries and compensation packages for the technology business development positions in the metro Denver region. It is important that my compensation be commensurate with this standard. My previous compensation was at the level you have offered. Based upon the skills and experience I bring, it would help me a great deal if we could discuss a higher base salary with an increased scope of responsibilities. Possibly this could include a director level title. Maintaining upward growth in my career is very important to me.

2. **Bonus Plan.** Thank you for providing me with a copy of the bonus plan. When we talk, I would like to clarify a few points that remain unclear to me.

3. **Vacation.** You have offered two weeks of paid vacation. I have been accustomed to three weeks of vacation with my previous two employers. Is this something we can discuss? Also, I have already planned and prepaid for two weeks of family vacation in June. In my case, could the six-month requirement for vacation be waived?

4. **Travel.** There is no mention of travel. What is your expectation in this area?

5. **Business Tools.** Does the company provide a cellphone, corporate calling card, corporate credit card (for business/entertainment expenses), a laptop, or reimbursement for high-speed Internet access while working from home?

6. **Stock Option Plan.** Am I eligible for a Stock Option Plan?

7. **Career Planning and Growth/Reviews:** Performance reviews were not mentioned. How will performance reviews be conducted? Do they occur routinely? Is there a plan in place for career planning and growth with regard to internal promotions? Does KPRZ Christian Radio favor promoting from within or do you routinely seek outside candidates for leadership roles?

8. **Professional Development / Continuing Education:** I don't believe we discussed the value KPRZ Christian Radio places on this area. Are professional association dues, certifications, and seminars included in your employee development program?

9. **Health Benefits:** As detailed in your attachment, employee health coverage begins on the first of the month, after the initial 30 days of employment. I understand the employer paid portion is $300 toward this benefit. Would it be possible for KPRZ Christian Radio to waive this 30-day waiting period?

10. **Life Insurance:** In your offer I noticed that executives are provided $50K in life insurance. Does an executive have the option of increasing this coverage, and if so, what are the amount limits?

11. **Miscellaneous:** As for the sick pay, personal leave, holidays, health club, 401K, and long-term disability, these appear standard.

12. **Start Date.** I have already made plans to spend the Christmas and New Years holidays with my family. Could we agree on a start date of January 10th, 2005?

In closing, Mr. Walton, let me express once again how delighted I am to receive your offer to join your team. I am looking forward to a long and mutually beneficial employment relationship with KPRZ Christian Radio. Please call me at your convenience to discuss these items.

Very truly,
Paul Williams

Paul speaking:

"Mr. Walton called me two days later to respond. He expressed how impressed he was by my letter. I knew then my career coach's strategy had been a sound one.

We talked through my letter item by item. First he discussed my base salary, indicating that he felt like $65K was fair. He also expressed that he understood I had been making the same salary in my previous position. A base of $67.5K was the best he could do given the firm's current budgetary constraints.

I countered with $70K. He really wanted to make something work, but he was hindered by his current budget requirements. Then, he made a suggestion I liked. He said 'Paul; we normally don't do hiring bonuses, especially in this economy. But in your case, and with your qualifications, here's what I'd like to do. With your track record, and your contacts in the industry and the Christian market, I know you'll bring in enough new business to more than justify a healthy raise in just a few months. Therefore, I'd like to offer you a base of $67.5K, and a signing bonus of $2.5K. That will be a total first-year compensation of $70K. In addition, I'll also put in writing that we will review your salary in six months.'

I could tell by his kind manner, and by his genuine struggle with the issues at hand, that he was going to be a fair employer, and committed to 'win-win' negotiations. This agreement helped me relax, and we proceeded through my list of talking points with the same professional, give-and-take process.

At the conclusion of our conversation, Mr. Walton said quite warmly, 'Paul, I believe we have a deal. I am privileged to extend our amended offer to you!'"

Here is what his final offer looked like:

KPRZ Christian Radio

4325 Main Street, Tustin, CA 92804

November 23rd, 2004

Mr. Paul Williams
365 Sky Ridge Lane
Colorado Springs, CO 80505

Dear Mr. Williams:

We are delighted to make you this offer of employment to join our team as director of business development. The essential duties are outlined in the job description we provided you during your last interview. You have come to us with exemplary references and a proven record of impressive business development achievements in the radio broadcasting industry.

We are pleased to offer you a base salary of $67.5K with a signing bonus of $2.5K, and a competitive bonus package, which you have already reviewed. As we mentioned before, you will be eligible for our personal performance bonus plan. This plan is tiered, based on achieving or exceeding individual and team revenue targets on a quarterly basis.

As part of your position, we will ask you to travel a maximum of 25% (one week per calendar month). We will also assure you that you will return to Denver by Friday night of each week, and not be expected to travel on Sunday.

Our company is committed to providing up-to-date technology business tools. To that end, each member of our business development team will be provided with a laptop, cellphone, corporate calling card, PDA (Blackberry), access to our corporate intranet, and reimbursement for high-speed Internet access.

While we have not finalized our employee stock ownership plan (ESOP), it is our heartfelt desire, and wholly within the corporate vision, to amply reward the contributions of team members who make this kind of commitment to KPRZ Christian Radio in its early stages.

In light of your and my discussions, I am pleased to announce that effective January 3rd 2005, KPRZ Christian Radio will reimburse up to $5K per employee per calendar year (prorated in the first year of initial employment) for professional memberships, continuing education, etc., for those at the director level and above. Please refer to our Addendum to the Employee Handbook, available on our intranet site, for eligibility for this new benefit, and for reimbursement forms.

We are confident you will find our employee benefits package quite competitive. Our company offers a choice of indemnity and HMO/PPO plans for family medical, dental and vision coverage. Your entire premium is paid by the company and in addition we will credit you up to $300 per month toward family coverage, so your actual out-of-pocket cost will vary depending on the coverage plans you choose. Finally, we will waive the 30-day waiting period before enrollment.

You will receive three weeks paid vacation annually. As per your request, and in light of our discussions, we will pay your two-week vacation in June, and waive our six-month employment rule. You will be eligible for five more vacation days in the year beginning June 11th, 2005. Additionally, you will receive 11 paid holidays annually. These holidays are published by human resources at the beginning of each calendar year.

Time is of the essence so we are hoping you will find this offer acceptable and begin your employment with us on Monday, January 10th, 2005. This offer expires at midnight, Tuesday, November 30th, 2004 unless extended in writing by an authorized agent.

Please sign and date the acceptance below and return it at your earliest convenience.

Very truly,
James Walton
Vice President, Sales & Marketing

I, Paul Williams, indicate by my signature below that I accept this final employment offer from KPRZ Christian Radio.

_____   _____
Paul Williams   Date

Paul speaking:

"The final offer from KPRZ Christian Radio was exactly what I wanted for my next position. I faxed a copy of my acceptance of the final offer to my coach and left a message for him to call me back.

When my coach returned my call, we reviewed my career goals and objectives. Together, we concluded that my job search was a complete success. I thanked him for his support, encouragement, direction and accountability. We ended our coaching relationship, but I knew that if I ever needed to go through this process again I could contact him at any time."

Strategy #50 Give the Lord Thanks & Praise for Direction in Your Career

"I will thank you, LORD, with all my heart;
I will tell of all the marvelous things you have done.
I will be filled with joy because of you.
I will sing praises to your name, O Most High." Psalm 9:1-2 (NLT)

After you have reached the end of your job search journey, set aside some time for thanksgiving and praise. Review your journal. Thank the Lord for his guidance and direction each step of the way. Make a closing journal entry documenting your journey's successful conclusion and celebrate your new position.

Then, take time to write a thank you note, letter or e-mail to each person who offered you encouragement, support, referrals, and network opportunities during your search. Tell them how they helped you and share your success with them too. You can use one of the sample thank you letters from Paul Williams' search in Chapter Seven as a guide.

Chapter Review

Milestone Three Tools-Negotiating & Accepting a Position

Strategy #46 Prepare Your Negotiations Worksheet
- Negotiable items
- Non-negotiable items

Strategy #47 Use Your Negotiations Preparation Worksheet

Strategy #48 Write Down Your Negotiations Questions

Strategy #49 Put Every Counter Offer in Writing

Strategy #50 Give the Lord Thanks and Praise for Direction in Your Career

Fifty Strategies—Discovering God's Blueprint for Your Career

#1   Understand the Job-Loss Cycle

#2   Accept Help from Others through Each Job-Loss Stage

#3   Commit To Daily Prayer and Meditation

#4   Develop a Plan to Cope with Your Job Loss

#5   Create and Maintain a Healthy Physical Lifestyle

#6   Plan a Spiritual Retreat

#7   Ask Others to Pray for Your Job Search

#8   Write Down Your Detailed Job-Search Action Plan

#9   Maintain a Positive Outlook during Your Search

#10 Uncover Your Talents

#11 Discover Your Gifts

#12 Discover Your Job Matches

#13 Create Your Personal Career & Education Inventory

#14 Build Your Confidence by Organizing Your Achievements, and Summarizing Your Education & Professional Development

#15 Utilize Your Functional Skills Checklist

#16 Prepare Your Functional Skills Summary

#17 Compose Compelling CAR Stories

#18 Complete Your Career History & Goals Worksheet

#19 Use the Industry Checklist to Target Your Search

#20 Select Your Industry Preferences and Focus Your Search Activity

#21 Plan the Scope of Your Search

#22 Identify the Geographic Scope of Your Search

#23 Broaden the Position Scope of Your Search

#24 Set Your Industry Scope Search Boundaries

#25 Determine the Size of Your Target Companies

#26 Define Your Search Activities

#27 Identify Your Career Obstacles

#28 Manage Your Career Obstacles with the Career Obstacles Checklist

#29 Understand Timing's Influence on Your Job Search

#30 Develop Your Activity & Scope Action Plan (ASAP)

#31 Create Your Activity and Scope Targets and Goals

#32 Access Internet Search Engines and Career Portals

#33 Conduct Informational Interviews—They Are Your Most Powerful Search Tool

#34 Compose Your Thirty-Second Commercial

#35 Set SMART Goals for Your Job-Search Activity

#36 Participate in a Network Group

#37 Join a Job Seekers' Group

#38 Get Job Interviews with Persuasive Résumés

#39 Use Different Résumé Styles for Optimum Success

#40 Write Compelling, Persuasive Job-Search Letters

#41 Obtain Essential Job-Search Equipment

#42 Dedicate an e-mail Account & Phone To Your Job Search

#43 Practice for all Your Interviews

#44 Utilize Your Interview Preparation Checklist

#45 Respond To Interview Questions with CAR Stories to Win Job Offers

#46 Prepare Your Negotiations Worksheet

#47 Use Your Negotiations Preparation Checklist

#48 Write Down Your Negotiations Questions

#49 Put Every Counter Offer in Writing

#50 Give the Lord Thanks and Praise for Direction in Your Career

Becoming a Christian

This guide is written for people who know Jesus Christ as their personal Savior and have committed to seeking his lordship over their lives. If you don't know him, or if you are unsure of your standing before God, please take time now to understand your options. All eternity is in the balance, and this is literally a life-or-death decision that you alone can make regarding your destiny.

God's Plan for Our Lives

When God created mankind, his desire was to have a loving, intimate relationship with his creation. He created us in his own image. *"Then God said, "Let us make people in our image, to be like ourselves. They will be masters over all life—the fish in the sea, the birds in the sky, and all the livestock, wild animals, and small animals. So God created people in his own image; God patterned them after himself; male and female he created them."* Genesis 1:26-27 (NLT)

Because God wanted us to have a choice, he gave us free will; the ability to make our own decisions and to take self-responsibility. He told Adam and Eve that they could choose to remain in fellowship with him or they could choose to be separated from him.

"The LORD God placed the man in the Garden of Eden to tend and care for it. But the LORD God gave him this warning: "You may freely eat any fruit in the garden except fruit from the tree of the knowledge of good and evil. If you eat of its fruit, you will surely die." Genesis 2:15-17 (NLT)

When Eve was tempted by Satan, in the form of a serpent, to eat of the fruit of the tree of knowledge of good and evil, she gave in and ate it. Then she shared the fruit with her husband, Adam, who also ate the fruit.

"Then the LORD God said, "The people have become as we are, knowing everything, both good and evil. What if they eat the fruit of the tree of life? Then they will live forever!" So the LORD God banished Adam and his wife from the Garden of Eden, and he sent Adam out to cultivate the ground from which he had been made." Genesis 3:22-23 (NLT)

We Are All Sinners

"When Adam sinned, sin entered the entire human race. Adam's sin brought death, so death spread to everyone, for everyone sinned." Romans 5:12 (NLT)

"For all have sinned; all fall short of God's glorious standard." Romans 3:23 (NLT)

Death is the Penalty for Our Sins

Our sinfulness separates us from God because he cannot be in the presence of sin. The price for our sin is the loss of an eternal, physical life and eternal separation from God. *"For the wages of sin is death, but the free gift of God is eternal life through Christ Jesus our Lord."* Romans 6:23 (NLT)

Jesus Christ Died in Our Place for Our Sins

God loved us so unconditionally that he wanted to give us another chance for an eternal relationship with him. Jesus was God in human form. He lived a sinless life so he was not guilty of sin himself. He did not have to die. Because of his sinlessness, he was able to become a substitute for you and me. He paid the price of death for our sin so that we wouldn't have to; he saved us from eternal separation from God.

"But God showed his great love for us by sending Christ to die for us while we were still sinners." Romans 5:8 (NLT)

"For God so loved the world that he gave his only Son, so that everyone who believes in him will not perish but have eternal life. God did not send his Son into the world to condemn it, but to save it." John 3:16-17 (NLT)

Forgiveness Requires Confessing Jesus Christ as Savior and Lord

Although God sent his son, Jesus, to die in our place for our sin; we still must individually receive his free offer of salvation and eternal life. The price for our sin has been paid—we are all forgiven—but we must individually choose to accept or reject this gift of salvation before our salvation is complete.

"Salvation that comes from trusting Christ—which is the message we preach—is already within easy reach. In fact, the Scriptures say, "The message is close at hand; it is on your lips and in your heart." For if you confess with your mouth that Jesus is Lord and believe in your heart that God raised him from the dead, you will be saved. For it is by believing in your heart that you are made right with God, and it is by confessing with your mouth that you are saved." Romans 10:8-10 (NLT)

Your Personal Decision

No one else can make this decision for you. It is your choice alone. God wants desperately to re-connect with you. He loves you and he has a wonderful plan for your life. He is waiting for you to accept him. If you want to accept his gift of salvation, eternal life and a personal relationship with the creator of the universe, you can do it today.

Just pray or talk to God right now. Tell him that you know you are a sinner and that you are separated from him. Thank him for sending his son, Jesus Christ to die for your sins. Receive Jesus Christ as your personal Savior and Lord by inviting him to fill your heart with the Holy Spirit and make you a new creature in Christ. Commit to seeking his Lordship in your life, living day-by-day and moment-by-moment under his guidance, seeking to fulfill his will for you in your life.

Appendix—Career Search Forms

The following section contains all the forms, worksheets, checklists and outlines you will need to manage your job search. Each one has been used in the main text to illustrate Paul Williams' search.

You can also use the Paul Williams sample résumé and letter formats earlier in this guide to develop your own. The chapters on résumés and job search letters both contain extensive information on style, formatting and grammar.

Make copies of these forms before using them so that you can modify your plans or add to them during the course of your job search. You might consider writing in pencil so that corrections and changes can be easily made to each document.

Job Search Checklist

☐ **Understanding the Job-Loss Cycle**

☐ **Discovering Job Matches**
Career Coach Assessment

☐ **Completing the Personal Career and Education Inventory**

☐ **Using the Functional Skills Checklist**

☐ **Creating CAR Stories**

☐ **Career History & Goals Worksheet**

☐ **Completing the Industry Checklist**

☐ **Factors Enhancing Your Job Search—SALT**
<u>Scope</u>
  Geographic Targets
  Position Targets
  Industry Targets
  Company Size
<u>Activity</u>
  Activity & Scope Action Plan (ASAP)
<u>Liabilities/Obstacles</u>
  Career Obstacles Checklist
<u>Timing</u>

☐ **Milestone One—Getting Job Interviews**
Writing Your Résumés
Résumé Styles
Crafting Your Cover Letters

☐ **Milestone Two—Winning Job Offers**
Preparing for Interviews

☐ **Milestone Three: Negotiating & Accepting a Position**
Negotiations Worksheet
Negotiations Preparation Checklist
Negotiations Questions

Personal Career and Education Inventory

Personal Career & Education Inventory

EDUCATION HISTORY		
High School: Eastern Regional High School		
City, State Voorhees, NJ	Graduation Date: 2003	
Trade School:		
City, State	Graduation Date:	
Technical School:		
City, State	Graduation Date:	
Community College:		
City, State		
Degree Awarded:	Graduation Date:	GPA:
College/University (undergraduate): University of Connecticut		
City, State Storrs, CT		
Major: Human Development & Family Studies	Minor:	
Degree Awarded: BA	Graduation Date: 2008	GPA: 3.67
College/University (graduate): Westminster Theological Seminary		
City, State Glenside, PA		
Major: Biblical Counseling	Minor:	
Degree Awarded: MA	Graduation Date: 2011	GPA: 3.52

EDUCATION HISTORY (Continued)

University (doctoral):

City, State

Major: Minor:

Degree Awarded: Graduation Date: GPA:

Internships: (dates and descriptions)

University (post-doctoral):

City, State

Certification: Graduation Date:

PROFESSIONAL LICENSES, CERTIFICATIONS

Type:

Licensing/Certifying Body:

Original Date of Licensure/Certification:

Type:

Licensing/Certifying Body:

Original Date of Licensure/Certification:

Work History

Next, gather and record data on your past employment. This will be a reverse chronological history that begins with your most recent position and goes back to your graduation from high school, college, or trade school. If you attended graduate school after working for a few years, go back as far as your undergraduate college graduation.

WORK HISTORY
Employer: The MENTOR Network.
City, State Broomall, PA
Start Date: 2011   **Termination Date:** N/A
Industry: Behavioral Health **Annual Revenue:** $ **Number of Employees:**
Job Title: Mobile Therapist **Direct Reports:** Program Manager
Compensation: $ 27/hr   **Budget Responsibility:** $ **P&L:** $
Immediate Supervisor: Karen Rentz
Title: Clinical Supervisor   **Phone:** 610 - 353 - 5332
Key Functional Skills: - Interpersonal Skill.   · Writing   · Communication
Duties & Responsibilities: Visit client's home/school to provide therapy.   · Coach effective parenting skills to parents.   · Document data, assessment, and plan.
Reason for Leaving:

WORK HISTORY (Continued)

Employer: The MENTOR Network

City, State Broomall, PA

Start Date: 2011   **Termination Date:** N/A

Industry: Behavioral Health   **Annual Revenue:** $ **Number of Employees:**

Job Title: Therapeutic Support Staff   **Direct Reports:** Program Manager

Compensation: $ 13/hr   **Budget Responsibility:** $ **P&L:** $

Immediate Supervisor: Karen Rentz

Title: Clinical Supervisor   **Phone:** 610—353—5332

Key Functional Skills: · Interpersonal skill
· communication
· writing

Duties & Responsibilities: · Visit clients at home/school to provide behavioral support
· Implement treatment plan · Transfer skills to caregiver
· Document data, assessment, plan

Reason for Leaving:

WORK HISTORY (Continued)

Employer: Amnion Crisis Pregnancy Centers

City, State Drexel Hill, PA

Start Date: 2011   **Termination Date:** N/A

Industry: Non-Profit Mental Health   **Annual Revenue:** $ **Number of Employees:**

Job Title: Intern Counselor   **Direct Reports:** Angel Halstead / Director

Compensation: $ N/A   **Budget Responsibility:** $ **P&L:** $

Immediate Supervisor: Michelle Alexandra

Title: Program Director   **Phone:** 610-622-9957

Key Functional Skills:
- Interpersonal
- Communication
- Writing

Duties & Responsibilities:
- Assess client's need in- or post- pregnancy
- Provide counseling and material assistance
- Refer clients to public services
- Document services provided

Reason for Leaving:

WORK HISTORY (Continued)

Employer: Church of Love In Philadelphia

City, State Erdenheim, PA

Start Date: 2010   **Termination Date:** 2011

Industry: Religious   **Annual Revenue:** $ **Number of Employees:**

Job Title: Youth Director   **Direct Reports:** Rev. David Lee / English Ministry Pastor

Compensation: $ 12,000/yr   **Budget Responsibility:** $ **P&L:** $

Immediate Supervisor: Rev. David Lee

Title: English Ministry Pastor   **Phone:** 215 - 601 - 1899

Key Functional Skills: Interpersonal
- Communication
- Planning/Organization

Duties & Responsibilities:
- Create bible study curriculum and teach it to youths.
- Plan, organize outreach events
- Counsel individual students as needs arise.

Reason for Leaving:
- To pursue desired career field.

WORK HISTORY (Continued)

Employer: University of Connecticut.

City, State Storrs, CT

Start Date: 2006   **Termination Date:** 2008

Industry: Research   **Annual Revenue:** $ **Number of Employees:**

Job Title: Research assistant   **Direct Reports:** Dr. Charles Super / Professor

Compensation: $ 8.50/hr   **Budget Responsibility:** $ **P&L:** $

Immediate Supervisor: Dr. Charles Super / Mary Sutherland

Title: Professor / PhD candidate   Phone: 860-486-1831

Key Functional Skills:
- Analyzing
- Organization
- Computer

Duties & Responsibilities:
- Code videos
- Attend weekly meetings
- Organize samples

Reason for Leaving:
- Graduation / Health.

WORK HISTORY (Continued)

Employer: New Hope Academy

City, State Marlton, NJ

Start Date: 2009   **Termination Date:** 2009

Industry: Education   **Annual Revenue:** $ **Number of Employees:**

Job Title: Teacher   **Direct Reports:** Rev. Alex Ahn

Compensation: $ 12.50/hr   **Budget Responsibility:** $ **P&L:** $

Immediate Supervisor: Rev. Alex Ahn

Title: Assistant Pastor   Phone: 617-504-1185

Key Functional Skills:

Duties & Responsibilities: · Create lesson plans for 4th grade Math and English. · Instruct 4th grade Math and English.

Reason for Leaving:

· Program ended.

WORK HISTORY (Continued)

Employer: Alpha Academy Christian Learning Center

City, State Moorestown, NJ

Start Date: 2006   **Termination Date:** 2006

Industry: Child care   **Annual Revenue:** $ **Number of Employees:**

Job Title: assistant Teacher   **Direct Reports:** Nina Alexander / Principal

Compensation: $ 8 /hr   **Budget Responsibility:** $ **P&L:** $

Immediate Supervisor: Nina Alexander

Title: Principal   **Phone:** 856-235-2252

Key Functional Skills:
- Maintain hygenes
- Helping physical needs
- Secure safety

Duties & Responsibilities:
- Provide direct care to infants and toddlers.
- Oversee children in preschool and kindergarten during lunch, nap and play time.

Reason for Leaving:
- Family emergency.

WORK HISTORY (Continued)

Employer: Rhode Island School of Design.

City, State Providence, RI

Start Date: 2004   **Termination Date:** 2006

Industry: Library.   **Annual Revenue: $**   **Number of Employees:**

Job Title: Library assistant   **Direct Reports:**

Compensation: $ 7.75/hr   **Budget Responsibility: $**   **P&L: $**

Immediate Supervisor:

          Title: Phone:

Key Functional Skills:
- Computer
- Organization

Duties & Responsibilities:
- Check in and out pictures.
- Register students
- Organize files
- Sort pictures

Reason for Leaving:

Military Service

If you served in the military on active duty, in the reserves or both, complete the following section. Record the service branch, your dates of service and your rank at discharge. Next, record a reverse chronological history of your rank and duties starting with your most recent position. If you completed any special training or received certifications during your military career, record those below.

Service Branch: _____   Service Dates: ___/___/___ to ___/___/___

Rank at Discharge: _____

<u>Reverse chronological history of rank and duties:</u>

Rank	Duties	Dates

<u>Special Military Training, Education & Certifications:</u>

School / Institution	Course / Program Title	Dates

Continuing Education & Professional Development

Review the past ten years and record any continuing education programs, professional development workshops or seminars that you have completed.

Provider	Course Name	Dates
Biblical Seminary	Certificate for Advanced Prof. Counseling	2011-2012

Honors, Awards & Professional Recognition

Record any honors, awards or professional recognition you have received during your high school, college or university experience and throughout your career. Include honor societies, production or performance awards, biographical sketches in publications like *Who's Who*, community service and professional association honors or awards.

Conferring Body	Type/Name/Description	Date Awarded
Univ. of Conn.	The National Honor Society of Phi Kappa Phi	2008-2009
	Tau Sigma National Honor society	2007-2008
	Phi Sigma Pi National Honor Fraternity	2007-2008
	New England Scholar	2007
	Dean's List	2006, 2007

Community Service

Record community service activities you have participated in over the past ten years. List the name of the group or activity. Describe your role and the dates you were involved.

Group/Activity	Description	Dates
Logan Hope Sumer Camp, Counselor		2010
Jubilee Pres. Church / Retreat, Counselor		2009, 2010
Grace Community Church/ Drepression Support Group/ Co-Leader		2009-2010
Univ. of Conn./ Faith Christian Fellowship / Small Group Leader		2007-2008
First Korean Pres. church / Vacation Bible Study / Assistant Director		2007
First Pres. Church of NJ / Sunday School Teacher		2003-2004
First Korean Pres. Church / Sunday School Teacher		2008

Charitable Activities

Describe your charitable activities over the past ten years. Record the names of each group or activity/event, and describe your role and the dates you participated.

Group/Activity	Description	Dates
Grace Comm. Church, Tanzania Mission Trip, Evengelist		2009
First Kor. Pres. Church, Thailand Mission Trip, Counselor		2007
First Kor. Pres. Church, Evitrea Mission Trip, Teacher		2003, 2005, 2006

Professional Associations

List any professional associations to which you belonged over the past ten years. Record the full name, the type of membership you held—Professional, Regular, Student, Active—and the dates of your membership.

Name	Membership Type	Dates

Leisure Activities

Caring for dog, Korean TV, Shopping, Cooking,

Functional Skills Checklist

Review the following checklist and identify your functional skills in each category. Place a "☑" next to each functional skill in each category within which you can document performance in your work or educational history.

Management Level—Check the area of management at which you see yourself.

☐ Executive Level Management   ☐ Entry-level Management

☐ Senior Level Management   ☐ Conducted Training

☑ Mid-Level Management   ☑ Completed Education

Management Skills

☑ Budgeting   ☐ Joint Ventures

☐ Business Planning   ☐ Labor Relations

☐ Business Re-engineering   ☐ Manager Development

☐ Change Management   ☐ Mergers & Acquisitions

☐ Consolidations   ☐ Methods & Measures

☐ Corporate Finance   ☐ Multi-Site Management

☐ Cost Control   ☐ Negotiations

☐ Cross-Functional Teams   ☐ Officer/Board Member

☑ Decision Making   ☐ Organizational Devel.

☐ Developing Policies   ☐ P&L Accountability

☐ Diversification   ☑ Project Management

☐ Divestitures   ☐ Resource Management

☐ Employee Evaluations   ☐ Restructuring

☐ Financing-Public/Private   ☐ Revenue Growth

☐ Government Relations   ☐ Staff Development

☐ Growth Strategies   ☐ Start-up Situations

☐ Hiring/Firing   ☐ Strategic Partnerships

☐ International Management   ☐ Strategic Planning

☐ Investor Relations   ☐ Supervision

☐ IPO Strategy/Positioning   ☐ Turnaround Situations

Operations Skills

- □ Assembly
- □ Automation Engineering
- □ Bidding
- □ Call Center Operations
- □ Configuration
- □ Construction
- □ Continuous Process Improvements
- □ Contract Management
- □ Control Systems
- □ Distribution/Transportation
- □ Document Control Management
- □ Environmental Issues
- □ Equipment Design
- □ Equipment Maintenance & Repair
- □ Equipment Management
- □ Facility Management/Leases
- □ Fleet Management
- □ Installation
- □ Inventory Control
- □ ISO 9000 series
- □ JIT (Just In Time Inventory)
- □ WIP (Work In Process)
- □ MRP (Material Resource Planning)
- □ Labor Control
- □ Lean Manufacturing (Toyota)
- □ Logistics
- □ Maintenance
- □ Labor Planning/Budgeting
- □ Manufacturing Engineering
- □ Materials Handling/Management
- □ Methods & Standards
- □ Multi-Shift Management

- □ New Product Development
- □ Operations Research
- □ Operations Supervision
- □ Order Processing
- □ Outsourcing
- □ Plant Design & Layout
- □ Policies & Procedures
- □ Process Control Supervision
- □ Process Engineering
- □ Production Planning
- □ Project Coordination
- □ Project Management
- □ Prototype Operations
- □ Purchasing/Procurement
- □ Quality Assurance/Control
- □ Safety Engineering
- □ Service Support
- ☑ Scheduling
- □ Shipping & Receiving
- □ Start-up Operations
- □ Supply Chain Management
- □ Theory of Constraints Mfg
- □ TQM (Total Quality Management)
- □ Traffic Management
- □ Troubleshooting
- □ Vendor Coordination
- □ Warehousing
- □ _____
- □ _____
- □ _____
- □ _____
- □ _____

Research & Development Skills

- ☐ Applied Research
- ☑ Basic Research
- ☐ Chemical Engineering
- ☐ Contract Administration
- ☐ Design and Specifications
- ☑ Diagnostics
- ☐ Electrical Engineering
- ☐ Engineering Support
- ☐ Environmental, Health, & Safety
- ☐ Feasibility Studies
- ☐ Field Studies
- ☐ Lab Management
- ☐ Lab/Facility Design & Construction
- ☐ Manufacturing/Engineering Liaison
- ☐ Mechanical Engineering
- ☐ Modeling
- ☐ New Equipment Design
- ☐ Patent Holder
- ☐ Process Engineering
- ☐ Product Applications
- ☐ Product Development
- ☐ Product Engineering

- ☐ Product Re-engineering
- ☐ Product Testing
- ☐ Program Development
- ☐ Project Management
- ☐ Prototype Development
- ☐ Quality Control
- ☐ R&D Management
- ☐ Regulatory Compliance
- ☐ Research Publications
- ☐ Security
- ☐ Service Development
- ☐ Simulation Development
- ☐ Software Tools
- ☐ Statistical Analysis
- ☑ Synthesizing
- ☐ Technical Writing
- ☐ Technology Evaluation
- ☐ _____
- ☐ _____
- ☐ _____
- ☐ _____
- ☐ _____

Sales and Marketing Skills

- ☐ Account Management
- ☐ Advertising
- ☐ Brand Management
- ☐ Budgeting/Expense Control
- ☐ Business Development
- ☐ Channel Marketing
- ☐ Collateral Development

- ☐ Compensation Plans
- ☐ Competitive Analysis
- ☐ Contract Negotiations
- ☐ Convention Planning
- ☐ Corporate Identity
- ☐ Customer Relations/Service
- ☐ Direct Sales

Sales and Marketing Skills (Continued)

- ☐ Distribution Channels
- ☐ Distributor Relations
- ☐ Ecommerce/B2B
- ☐ Field Liaison
- ☐ Field Sales (Outside Sales)
- ☐ Forecasting
- ☐ Goal Setting
- ☐ Image Development
- ☐ Import/Export
- ☐ Incentive Programs
- ☐ Inside Sales
- ☐ International Business Development
- ☐ International Expansion
- ☐ Logo Development
- ☐ Market Research & Analysis
- ☐ Market Rollout
- ☐ Marketing Communications
- ☐ Marketing Plans
- ☐ Marketing Promotions
- ☐ Media Buying/Evaluation
- ☐ Media Relations
- ☐ Merchandising
- ☐ Multimedia Presentations
- ☐ New Account Sales
- ☐ New Product Development
- ☐ On-line Marketing & Advertising
- ☐ Packaging
- ☐ Pricing
- ☐ Product Demonstrations
- ☐ Product Introduction/Launch
- ☐ Product Line Development
- ☐ Product Management

- ☐ Product Publishing/Sales
- ☐ Product Sourcing
- ☐ Product Specifications
- ☐ Proposal Writing
- ☐ Radio Media
- ☐ Sales Administration
- ☐ Sales Analysis
- ☐ Sales Forecasting
- ☐ Sales Kits
- ☐ Sales Management
- ☐ Sales Presentations
- ☐ Sales Promotions
- ☐ Sales Recruiting
- ☐ Sales Support
- ☐ Sales Training
- ☐ Showrooms
- ☐ Strategic Alliances/Partnerships
- ☐ Strategic Planning
- ☐ Supply Chain Analysis
- ☐ Supply Chain Management
- ☐ Survey Design
- ☐ Technical Sales Support
- ☐ Telemarketing
- ☐ Television Media
- ☐ Territory Development
- ☐ Tradeshows
- ☐ Trend Analysis
- ☐ Video Productions
- ☐ _____
- ☐ _____
- ☐ _____
- ☐ _____

Corporate Communications Skills

- ☐ B to B Communication
- ☐ Community Affairs/Relations
- ☐ Corporate Image
- ☐ Corporate Philanthropy
- ☐ Corporate Publications
- ☐ Corporate Relations
- ☐ Educational Programs
- ☐ Employee Communications
- ☐ Employee Newsletters
- ☑ Event Planning
- ☐ Fund-Raising
- ☐ Government Affairs/Relations
- ☐ Industry/Association Relations
- ☑ Internet Communications

- ☐ Investor Collateral
- ☑ Multimedia Presentations
- ☐ Press Releases
- ☐ Proposal Writing
- ☐ Public Relations
- ☑ Public Speaking
- ☐ Risk-Management Communication
- ☐ Shareholder Relations
- ☐ Speech Writing
- ☐ Trade Relations
- ☐ Web Site Development-html
- ☐ _____
- ☐ _____
- ☐ _____

Human Resources Skills

- ☐ Affirmative Action
- ☐ Arbitration/Mediation
- ☐ Benefits Vendor Management
- ☐ Career Counseling
- ☐ Career Development
- ☐ Classified Advertisements
- ☐ Company Orientation
- ☐ Compensation & Benefits
- ☐ Computer-Based Training
- ☐ Corporate Culture & Change
- ☐ Cost-Benefit Analysis
- ☐ Course Development
- ☐ Diversity
- ☐ Downsizing
- ☐ EEOC Compliance

- ☐ Employee Coaching
- ☐ Employee Communications
- ☐ Employee Discipline
- ☐ Employee Relations
- ☐ Employee Selection
- ☐ Executive Recruiting
- ☐ Grievances
- ☐ HR Generalist
- ☐ HRIS
- ☐ Human Resources Management
- ☐ Industrial Relations
- ☐ Interactive Training (Internet)
- ☐ International Employees
- ☐ Job Analysis
- ☐ Job Competencies

Human Resources Skills (Continued)

- ☐ Labor Negotiations
- ☐ Organizational Development
- ☐ Outplacement
- ☐ Performance Measurement
- ☐ Policies & Procedures
- ☑ Psychological Assessment
- ☐ Records Management
- ☐ Recruiting
- ☐ Relocation
- ☐ Salary Administration
- ☐ Succession Planning

- ☐ Team-Building
- ☐ Training
- ☐ Training Administration
- ☐ Union Coordination
- ☐ Wage/Rate Analysis
- ☐ Workers' Compensation
- ☐ Workforce Forecasting/Planning
- ☐ Workforce Security
- ☐ _____
- ☐ _____
- ☐ _____

Finance Skills

- ☐ Accounting Management
- ☐ Accounts Payable
- ☐ Accounts Receivable
- ☐ Acquisitions & Mergers
- ☐ Actuarial/Rating Analysis
- ☐ Angel Funding
- ☐ Auditing
- ☐ Banking Relations
- ☐ Budget Control
- ☑ Budgeting
- ☐ Capital Budgeting
- ☐ Capital Investment
- ☐ Cash Management
- ☐ Cost Accounting
- ☐ Cost Control
- ☐ Credit/Collections
- ☐ Debt Negotiations
- ☐ Economic Studies

- ☐ Equity/Debt Management
- ☐ Feasibility Studies
- ☐ Financial Analysis
- ☐ Financial Planning
- ☐ Financial Reporting
- ☐ Financial Software Packages
- ☐ Financing
- ☐ Forecasting
- ☐ Foreign Exchange
- ☐ General Ledger
- ☐ Insurance
- ☐ Internal Controls
- ☐ Investor Relations
- ☐ IPOs
- ☐ Lending
- ☐ Lines of Credit
- ☐ Management Reporting
- ☐ New Business Development

Finance Skills (Continued)

- ☐ Operations Research/Analysis
- ☐ Payroll
- ☐ Pension & Fund Management
- ☐ Pricing/Forecast Modeling
- ☐ Private Placements
- ☐ Profit Planning
- ☐ Risk Management
- ☐ Road Shows
- ☐ SEC Reporting
- ☐ Special Reports

- ☐ Stockholder Relations
- ☐ Systems Installation/Training
- ☐ Taxes
- ☐ Treasury
- ☐ VC/Investor Presentations
- ☐ Venture Capital Relations
- ☐ _____
- ☐ _____
- ☐ _____
- ☐ _____

Administrative Skills

- ☐ Concierge
- ☐ Construction
- ☐ Contract Negotiations
- ☐ Credit Transactions
- ☐ Customer Service
- ☐ Equipment Purchasing
- ☐ Facility Management
- ☐ Forms and Methods
- ☐ HVAC
- ☐ Leases
- ☑ Library
- ☐ Logistics
- ☐ Mailroom
- ☑ Office Equipment
- ☐ Office Management

- ☐ Office Relocations
- ☐ Office Staff Training/Supervision
- ☐ Parking
- ☐ Policies & Procedures
- ☐ Project Management
- ☐ Real Estate
- ☐ Reception
- ☐ Records Management
- ☐ Security
- ☐ Space Planning
- ☐ Telecommunications
- ☐ Utilities
- ☐ _____
- ☐ _____
- ☐ _____

Legal Skills

- Anti-Piracy Investigation
- Antitrust
- Board of Director Affairs
- Case Management
- City, County, State Issues
- Contract Administration/Mgmt
- Copyrights & Trademarks
- Corporate Secretary
- Documentation
- EEO, OSHA, EPA, FDA, etc.
- Employment Law
- Federal Issues
- Financial Regulations
- Government Contracts
- Government/Legislative Affairs
- Incorporation
- Intellectual Property
- International Agreements
- Labor Issues
- Leases & Records
- Legislative Affairs
- Licensing
- Litigation
- Lobbying
- Mergers & Acquisitions
- Patents
- Political Relations
- Purchase Agreements
- Real Estate Law
- Regulatory Compliance
- Safety Regulations
- Securities Registration
- Shareholder Proxies
- Stock Administration
- Taxes
- Transactions

Information Systems/Information Technology/Electrical Engineering/Internet Skills

- Analog Design
- Algorithm Development
- Applications Database Admin.
- Applications Development
- ASP Applications Systems Provider
- Broadband Networks
- Business Systems Planning
- Cabling
- Capacity Planning
- Chip Design
- CRM-(Client Relationship Mgmt)
- Computer-Aided Design
- Computer Architecture
- Computer Configuration
- Computer Interface
- Computer Operations
- Computer Selection
- Computer Systems Conversion
- Data Center Operations
- Data Mining
- Data Processing Management
- Data Security
- Database Administration
- Database Development

Information Systems/Information Technology/Electrical Engineering/Internet Skills (Continued)

- ☐ Desktop Publishing
- ☐ Desktop Video Publishing
- ☐ Diagnostics
- ☐ Digital Design
- ☐ Digital Signal Processing
- ☐ Distributed Processing
- ☐ Ecommerce/B2B
- ☐ EDI (Electronic Data Interface)
- ☐ EAP (Enterprise Asset Management)
- ☐ Enterprise Level Applications
- ☐ ERP (Enterprise Resource Planning)
- ☐ Equipment Selection
- ☐ Field Support Engineering
- ☐ Game Design
- ☐ Graphics
- ☐ Hardware Management
- ☐ HTML/XML
- ☐ Information Management
- ☐ Information Technology Administration
- ☐ Integration Software
- ☐ Intranet Development
- ☐ Languages-Java, C+++, etc.
- ☐ Linear Programming
- ☐ Linux Operating System
- ☐ Methodology Engineering
- ☐ Microprocessors
- ☐ Modeling
- ☐ Multiplexors
- ☐ Network Engineering
- ☐ Network Operations Management
- ☐ Object-Oriented Development
- ☐ Office Automation
- ☐ Performance Monitoring
- ☐ Peripheral Equipment
- ☐ Portal Design/Development
- ☐ Process Development

- ☐ Programming/Coding
- ☐ Project Management
- ☐ Release Management
- ☐ Software Customization
- ☐ Software Development
- ☐ Software Engineering
- ☐ Spreadsheets
- ☐ Supplier Integration
- ☐ Systems Analysis
- ☐ Systems Applications
- ☐ Systems Development
- ☐ Systems Design
- ☐ Systems Testing
- ☐ Systems/Software Installation
- ☐ Systems/Software Training
- ☐ Technical Evangelism
- ☐ Technical Support/Help Desk
- ☐ Technical Writing
- ☐ Telecommunications
- ☐ Test Engineering
- ☐ Tracking Systems
- ☐ Unix
- ☐ Usability Engineering
- ☐ User Education/Documentation
- ☐ User Interface
- ☐ Vendor Relations
- ☐ Vendor Sourcing
- ☐ Voice & Data Communications
- ☐ Web Development/Graphic Design
- ☐ Web Site Content Writer
- ☐ Web Site Editor
- ☐ Wireless Systems
- ☑ Word Processing
- ☐ _____
- ☐ _____
- ☐ _____

Pastoral & Ministry Skills

- ☐ Preaching
- ☐ Leading Worship
- ☑ Missions
- ☑ Evangelism
- ☐ Church Administration
- ☑ Fund-raising
- ☐ Wedding Ceremonies
- ☐ Funeral Ceremonies
- ☑ Visitation
- ☑ Christian Education

- ☑ Curriculum Design
- ☑ Program Director
- ☑ Children
- ☑ Youth
- ☑ Adult
- ☐ Spiritual Direction
- ☑ Personal & Spiritual Development
- ☐ Stewardship
- ☐ Church Architecture
- ☐ Church Planting

Ministry Specializations

- ☐ Death & Dying
- ☑ Family Life Education
- ☑ Youth
- ☑ Singles
- ☐ Divorce Recovery
- ☐ Step-families
- ☐ Single Parents
- ☑ Children
- ☑ Adults
- ☑ Women
- ☐ Men
- ☐ Fathers
- ☐ Seniors
- ☐ Music
  - ☐ Choir Director
  - ☐ Organist
  - ☐ Pianist

- ☐ Singing
- ☑ Creative Arts
- ☑ Painting
- ☐ Drama
- ☐ Dance
- ☑ Pastoral Counseling
  - ☐ Crisis
  - ☑ Family
  - ☐ Pre-marital
  - ☐ Marital
  - ☐ Group
  - ☐ Addictions
- ☑ Church School
  - ☐ Administration
  - ☑ Teaching
  - ☑ Testing
  - ☑ Teacher Training

Ministry Specializations (Continued)

- ☐ Conference Leadership
- ☑ Camp Ministry
  - ☑ Program Director
  - ☑ Administration
  - ☑ Recreation
- ☐ Chaplaincy
  - ☐ Hospital
  - ☐ Military
  - ☐ School
  - ☐ Corporation

- ☐ Correctional Institution
- ☐ Hospice
- ☐ Camp
- ☑ Outreach Ministries
  - ☐ Inner City
  - ☐ Mothers of Preschoolers
  - ☑ Campus
  - ☐ Alzheimer's Day Care
  - ☑ Pre-school

Functional Skills Summary

Budgeting	Multimedia Presentation	Visitation
Decision Making	Public Speaking	Christian Education
Project Management	Psychological Assessment	Personal & Spiritual Dev.
Scheduling	Library	Youth, Children, Singles, Women
Basic Research	Office Equipment	Family
Diagnostics	Word Processing	Painting, Creative Arts
Synthesizing	Missions	Pastoral Counseling
Event Planning	Evangelism	Church School
Internet Communication	Fund-raising	Camp Ministry
		Outreach Ministry

CAR Stories

Functional Skill: Psychological assessments

Employer: The MENTOR   Position: Mobile Therapist

Challenges

It was challenging to asses client's therapeutic issues when client did not display behaviors at home setting and the parent did not open up about client's behaviors at home.

Actions

I established rapport with the family by showing care, and being consistant with support.

Results

The parent began to share her concerns about client's behaviors.

Functional Skill: Family Education

Employer: The MENTOR   Position: Mobile Therapist

Challenges

It was challenging to help families see their ineffective parenting strategies and unhealthy home environment that exacerbate client's problem and they became defensive.

Actions

I frequently communicated with my team members and supervisors about the issue and worked on building trusting relationship with family by pointing out their strengths while addressing issues.

Results

I brought in support from the team and the family became more receptive to my suggestions.

Functional Skill: <u>Youth Ministry</u>
Employer: <u>Church of Love</u>   Position: <u>Youth Director</u>

Challenges
It was challenging to establish trusting relationship with students & motivate them towards a goal. and

Actions
I tried to maintain close contact with all students by having one-on-one meetings regularly, hosting meetings at my place, making visitations, and appointing leaders and roles to help them feel ownership.

Results
Most of students regularly participated in events and some of them actively helped out in the process. They also opened up their personal lives.

Functional Skill: <u>Children Ministry.</u>
Employer: <u>New Hope Academy</u>   Position: <u>Teacher.</u>

Challenges
It was challenging to stimulate interests in students in class and help them achieve the lesson goals without losing them in process.

Actions
I prepared interactive teaching materials to draw students' participation and promoted learning through practical experience.

Results
Students displayed interest in lesson subjects and achieved academic goals.

Functional Skill: Basic Research

Employer: Univ. of Conn.   Position: Research Assistant

Challenges

The Job involved watching 30 minutes of videos for five times to complete coding for one sample. The project was backed up before I came in.

Actions

I spent my work hours in coding diligently to catch up with the goal.

Results

I managed to finish the project by the due time and helped PhD candidate to analyze and present the data.

Functional Skill: Event Planning

Employer: Church of Love   Position: Youth Director

Challenges

I was challenged to plan and organize outreach and recreational activities every month while students lived far away from each other (25 mile radius) and did not have transportations.

Actions

I worked to come up with time and place that will accommodate all students and arranged rides every time, usually picking up/dropping off students myself.

Results

All events happened on scheduled time and had a good turn-outs.

Functional Skill: <u>Multimedia Presentation</u>

Employer: <u>Church of Love</u>   Position: <u>Youth Director</u>

Challenges

I was challenged to make multimedia presentations every week to present Bible study materials to students in interactive and engaging ways that stimulate their interests.

Actions

I used Mac keynote program to make presentations visually appealing, effectively communicating, and interesting by using images, videos, and texts.

Results

Students paid better attention to the material than when it was presented in pure oral or on paper forms.

Functional Skill: <u>Public Speaking</u>

Employer: <u>Church of Love</u>   Position: <u>Youth Director</u>

Challenges

5 sermons

I was challenged to preach at a retreat within scheduled time and had only 1 week to prepare.

Actions

I typed manuscripts and practiced it several times to speak naturally and encouragingly to students. I included questions that will stimulate interaction and self-reflections.

Results

I was able to carry out planned material within time limit and got students' attention.

Functional Skill: <u>Women's Ministry</u>

Employer: <u>Amnion</u>   Position: <u>Counselor.</u>

Challenges

counseling

<u>I was challenged to provide ∧ services to women in</u>

<u>crisis pregnancy</u>

Actions

<u>I worked towards providing safe and comforting</u>

<u>environments for women when they came in to</u>

<u>counseling room by attentively listening to their</u>

<u>stories, empathizing, validating, and support them</u>

<u>with making choices.</u>

Results

<u>Women got chances to share their stories and receive</u>

<u>emotional support they need.</u>

Functional Skill: <u>Church School</u>

Employer: <u>New Hope Academy</u>   Position: <u>Teacher.</u>

Challenges

<u>I was challenged to design lesson plans that will help</u>

<u>students to be prepared for next school year</u>

<u>without assistant.</u>

Actions

<u>I utilized books and internet resources to</u>

<u>create lesson plans that will be engaging and</u>

<u>interesting, yet help students achieve academic</u>

<u>standards.</u>

Results

<u>Students achieved their academic goals.</u>

Functional Skill: _____

Employer: _____   Position: _____

Challenges

_____
_____
_____
_____

Actions

_____
_____
_____
_____

Results

_____
_____
_____
_____

Functional Skill: _____

Employer: _____   Position: _____

Challenges

_____
_____
_____
_____

Actions

_____
_____
_____
_____

Results

_____
_____
_____
_____

Functional Skill: _____

Employer: _____   Position: _____

*C*hallenges

_____
_____
_____
_____

*A*ctions

_____
_____
_____
_____

*R*esults

_____
_____
_____
_____

Functional Skill: _____

Employer: _____   Position: _____

*C*hallenges

_____
_____
_____
_____

*A*ctions

_____
_____
_____
_____

*R*esults

_____
_____
_____
_____

Career History & Goals Worksheet

1. List the titles you have held in order of responsibility and seniority, beginning with the highest level position first. Go back ten years in your work history.

<u>Job Titles</u>

1. Youth Director
2. Assistant Director
3. Mobile Therapist
4. Teacher
5. Therapeutic Support Staff
6. Assistant Teacher
7. Research Assistant
   Library Assistant

2. Categorize the company sizes you have worked in throughout your career. Record the company name in the chart below under the correct heading.

Small-size Company (Up to $100M revenue)	Medium-size Company ($100M to $1B revenue)	Large-size Company ($1B plus revenue)

3. Describe your career objective for your next position in one sentence. For example: *To obtain a full-time position as a Sales Manager in a small-size company in the consumer products or packaged goods industry in the Western United States.*

To obtain a full-time position as a counselor in a counseling center in the mental health industry.

4.   Outline your short-term, medium-term, and long-term position objectives. Remember that the company size will influence the title of your position. You may choose to target different positions in different size companies within each objective. Research various companies within each company size category in the industries you are targeting. Determine the titles used and the career progression within each company to guide your goal setting in this activity.

A.   <u>Short-Term Position Objective</u> (next position)

Sales Manager, large-size company

Sales Director, medium-size company

Vice President—Sales, small-size company

1.   <u>Counselor</u>
2.   <u>Therapist</u>
3.   _____
4.   _____

B. <u>Medium-Term Position Objective</u> (Next promotion in two to three years)

Sales Director, large-size company

Vice President—Sales, medium-size company

Top Sales Executive, small-size company

1.   <u>Counselor</u>
2.   <u>Therapist</u>
3.   _____
4.   _____

C. <u>Long-Term Position Objective</u> (Second promotion in five to seven years)

Vice President—Sales, large-size company

Top Sales Executive, medium or small-size company

Own my own business

1.   <u>Clinical Supervisor</u>
2.   <u>Faculty</u>
3.   _____
4.   _____

5. Place a ☑ next to each industry in the following checklist, within which you have industry experience. Highlight the industries you would like to explore pursuing in your job search.

Industry Checklist

Aerospace & Defense

☐ Aerospace/Defense-Major Diversified

☐ Aerospace/Defense-Products

☐ Aerospace/Defense-Maintenance & Service

Automotive & Transport Equipment

☐ Auto Manufacturers

☐ Trucks, Buses & Other Vehicles

☐ Auto Parts

☐ Recreational Vehicles

☐ Motorcycles & Other Small-Engine Vehicles

☐ Pleasure Boats

☐ Shipbuilding & Related Services

☐ Rail & Trucking Equipment

Banking

☐ Money Center Banks

☐ Banking-Northeast

☐ Banking-Mid-Atlantic

☐ Banking-Southeast

☐ Banking-Midwest

☐ Banking-Southwest

☐ Banking-West

☐ Banking-US Territories

☐ Banking-Canada

☐ Banking-Europe

☐ Banking-Asia & Australia

☐ Banking-Latin America, Middle East & Africa

☐ Other Banking Services

Chemicals

☐ Diversified Chemicals

☐ Basic & Intermediate Chemicals & Petrochemicals

☐ Agricultural Chemicals

☐ Specialty Chemicals

☐ Plastics & Fibers

☐ Paints, Coatings & Other Finishing Products

Computer Hardware

☐ Diversified Computer Products

☐ Large-Scale Computers

☐ Personal Computers

☐ Miscellaneous Computer-Based Systems

☐ Data Storage Devices

☐ Networking & Communication Devices

☐ Computer Peripherals

☐ Electronic Business Equipment

Computer Software & Services

☐ Diversified Software

☐ Multimedia Production, Graphics & Publishing Software

☐ Entertainment & Games Software

☐ Educational Software

☐ Document Management Software

☐ Database & File Management Software

☐ Corporate, Professional & Financial Software

☐ Manufacturing & Industrial Software

☐ Engineering, Scientific & CAD/CAM Software

☐ Networking & Connectivity Software

☐ Communications Software

☐ Internet & Intranet Software & Services

☐ Other Application Software

☐ Development Tools, Operating Systems & Utility Software

☐ Security Software & Services

☐ Information Technology Consulting Services

☐ Data Processing Software & Services

☐ Miscellaneous Computer Services

☐ Computer Products Distribution & Support

Conglomerates

- ☐ Conglomerates
- ☐ Trading Companies

Consumer Products-Durables

- ☐ Appliances
- ☐ Home Furnishings
- ☐ Housewares & Accessories
- ☐ Lawn & Garden Equipment & Small Tools & Accessories
- ☐ Office & Business Furniture & Fixtures
- ☐ Consumer Electronics
- ☐ Toys, Games & Other Recreational Goods
- ☐ Sporting Goods
- ☐ Professional Sports Gear & Apparel
- ☐ Jewelry, Watches & Clocks
- ☐ Photographic Equipment & Supplies
- ☐ Miscellaneous Durable Consumer Goods

Consumer Products-Non-Durables

- ☐ Apparel-Clothing
- ☐ Apparel-Footwear & Accessories
- ☐ Personal Care Products
- ☐ Cleaning Products
- ☐ Business Forms & Other Office Supplies
- ☐ Miscellaneous Non-Durable Consumer Goods
- ☐ Luxury Goods

Diversified Services

- ☐ Advertising
- ☐ Marketing & Public Relations Services
- ☐ Telemarketing, Call Centers & Other Direct Marketing
- ☐ Market & Business Research Services
- ☐ Accounting, Bookkeeping, Collection & Credit Reporting
- ☐ Staffing, Outsourcing & Other Human Resources
- ☐ Management Consulting Services

- ☐ Printing, Photocopying & Graphic Design
- ☐ Building Maintenance & Related Services
- ☐ Miscellaneous Business Services
- ☐ Legal Services
- ☐ Security & Protection Products & Services
- ☐ Car & Truck Rental
- ☐ Personal Services
- ☐ Consumer Services
- ☑ Child Care Services & Elementary & Secondary Schools
- ☐ Education & Training Services
- ☐ Colleges & Universities
- ☐ Technical & Scientific Research Services
- ☐ Charitable Organizations
- ☐ Membership Organizations
- ☐ Foundations & Cultural Institutions

Drugs

- ☐ Drug Manufacturers-Major
- ☐ Drug Manufacturers-Other
- ☐ Drugs-Generic
- ☐ Drug Delivery Systems
- ☐ Vitamins, Nutritionals & Other Health-Related Products
- ☐ Biotechnology-Medicine
- ☐ Biotechnology-Research
- ☐ Diagnostic Substances
- ☐ Drugs & Sundries-Wholesale

Electronics & Miscellaneous Technology

- ☐ Semiconductor-Broad Line
- ☐ Semiconductor-Memory Chips
- ☐ Semiconductor-Specialized
- ☐ Semiconductor-Integrated Circuits
- ☐ Semiconductor Equipment & Materials
- ☐ Diversified Electronics
- ☐ Computer Boards, Cards & Connector Products

Electronics & Miscellaneous Technology (Continued)

- ☐ Miscellaneous Electronics
- ☐ Scientific & Technical Instruments
- ☐ Electronic Test & Measurement Instruments
- ☐ Contract Electronics Manufacturing
- ☐ Electronics Distribution

Energy

- ☐ Integrated Oil & Gas
- ☐ Oil & Gas Exploration & Production
- ☐ Oil & Gas Refining & Marketing
- ☐ Oil & Gas Equipment
- ☐ Oil & Gas Services
- ☐ Oil & Gas Pipelines & Storage
- ☐ Petroleum Product Distribution

Financial Services

- ☐ Investment Banking & Brokerage
- ☐ Asset Management
- ☐ Royalty Trusts
- ☐ Investment Firms
- ☐ Closed-End Investment Funds
- ☐ Venture Capital Firms
- ☐ Consumer Loans
- ☐ Mortgage Banking & Related Services
- ☐ Commercial Lending
- ☐ Leasing
- ☐ Miscellaneous Financial Services
- ☐ Services to Financial Companies

Food, Beverage & Tobacco

- ☐ Diversified Foods-Major
- ☐ Diversified Foods-Other
- ☐ Agricultural Operations & Products
- ☐ Agricultural Services
- ☐ Agriculture-Biotechnology
- ☐ Grains, Breads & Cereals

- ☐ Meat Products
- ☐ Dairy Products
- ☐ Canned & Frozen Foods
- ☐ Other Processed & Packaged Goods
- ☐ Sugar & Confectionery
- ☐ Miscellaneous Food Products
- ☐ Food Wholesale-to Grocers
- ☐ Food Wholesale-to Restaurants
- ☐ Beverages-Brewers
- ☐ Beverages-Wineries
- ☐ Beverages-Distillers
- ☐ Beverages-Bottlers & Wholesale Distributors
- ☐ Beverages-Soft Drinks
- ☐ Tobacco Products

Health Products & Services

- ☐ Medical Instruments & Supplies
- ☐ Medical Appliances & Equipment
- ☐ Health Care Plans
- ☐ Long-Term Care Facilities
- ☐ Hospitals
- ☑ Specialized Health Services
- ☐ Home Health Care
- ☐ Medical Laboratories & Research
- ☐ Medical Practice Management & Services
- ☐ Medical Products Distribution

Insurance

- ☐ Multi-line Insurance
- ☐ Life Insurance
- ☐ Accident & Health Insurance
- ☐ Property & Casualty Insurance
- ☐ Surety, Title & Miscellaneous Insurance
- ☐ Insurance Brokers
- ☐ Reinsurance

Leisure

- □ Lodging
- □ Travel Agencies, Tour Operators & Other Travel Services
- □ Gambling Resorts & Casinos
- □ Gaming Activities
- □ Gaming Equipment & Services
- □ Sporting Activities
- □ Professional Sports Teams & Organizations
- □ Restaurants
- □ Specialty Eateries & Catering Services
- □ Miscellaneous Entertainment
- □ Adult Entertainment

Manufacturing

- □ Diversified Machinery
- □ Agricultural Machinery
- □ Construction, Mining & Other Heavy Machinery
- □ Material Handling Machinery
- □ Miscellaneous General & Special Machinery
- □ Industrial Automation Products & Industrial Controls
- □ Machine Tools, Components & Accessories
- □ Hardware & Fasteners
- □ Metal Fabrication
- □ Fluid Control Equipment, Pumps, Seals & Valves
- □ Pollution & Treatment Controls & Filtration Products
- □ Food Service Equipment
- □ Turbines, Transformers & Other Electrical Generation Equipment
- □ Wire & Cable
- □ Miscellaneous Electrical Products
- □ Lighting & Other Fixtures
- □ Textile Manufacturing
- □ Packaging & Containers
- □ Rubber & Plastic Products
- □ Glass & Clay Products
- □ Paper & Paper Products
- □ Miscellaneous & Diversified Industrial Products
- □ Industrial Equipment & Products Distribution

Materials & Construction

- □ Diversified Building Materials
- □ Lumber, Wood Production & Timber Operations
- □ Aggregates, Concrete & Cement
- □ Plumbing & HVAC Equipment
- □ Miscellaneous Building Materials
- □ Manufactured Buildings
- □ Engineering & Architectural Services
- □ Heavy Construction
- □ Specialty Contracting & Industrial

Maintenance

- □ Waste Management & Recycling
- □ Environmental Services

Media

- □ Media—Major Diversified
- □ TV Broadcasting
- □ Television Production, Programming & Distribution
- □ Radio Broadcasting & Programming
- □ Motion Picture & Video Production & Distribution
- □ Movie Theaters
- □ Music Production & Publishing
- □ Movie, Television & Music Production Services & Products
- □ Publishing-Newspapers
- □ Publishing-Periodicals
- □ Publishing-Books
- □ Publishing-Other
- □ Information Collection & Delivery Services
- □ Internet & On-line Content Providers

Metals & Mining

- ☐ Diversified Mining & Metals
- ☐ Copper
- ☐ Aluminum
- ☐ Coal
- ☐ Gold & Silver & Other Precious Metals
- ☐ Diamonds & Other Precious Stones
- ☐ Industrial Minerals & Metals
- ☐ Steel Production
- ☐ Miscellaneous Mining & Metals Processing
- ☐ Metals & Alloys Distribution

Real Estate

- ☐ REIT-Diversified & Miscellaneous
- ☐ REIT-Office
- ☐ REIT-Health Care Facilities
- ☐ REIT-Hotel/Motel
- ☐ REIT-Industrial
- ☐ REIT-Residential
- ☐ REIT-Retail
- ☐ REIT-Mortgage Investment
- ☐ Property Investment & Management
- ☐ Real Estate Development
- ☐ Residential Construction
- ☐ Miscellaneous Real Estate Services

Retail

- ☐ Clothing, Shoe & Accessory Retailing & Wholesaling
- ☐ Department Stores
- ☐ Discount & Variety Retailing
- ☐ Drug, Health & Beauty Product Retailing
- ☐ Grocery Retailing
- ☐ Convenience Stores & Gas Stations
- ☐ Consumer Electronics & Appliance Retailing
- ☐ Building Materials & Gardening Supplies Retailing & Wholesale

- ☐ Home Furnishings & Housewares Retailing
- ☐ Auto Parts Retailing & Wholesale
- ☐ Non-Store Retailing

Specialty Retail

- ☐ Sporting Goods Retailing
- ☐ Toy & Hobby Retailing & Wholesale
- ☐ Jewelry Retailing & Wholesale
- ☐ Music, Video, Book & Entertainment
- ☐ Software Retailing & Dist.
- ☐ Computer & Software Retailing
- ☐ Office Products Retailing & Distribution
- ☐ Auto Dealers & Distributors
- ☐ Miscellaneous Retail
- ☐ Miscellaneous Wholesale

Telecommunications

- ☐ Switching & Transmission Equipment
- ☐ Communications Processing Equipment
- ☐ Wireless, Satellite & Microwave Communications Equipment
- ☐ Wireless Communications Services
- ☐ Long-Distance Carriers
- ☐ Local Telecom & Private Transmission Services
- ☐ Diversified Telecom Service Providers
- ☐ Cable TV & Satellite Systems
- ☐ Internet & On-line Service Providers
- ☐ Miscellaneous End-User Communications Services
- ☐ Miscellaneous Services to Communication Providers

Transportation

- ☐ Airlines
- ☐ Air Services, Other
- ☐ Air Delivery, Freight & Parcel Services
- ☐ Trucking
- ☐ Shipping
- ☐ Railroads

Transportation (Continued)

- ☐ Bus, Taxi & Other Passenger Services
- ☐ Logistics & Other Transportation Services

Utilities

- ☐ Diversified Utilities
- ☐ Electric Utilities
- ☐ Independent Power Producers & Marketers
- ☐ Gas Utilities
- ☐ Water Utilities
- ☐ Alternative Energy Sources

Ministry Industries

- ☐ Church, Pastoral

- ☐ Missions, Field Work
- ☐ Missions, Board Administration
- ☐ Denominational Leadership
- ☐ Schools, Pre-school
- ☐ Schools, Elementary
- ☐ Schools, Secondary
- ☐ College/University/Seminary
- ☐ Correctional Institutions
- ☐ Military, Chaplaincy
- ☐ Parachurch Organizations
- ☐ Media, Television, Radio, Film
- ☐ Creative Arts, Singing, Dance, Musician

6. List your industry preferences for your job search (those highlighted above)

College/Universities

Long-term care facilities

Hospitals

Specialized health services

Missions, Field work

Parachurch Organization

Career Obstacles Checklist

Place an "X" in the column that best describes how you perceive each career obstacle listed in the checklist below. For each obstacle that you check as "YES" or "UNSURE," write a note in the space below it describing why you have this perception.

CAREER OBSTACLES	YES	UNSURE	NO
No Previous Work History			X
Currently Unemployed			X
Discharged From Position			X
Disabilities			X
My Gender is Nontraditional for My Career			X
Pregnancy			X
Obesity			X
Limited Geographic Constraints			X
No College Degree or Graduate Degree			X
No Professional Licenses/Certifications	X		

Most of places look to hire person with licensure and master's degree isn't enough.

CAREER OBSTACLES	YES	UNSURE	NO
Age Concerns			X
Dependent-Care Responsibilities			X
Perceived as Lacking Direction or Career Planning			X
Perceived as Specialist in My Field			X
Perceived as Generalist in My Field			X
Limited Line Experience			
Limited Staff Experience			
Lacking Titles That Represent My Scope of Responsibilities			X
Lacking Upward Mobility in My Career		X	
Counselors and Therapists usually do not have promotions unless they are called to faculty at educational institution			
Left Short-Term Position		X	
I haven't have that much experience w/ any of the jobs I held.			
Frequently Changed Jobs			X

CAREER OBSTACLES	YES	UNSURE	NO
Left A Company That Was in Financial Difficulty			X
Left A Company That Had A Poor Reputation			X
Adverse Personal Credit Report			X
References Unfavorable		X	
I didn't really invest in building good relationships with supervisors			

Now, return to the section on career obstacles in the main text and read about those obstacles you checked as "YES" or "UNSURE" and develop your strategies for overcoming them in your job search.

ASAP Goals & Tracking Worksheet

Target Activity & Daily Goals	Weekly Goals	Monthly Goals
Résumé Distribution Services (Electronic) (7%)		
1. I will distribute my résumé to targeted employers on a _____ basis.	3	12
2. I will distribute my résumé to targeted recruiters on a _____ basis.	2	8
Résumé Distributions (First-Class Mail) (7%)		
1. I will distribute my résumé to _____ targeted employers.	3	12
2. I will spend _____ minutes daily in follow-up activities.		
Responding to Job Openings in Trade Journals (7%)		
1. I will spend _60_ minutes daily researching and applying to openings.	300	
2. I will spend _15_ minutes daily following up on openings applied to earlier.	75	
Applying via On-line Job Boards (10%)		
1. I will spend _60_ minutes daily researching and applying to openings	300	
2. I will spend _15_ minutes daily following up on openings applied to earlier.	75	
Applying to Company Web site Job Boards (10%)		
1. I will spend _60_ minutes daily researching and applying to openings.	300	
2. I will spend _15_ minutes daily following up on openings applied to earlier.	75	
Contacting Recruiters (15%)		
1. I will spend _60_ minutes daily researching & applying to recruiter Web sites.	300	
2. I will spend _15_ minutes daily sending e-mails with my résumé to recruiters.	75	
3. I will spend _15_ minutes daily calling recruiters to follow-up on Web site applications and e-mails.	75	
Contacting Investment Firms (15%)		
1. I will spend _____ minutes daily researching investment firms on-line and making contact via e-mail, mail or phone.		
2. I will spend _____ minutes daily in follow-up activities (e-mail, mail, or phone).		
Networking Family Members (33%)		
1. I will spend _30_ minutes daily contacting family members via e-mail, mail or phone.	150	
2. I will spend _15_ minutes daily in follow-up activities via e-mail, mail or phone.	75	

Target Activity & Daily Goals	Weekly Goals	Monthly Goals
Networking Friends & Acquaintances (33%)		
1. I will spend _30_ minutes daily contacting friends & acquaintances via e-mail, mail or phone.	150	
2. I will spend _15_ minutes daily in follow-up activities via e-mail, mail or phone.	75	
Networking Co-workers & Colleagues (33%)		
1. I will spend _30_ minutes daily contacting co-workers and colleagues via e-mail, mail or phone.	150	
2. I will spend _15_ minutes daily in follow-up activities via e-mail, mail or phone.	75	
Networking Former Employers & Supervisors (33%)		
1. I will spend _30_ minutes daily contacting former employers & supervisors via e-mail, mail or phone.	150	
2. I will spend _15_ minutes daily in follow-up activities via e-mail, mail or phone.	75	
Networking Alumni (33%)		
1. I will spend _30_ minutes daily contacting alumni via e-mail, mail or phone.	150	
2. I will spend _15_ minutes daily in follow-up activities via e-mail, mail or phone.	75	
Networking Professional Associations (33%)		
1. I will spend _30_ minutes daily contacting professional members via e-mail, mail or phone.	180	
2. I will spend _15_ minutes daily in follow-up activities via e-mail, mail or phone.	75	
Networking Clubs (33%)		
1. I will spend _30_ minutes daily contacting networking members via e-mail, mail or phone.	150	
2. I will spend _15_ minutes daily in follow-up activities via e-mail, mail or phone.	75	
Networking Religious Affiliations (33%)		
1. I will spend _30_ minutes daily contacting members of my religious group via e-mail, mail, or phone.	150	
2. I will spend _15_ minutes daily in follow-up activities via e-mail, mail or phone.	75	
Direct Mail to Employers (Letter Résumé, Value-Proposition Letter & Industry Influential Letter) (47%)		
1. I will spend _60_ minutes daily researching target companies in my targeted industries and geographic regions.	300	
2. I will spend _60_ minutes daily writing letters based on my research, to target companies in my targeted industries and geographic regions.	300	
3. I will spend _15_ minutes daily in follow-up activities via e-mail, mail or phone.	75	—

Target Activity & Daily Goals	Weekly Goals	Monthly Goals
Informational Interviewing (60%)		
1. I will spend _60_ minutes daily researching influential leaders and executives in my targeted industries and geographic regions.	300	
2. I will conduct informational interviews via e-mail, telephone or in-person.	1	4
3. I will spend _15_ minutes daily in follow-up activities via e-mail, mail or phone.	75	

Interview Preparation Checklist

Interview Preparation Checklist

☐ 1. <u>Reviewed research</u>

  ☐ Company history (revenue growth/decline, expansions, mergers/acquisitions)

  ☐ Company culture (mission, vision, values, dress code)

  ☐ Products/services (new launches, market leaders)

  ☐ Key executives (bios, titles)

  ☐ Media releases

  ☐ Major customers

☐ 2. <u>Reviewed position description</u>

  ☐ Chose CAR stories supporting fit for each essential skill

  ☐ Identified potential career obstacles

☐ 3. <u>Prepared list of anticipated questions</u>

  ☐ Practiced answering questions using CAR stories

  ☐ Prepared to respond to career obstacles with examples of similar skills or accomplishments which are highly transferable

☐ 4. <u>Practiced thirty-second commercial</u>

  ☐ Focused on strengths relevant to position

  ☐ Tailored positioning statements to position

☐ 5. <u>Role-played interview with coach or family member/friend</u>

  ☐ Videotaped or audiotape recorded role-play

  ☐ Debriefed the recording

  ☐ Repeated role-play, incorporating feedback from debriefing

---

Negotiations Worksheet

Negotiations Worksheet

Non-negotiable items:

1. Health Insurance
2. Paid Time Off
3. No work on Sunday .
4.
5.
6.

Negotiable items:

1. Work Schedule
2. 401K
3. Salary $25 - $30
4.
5.
6.
7.
8.
9.
10.

Negotiations Preparation Checklist

Negotiations Preparation Checklist

☐ 1. <u>Company history</u>

    ☐ (1) Revenue growth or decline?

    ☐ (2) History of layoffs or acquisitions?

    ☐ (3) Business structure

        ☐ (a)   Family-owned and operated

        ☐ (b)   Closely held private corporation

        ☐ (c)   Publicly traded company

☐ 2. <u>Industry history</u>

    ☐ (1) Growth, stable, declining?

    ☐ (2) Future projections?

☐ 3. <u>Salary ranges for position being offered</u>

    ☐ (1) Salary.com reports

    ☐ (2) Salaryexpert.com reports

☐ 4. <u>Cost-of-living factors if relocating</u>

    ☐ (1) Moving.com reports

☐ 5. <u>Relocation assistance package</u>

☐ 6. <u>Growth potential for me in the company</u>

    ☐ (1) Career-path planning

    ☐ (2) Professional-development resources

☐ 7. <u>Employee benefits</u>

    ☐ (1) Family coverage for medical/dental/vision/disability insurance

    ☐ (2) Vacation/personal paid leave

    ☐ (3) Stock options

    ☐ (4) Bonus program

    ☐ (5) Paid holidays

    ☐ (6) Employee assistance program

    ☐ (7) Medical spending accounts

    ☐ (8) Retirement plan, vesting period, employer matching funds

    ☐ (9) Family-leave policy

    ☐ (10)Bereavement-leave policy

    ☐ (11)Health and wellness program or benefits

☐   8. <u>Employee expense-reimbursement policy</u>

    ☐   (1) Corporate credit card

    ☐   (2) Corporate calling card

    ☐   (3) Cellphone provided

    ☐   (4) Laptop provided

☐   9. <u>Travel required? What percentage? How long is average trip?</u>

☐   10. <u>Title—Is it negotiable?</u>

☐   11. <u>Executive Benefits</u>

    ☐   (1) Stock grants

    ☐   (2) Country club membership

    ☐   (2) Car

    ☐   (3) Airline club memberships

    ☐   (4) Limousine service

    ☐   (5) Business-class airline travel overseas

    ☐   (6) Use of corporate jet

☐   12. _____

☐   13. _____

☐   14. _____

Negotiations Questions

Negotiations Questions

1. What is heath insurance coverage like?

2. Do you have paid time off? How many day?

3. I would like to take 1-2 weeks off in Summer to participate in mission trip. Would it be possible?

4. I cannot work on Sunday because of my religeous duty. Does the position require Sunday?

5.

6.

7.

8.

9.

Biography—John S. Lybarger, MBA, PhD

Dr. John Lybarger has over 18 years of experience in leadership and organizational development. He is the president and founder of Lybarger & Associates Inc., a career coaching and leadership training firm specializing in designing career and leadership pathways for men and women.

He has worked with clients in Qwest (formerly US West); MediaOne, AT&T Broadband, Covad Communications, Ryder, Frito-Lay, Procter & Gamble, Jacuzzi, Nabisco, Schlumberger, Kodak, Rockefeller Center, Radio City Music Hall, Six Flags, Hilton, The Home Depot, Charles Schwab, Fidelity, BankBoston, FMC Corporation, Computer Science Corporation, Adobe, and IBM. Additionally, he has worked with most federal government agencies through the Office of Personnel Management as an adjunct faculty member of the Western Management Development Center in Aurora, Colorado.

Dr. Lybarger has conducted more than 600 executive coaching sessions, utilizing assessments, improving individual performance, increasing job match, reducing workplace conflict, and strengthening team relationships in the public and private sectors. He has facilitated more than 50 mediation sessions, improving dispute resolution and reducing litigation expenses. He has facilitated more than 500 training programs with more than 7,000 participants, from front-line employees to senior executives.

He earned a PhD in psychology and a Master of Business Administration in human resource development from California Coast University, a Master of Science in counseling from California State University at Fullerton and a Bachelor of Science in Christian education from Biola University. Dr. Lybarger holds the following licensures and credentials: Marriage and Family Therapist license (California); Certified Paralegal (General Practice) from the ABA-approved Denver Paralegal Institute, and Certified Business Mediator from the Center for Solutions Training Institute in Denver.

Dr. Lybarger is profiled in *Who's Who in the World, Who's Who in America, Who's Who in the West, Who's Who in Finance, and Who's Who in American Education*. He is a former faculty member of Loma Linda University's School of Medicine.

Active in professional associations, Dr. Lybarger is a professional member of the American Counseling Association and the National Career Development Association. He has been featured in many media interviews (radio, television and print including, *Inc. Magazine, Business Week*, and *The Denver Business Journal*) in the United States, Canada, Australia and the United Kingdom. He is the co-author of the book, "*Coaching Tips for Job Seekers—Keys and Secrets for Success!*" and various journal articles on customer service, sexual harassment, spirituality and addiction issues.

Web site: www.lybargerassociatesinc.com
E-mail: john@lybargerassociatesinc.com
Phone: (303) 421-8080

Biography—William L. Donelson, MDiv

Mr. Donelson brings outstanding leadership, extensive management experience, and superior verbal and written communication skills to his career coaching practice. He has consulted with over 500 executives from Global and Fortune 1000 companies, blue chip firms, and government organizations, as well as smaller businesses both public and private, assisting them with résumé writing, career search strategies, and interviewing and negotiations techniques.

His diverse career experiences in human resources management, organizational development, and public speaking give him a unique perspective as he consults with clients from a broad spectrum of industries and experiences. His clients have come from companies like Oracle, SAP, Nortel Networks, J.D. Edwards, ING, International Truck and Engine, SunTrust, MCI, Sprint, Kellogg, AstraZeneca, Kodak, the Department of Justice and the Department of Defense.

Mr. Donelson was previously a Senior Vice President at McKenzie Scott Partners. He joined the firm in 1998, after a successful career in human resources management and consulting with a regional firm in Denver. In this role, he consulted with businesses, groups, and individuals, on a variety of interpersonal and organizational development issues. He facilitated seminars, workshops, and teambuilding retreats that improved productivity, increased profitability and enhanced and team performance.

Mr. Donelson founded a nonprofit corporation providing consulting and strategic leadership direction to other nonprofits throughout the Western United States in the areas of staff development, board leadership, and fundraising campaign strategies. He also served as a board member for local, regional, and national nonprofit organizations.

He moved to Colorado from Wyoming and served as business manager and controller for a $40 million commodity-trading firm (which owned a locally-prominent western art gallery). Prior to his relocation, he successfully launched, operated, and sold several franchise businesses in Wyoming. His early career included serving as a controller and finance manager for a network of automotive dealerships.

After receiving his master's degree in counseling from Denver Seminary, he became a Licensed Professional Counselor in Colorado. He obtained his Bachelor of Science degree in accounting from the University of Wyoming, where he was an outstanding graduate of the College of Commerce and Industry, and a student representative of his college in the University of Wyoming Student Senate. Mr. Donelson is profiled in *Who's Who in American Colleges and Universities* and he is the co-author of "*Coaching Tips for Job Seekers—Keys and Secrets for Success!*

E-mail: billdonelson@msn.com
Phone: (303) 985-3020